Afro-Centered Futurisms in Our Speculative Fiction

BLACK LITERARY AND CULTURAL EXPRESSIONS

Bloomsbury's **Black Literary and Cultural Expressions** series provides a much-needed space for exploring dimensions of Black creativity as its local expressions in literature, music, film, art, etc., interface with the global circulation of culture. From contemporary and historical perspectives, and through a multidisciplinary lens, works in this series critically analyze the provenance, genres, aesthetics, intersections, and modes of circulation of works of Black cultural expression and production.

Series Editors
Toyin Falola and Abimbola A. Adelakun, University of Texas at Austin, USA

Advisory Board
Nadia Anwar, University of Management and Technology, Lahore, Pakistan
Adriaan van Klinken, University of Leeds, UK
Alain Lawo-Sukam, Texas A&M University, USA
Nathaniel S. Murrell, University of North Carolina, Wilmington, USA
Mukoma wa Ngugi, Cornell University, USA
Bode Omojola, Mount Holyoke and the Five College Consortium, USA
Nduka Otiono, Carleton University, Canada
Bola Sotunsa, Babcock University, Nigeria
Nathan Suhr-Sytsma, Emory University, USA

Volumes in the Series:
Wole Soyinka: Literature, Activism, and African Transformation by Bola Dauda and Toyin Falola
Social Ethics and Governance in Contemporary African Writing: Literature, Philosophy, and the Nigerian World by Nimi Wariboko

The Birth of Breaking: Hip Hop History from the Floor Up
by Serouj "Midus" Aprahamian
Literature of the Somali Diaspora: Space, Language and Resistance in Somali Anglophone and Italian Novels by Marco Medugno
The Decolonizing Work of Jessica Huntley: The Political Roots of a Radical Black Activist by Claudia Tomlinson
Afro-Centered Futurisms in Our Speculative Fiction edited by Eugen Bacon
Chinua Achebe: Narrating Africa in Fictions and History by Toyin Falola
Irony, Agency and the Global Imaginary in Contemporary Nigerian and Kenyan Literature by Penny Cartwright (forthcoming)
In Conversation with Denise Ferreira da Silva: New Methodologies for Race, Ethnic and Decolonial Studies edited by Julietta Hua and rashné limki (forthcoming)

Afro-Centered Futurisms in Our Speculative Fiction

Edited by Eugen Bacon

BLOOMSBURY ACADEMIC

NEW YORK · LONDON · OXFORD · NEW DELHI · SYDNEY

BLOOMSBURY ACADEMIC
Bloomsbury Publishing Inc
1385 Broadway, New York, NY 10018, USA
50 Bedford Square, London, WC1B 3DP, UK
29 Earlsfort Terrace, Dublin 2, Ireland

BLOOMSBURY, BLOOMSBURY ACADEMIC and the Diana logo
are trademarks of Bloomsbury Publishing Plc

First published in the United States of America 2024

Copyright © Eugen Bacon, 2025
Each chapter © Contributors, 2025

Cover design by Eleanor Rose
Cover image © katyau / iStock / Getty Images

All rights reserved. No part of this publication may be reproduced or
transmitted in any form or by any means, electronic or mechanical, including
photocopying, recording, or any information storage or retrieval system,
without prior permission in writing from the publishers.

Bloomsbury Publishing Inc does not have any control over, or responsibility for,
any third-party websites referred to or in this book. All internet addresses given
in this book were correct at the time of going to press. The author and publisher
regret any inconvenience caused if addresses have changed or sites have ceased
to exist, but can accept no responsibility for any such changes.

A catalogue record for this book is available from the British Library.

A catalog record for this book is available from the Library of Congress.

ISBN: PB: 979-8-7651-1467-4
        HB: 979-8-7651-1466-7
        ePDF: 979-8-7651-1469-8
        eBook: 979-8-7651-1468-1

Series: Black Literary and Cultural Expressions

Typeset by Integra Software Services Pvt. Ltd.

To find out more about our authors and books visit www.bloomsbury.com
and sign up for our newsletters.

For
Our
Mother.
Africa

Contents

Preface	x
The Structure of This Book	xii

1 Suyi Okungbowa: Afrocentric Futurisms—The Case for an Inclusive Expression, *Nigeria/Canada* — 1

2 Stephen Embleton: Cosmologies and Languages Building Africanfuturism, *South Africa/UK* — 23

3 Eugen Bacon: An Afrofuturistic Dystopia and the Afro-irreal, *Tanzania/Australia* — 41

4 Nuzo Onoh: The Power of African Spirituality in Africanfuturism, *Nigeria/UK* — 59

5 Shingai Njeri Kagunda: Black-Futurisms Vs. Systems of Domination, *Kenya* — 77

6 Cheryl S. Ntumy: Faith and Fantasy—Afrofuturist and Africanfuturist Spirituality, *Ghana* — 97

7 Xan van Rooyen: Queer Imaginings in Africanfuturism Inspired by African History, *South Africa/Finland* — 119

8 Aline-Mwezi Niyonsenga: Afrofuturism and Exploring Cultural Identity as a Process of Becoming, *Rwanda/Australia* — 137

9 Tobi Ogundiran: Fabulist Imaginings in Tales of the Dark and Fantastic, *Nigeria/USA* — 151

10 Dilman Dila: A Vision for Direct Democracy in Yat Madit, *Uganda* — 163

11 Nerine Dorman: A Gaze at Post-Colonial Themes That Re-Envision Africa, *South Africa* — 191

12 Denouement: Autoethnography—The Self-As-Research, Eugen Bacon, *Tanzania/Australia* — 207

Acknowledgments	224
Index	226

Preface

There's an animal tacked in my hair, and it hangs like a mirror I can't see.
It's full of silence, shadows, asking are we caged, or free? Sometimes
It licks my skin but doesn't disturb me. When I reach up to touch it,
I can't remember where it is, if it is. Perhaps it's more cunning
Than I thought, hiding its pawprints. Patiently waiting to
Catch me with reflections of ebony nights, white stars,
Burnt-orange dust. I know and I don't, the hum of
Rain on a tin roof. The taste of my grandma's
Sweetened mangoes—moulded like
A donkey's ear plucked fresh from
A tree that's a silhouette above
My mother's bones.

—*"An Earnest Blackness"*

"An Earnest Blackness" by Eugen Bacon—illustrated by Elena Betti[1]

---

[1]Bacon, Eugen (2021), "An Earnest Blackness," in *Saving Shadows*, p. 90, Alconbury Weston: NewCon Press.

The Structure of This Book

This vibrant book explores virgin ground in its "voice from the grassroots" positioning that enwraps writerly perspectives from Afrodescendant peoples with lived experience from the continent, in critical conversations on Afrofuturism and Afro-centered futurisms. It interrogates in its chapters the nature of Afrocentric fiction in a fun and playful way, interspersing scholarly dissertation with creative artefacts on language, song, belief, and spirituality. It casts a crucial gaze on definitions, including Africanfuturism, Africanjujuism, Afrocentric, Afrodescendant, Afrofuturism, Afropantheology, Afrosurrealism, Afro-irreal, autoethnography, Black speculative fiction, Black writing, decolonization, ethnography, futurisms, othering, and more, together with the holistic umbrella of speculative fiction.

The goal of this approachable book is to negotiate and create a critical awareness of black speculative fiction contextualized in Afrocentric futurisms. It scrutinizes the characteristics of "futurisms" from an African gaze, and is a valuable resource for students, academics, creators, commentators, and consumers of contemporary speculative fiction—including general adult readers of African writing and speculative fiction.

Afro-Centered Futurisms in Our Speculative Fiction is not simply a "Now, listen … " book—spoken with the sagely tone of an ancient woman in the village, grained with a hint of exasperation: she has seen enough. Indeed, it seeks to correct misconceptions of African writing, and the works of Afrodescendant peoples, but it's also a vital study that offers, creatively, unique perspectives anchored with immense potential to hearten a diverse readership. It fosters critical awareness of Afro-centered fiction, including works by award-winning African writers. Contributing authors have featured in major genre and literary awards, including the Bram Stoker, World Fantasy, British Fantasy, Philip K. Dick, Shirley Jackson, British Science Fiction Association, Locus, Ignyte, Nommo, Victorian Premier's Literary and Otherwise Awards, the Commonwealth Short Story Prize, and other awards.

Chapter by Chapter Synopsis

Chapter 1. Suyi Okungbowa: Afrocentric Futurisms—The Case for an Inclusive Expression, Nigeria/Canada: A conversation on futurisms in African writing, with focus on (i) the historiography of the diverse and unitary expressions we use to describe our speculative work, including making a case for inclusive collective terminology, and (ii) how authors and scholars in this volume carry on this tradition through their works and excerpted herein.

Chapter 2. Stephen Embleton: Cosmologies and Languages Building Africanfuturism, South Africa/UK: A close gaze at the use of language in Embleton's James Currey Fellowship-winning novel *Bones & Runes,* and the world of Sauúti, a five-planet system in a world deeply rooted in African mythology, language, and culture, from a founding collective of African creators.

Chapter 3. Eugen Bacon: An Afrofuturistic Dystopia and the Afro-irreal, Tanzania/Australia: Exemplars from Bacon's Afrofuturistic dystopian novel *Mage of Fools,* and Afro-irreal collection of black speculative short stories, *Chasing Whispers.*

Chapter 4. Nuzo Onoh: The Power of African Spirituality in Africanfuturism, Nigeria/UK: The paradox between the past and the future in Igbo philosophy and Africanfuturism, and application in Onoh's masterful African horror novel *A Dance for the Dead.*

Chapter 5. Shingai Njeri Kagunda: Black-Futurisms Vs. Systems of Domination, Kenya: Kagunda takes an intimate gaze at dark fiction and the Afrosurreal as a resistance to capitalism.

Chapter 6. Cheryl S. Ntumy: Faith and Fantasy—Afrofuturist and Africanfuturist Spirituality, Ghana: Ntumy reflects on her closer identification with Africanfuturism rather than Afrofuturism in her works, with relevance to the diverse and complex beliefs of African peoples.

Chapter 7. Xan van Rooyen: Queer Imaginings in Africanfuturism Inspired by African History, South Africa/Finland: This chapter is a brief exploration of how to resurrect the ancient and traditional queerness present across the

African continent, eroded and erased by Western hegemony as we move toward an African-inspired post-gender society.

Chapter 8. Aline-Mwezi Niyonsenga: Afrofuturism and Exploring Cultural Identity as a Process of Becoming, Rwanda/Australia: An exploration of the self and morphing identities through the application of futurism in Aline-Mwezi's speculative novelette *Fell Our Selves.*

Chapter 9. Tobi Ogundiran: Fabulist Imaginings in Tales of the Dark and Fantastic, Nigeria/USA: Ogundiran discusses surrealism in his duology *Jackal, Jackal.*

Chapter 10. Dilman Dila: A Vision for Direct Democracy in Yat Madit, Uganda: An exploration of Dila's world of Yat Madit, a governance system modeled on nations without centralized governments or kingships, an AI that enables a vision for direct democracy.

Chapter 11. Nerine Dorman: A Gaze At Post-colonial Themes That Re-envision Africa, South Africa. Nerine Dorman offers a gaze at post-colonial themes in her fiction that re-envisions what Africa might have turned out to be.

Chapter 12. Denouement: Auto-Ethnography—The Self-As-Research, Eugen Bacon, Tanzania/Australia: In this closing chapter, editor Eugen Bacon contextualizes ethnographic writing with the self-as-research. It refocuses attention to the autoethnographic nature of each author's chapter. With self-examples, the author also discusses the process of writing autobiographical creative fiction in a self-reflective autoethnographic account. Bacon also situates the chapters in this book alongside ethnographic exploration of the self and identity through Afro-centric fiction, rooted in practice and from the integral gaze of award-winning African voices.

Upon reading each chapter, it's imperative for the reader to recognize the importance of naming in the African culture. It is this very importance that informs each chapter's approach, each author's positioning relative to identity and definitions (aka naming).

The intent of this book is *not* to settle on an all-inclusive term that foregrounds the relationship between the continent and its diasporas. As Xan van Rooyen and I reiterate in our chapters, Africa is not a country. According to Worldometer (2024), Africa has a population of over 1.482 billion, an equivalent of 17.89 percent of the total world population. The continent, with a total of fifty-four countries today and over 3,000 spoken languages, is large and highly diverse in geography, traditions, and linguistics. Tanzania, my home country, alone has over 120 dialects (Tomedes 2024). There are distinctions across east and west, and south and north, and central of the continent. Even just within East Africa, for example, there are Bantus and Cushites and Nilotes—all uniquely distinct peoples in many ways, including in their features and dialects and foods and beliefs and traditions.

Homogeneity is not an option.

There's no overall voice that's a guide map. But we can co-exist, be one people—evidencing itself in the authorial, cultural identity and narratological diversity herein.

The structure of this book allows distinct authors to reconnoitre how they autoethnographically situate Africa in their writings, how—through storytelling and narratology—they embrace or interrogate their cultural identities, mis/identities, and multiplicities.

This book is a relevant discussion for publishers, writers, and readers, for all players in literary production on the continent, in the wider African diasporas, and globally, and it is relevant yesterday, today, and tomorrow. It petitions, openly and between the lines, for understanding: each author is a sum of the self and the other, and each tenderly finds affinity with some names (definitions) or contexts, and each closely hugs a choice on how to align their individual and societal totality with their fiction.

This book is a gift—to you, me, us; it's the self-as-research. An inner gaze into the speculative author's heart, mind, and self.

References

Tomedes (2024), "An Introduction to the Languages of Tanzania," *tomedes.com.* [online] Available at < https://www.tomedes.com/translator-hub/tanzania-language> [Accessed February 21, 2024].

Worldometer (2024), "Africa Population," *worldometers.infor.*, [online] Available at <https://www.worldometers.info/world-population/africa-population/> [Accessed February 21, 2024].

1

Suyi Okungbowa: Afrocentric Futurisms—The Case for an Inclusive Expression, *Nigeria/Canada*

Bio

Suyi Okungbowa is an Assistant Professor of Creative Writing at the University of Ottawa in Ontario, Canada. He is the award-winning author of multiple published works, most recently *Lost Ark Dreaming*, *Warrior of the Wind* and *Son of the Storm*. His shorter stories and essays have appeared internationally in various periodicals and anthologies. He earned his MFA in Creative Writing at the University of Arizona.

In this chapter, I will put forward the case for "Afrocentric Futurisms" as an inclusive expression for describing the speculative work of Afrodescendants by looking at a historiography of the diverse descriptors employed so far and integrating discussions about the works collected in this volume (and their authors).

Keywords: Africanfuturism, Afrocentric Futurisms, Afrodescendant, Afrofuturism, Blackness

An Intersection of Imagining

Imagining alternative ways of existence has always been embedded in the stories we—Africans and those descended from them, henceforth referenced as Afrodescendants—tell of ourselves. We have always pined for, and therefore imagined, better ways to exist, both those we have been able to bring to being and those we yet have not. We have redefined and re-shaped our own realities by telling stories about who we are, re-imagining who we used to be, and speculating about who we may become.

There is no singular accepted history that outlines how Afrodescendant peoples have collectively referred to such stories using their own terminology. Early attempts at this were often ethnographical approaches by external forces—imperial and otherwise—to simply append "African-" and "Afro-" prefixes to storytelling about Afrodescendant peoples. The ensuing expressions—*African folk tales, African legends, African science fiction*—often proved insufficient and lacking context. Later, during the 1950s and 1960s global movements for Black liberation—occurring as anti-colonial sentiments on the African continent and as anti-segregation movements in the diasporas—the "African-" and "Afro-" prefixes were often substituted for "Black" as a statement toward the growing Pan-African and Black solidarity movements that aimed to join hands between the continent and its diasporas.

Despite these attempts, Ytasha Womack's 2013 monograph, *Afrofuturism: The World of Black Sci-Fi and Fantasy Culture*, is understood to be the first book-length survey of the field that attempts to define the speculative work of Afrodescendants. It imagines this collective body of work as "an intersection of imagination, technology, the future, and liberation" wherein "Afrofuturists redefine culture and notions of blackness for today and the future" by infusing "elements of science fiction, historical fiction, speculative fiction, fantasy, Afrocentricity, and magic realism with non-Western beliefs" (2013: 9). Since then, others have made similar attempts, including Sofia Samatar's "Toward a Planetary History of Afrofuturism" (2017), which problematizes Womack's approach by highlighting its seamless absorption of artists writing from an African/non-diasporan lens (Nnedi Okorafor, Wanuri Kahiu, amongst others), "without a discussion of how their relationship to the African continent, obviously different from that of most artists in the diaspora, informs their engagement with the field." Samatar insisted that "the lack of attention to the diverse streams of Afrofuturism threatens not only to obscure possibilities for rich discussions, but to imply a development narrative that assumes there were no African futurists before 2000." Samatar's argument that peoples of African descent are much too diverse for there to be singular terminology that efficiently encapsulates (and therefore can be employed to reference) their work, has served as the basis for arguments that have come after. In the "Speculative and Science Fiction" issue of *African Literature Today* (Egbunike and Nwankwo 2021), series editors Chimalum Nwankwo and Louisa Egbunike highlight how the authors of their volume offer up "multiple critical lenses through which to read a broad range of fiction" (p. 7), a move that eschews collective definition on the basis of collective identity, namely Africanness or Blackness.

However, with the growth of institutions of thought and education, and institutions of storytelling and publication, we have witnessed the global proliferation of stories and speculative thought that would have once been local only. With this proliferation has arisen the need for collective terminology to employ in the discussion of stories that share similar points of origin, identity, and thematic or other concerns. Continued institutional growth in the study of Africanist and Afrodescendant perspectives in storytelling, and the shifting tides of contemporary literary criticism to recognize these narratives and engage with their origins, has therefore increased the desire for even broader terminology that could contain the various iterations of Afrodescendant speculative stories. Of this desire was born the new and more favored expressions that have largely stuck to this day, and which are now more or less employed within academic, literary, and public circles alike.

The most proliferated of these is *Afrofuturism*, coined by Mark Dery in 1994, in his seminal interview, "Black to the Future: Interviews with Samuel R Delany, Greg Tate, and Tricia Rose." *Africanfuturism* (and its sister term, *Afrojujuism*), coined by Nnedi Okorafor, followed many years later, in an attempt to decenter the experiences, concerns, and speculative thought of the African-American self (largely resident in North America) and favor those of the African self (largely resident on the African continent). Other nascent terms like *Afropantheology* (Ekpeki and Omenga's 2023 attempt to further turn the focus to cosmological and spiritual thought systems that embody the Africanist consciousness, and the stories that spring out of that) continue to arise. Even older terms have taken on new light: *Afrosurrealism*, for instance, once the domain of diaspora actors like Amiri Baraka (coined in an introduction to the 1974 book *Ark of Bones and Other Stories* by Henry Dumas) has now found new orientation to encompass continental concerns through the work of contemporary authors like Lisa Yvette Ndlovu and Eugen

Bacon, who expands this into *Afro-irrealism*—further bending the fantastical into a coherent, potentially believable, "impossibility," as covered in her chapter in this book.

To understand the reason for the proliferation of these terms, and the continuing fractionation of expressions for referencing and discussing speculative thought and stories that center the Afrodescendant self, we must first understand why the authors and scholars in this broad field desire and insist upon specificity rather than umbrella terminology. What concerns undergird the favoring of silos over collectives? Is there value in moving in the opposite direction, in investing in an inclusive expression that allows *both* the silo and the collective, the specific and the general, to exist? If there is, what will that be?

This introduction—and in tandem, the various contributions to this volume—make the case for why there is the need for an appropriately broad yet inclusive expression that will allow authors, scholars, and thinkers to discuss Afrodescendant speculative thought collectively, while recognizing the need for narrower terms that, at the same time, allow purveyors of speculative stories to employ specific naming in their areas focus.

What's In a Name?

To understand the perceived inadequacy of the terms currently employed in collectively describing speculative stories centering the Afrodescendant, we must first understand how we arrived at them, which in turn requires a disquisition of the terms themselves that form the basis of their coinage.

Africanness and Blackness

Africanness and *Blackness*, while closely related terms, do not always mean the same thing. Terms like "African" or "Black," used on their own and without qualification, have quite limited meaning. Peoples of African descent, however close to or removed from their continent of origin by space and/or time, are more diverse than a single label can allow. To discuss peoples of African descent will require employing specific identity loci and their attendant concerns. We may do this, say, via the locus of the geographical (e.g., continental versus diasporic, or by examining intra-continental or intra-national differences, etc.); or via a racial locus (i.e., divisions based on skin shade, predominantly imposed by colonial and imperial forces); or via the ethnic or ethno-religious locus (i.e., differences within the populations themselves based on language or cultural values or faith/religious or other factors); etc. This kind of diversity, even within the confines of a specific locus, renders terms such as "African" or "Black" nebulous without further qualification. So, while we may say "African" or "Black," or employ other variations of these terms thereof, consider that they do not address or represent all iterations of said Africanness or Blackness.

Africanness as a concept references *origin, relationship or affinity with the continent of Africa*, including (but not always) phenotypic attributes understood to have origins in the continent of Africa, e.g., darker skin shades. This understanding accepts the "multiplicities, changeability and particularity" of the various African selves, and refuses "static singularity" and "a homogenising visual centre" (Ngwena 2018: 2). In this way, Africanness, by its very distinction, rejects the historical singularity that the allied term, *Blackness*, was meant to impose (in its application by various imperial forces). Though both these terms have shifted in meaning in contemporary usage, a useful way to consider the contemporary relationship between Africanness and Blackness is to understand that not all who identify as Africans also identify as Black, whether through racial, ethnic, or other identities (e.g., Africans of Arab, European or Asiatic descent).

Blackness as a concept leans toward the ethnic and cultural heritage affiliated with the racial category of the historical Negro, an attempt to corral all selves that have historically existed within this category, regardless of their proximity to or degree of removal—by time or distance—from the continent of Africa. And yet, while *Black* as a descriptive term may reference the phenotypical presentation of the historical Negro, Blackness does not always reference physical characteristics. In many areas of North America, for instance, *Black* may be employed in describing persons of multi-racial origin, pointing toward a socio-cutural embodiment of Blackness rather than physical appearance. In Australia and its affiliated Pacific Islands, "black" or "blak" is often employed as a self-descriptor within First Nations groups, most of which have limited documented cultural commonality with people of the African diaspora, as well as differing genetic and phenotypic characteristics (Common Ground 2019). "Black," therefore, as a social, ethnic and racial category, does not always describe all people of African descent, and does not cover peoples of other racial categories who have become African through migration, residency and other historical and contemporary forms of affiliation.

Speculative Stories

References to *stories* in this chapter include all forms of storytelling across the artistic spectrum of literature, film, TV, visual art and graphic illustrations, oral tales, etc. regardless of the medium of delivery.

Speculative, as a qualifier to these stories, will describe everything across the spectrum of storytelling that involves the imagination of an alternative reality outside of what is currently, and predominantly, known and proven. Science fiction, fantasy, horror, utopias and dystopias, alternate histories, the spiritual and supernatural, fabulism and fairy tales, apocalyptic and post-apocalyptic fiction, superhero fiction, etc. all fall under this umbrella.

Futurism

Futurism describes a "cross-disciplinary artistic movement" concerned with the future and conditions that may shape its arrival (Maurits 2019: 131). The first European iteration began in Italy in 1909, with the publication of Filippo Marinetti's *Manifesto of Futurism*, which quickly devolved into a "state-sponsored cultural form" under Mussolini (2019: 131). Futurist principles were also employed in the art of other countries like Japan (under the Meiki regime in 1868), "Sweden (Per Lagerkvist), China (Hu-shi, Kuo-Mo-jo), Brazil (Anita Malfatti), Peru (Alberto Hidago), and Argentina (Emilio Petorutti)" (2019: 132). Contemporary futurism projects have evolved past those nationalist roots, and are often less deeply steeped in technological revolutions. Instead, their manifestos function more as vehicles for decolonial projects and frameworks for decolonized imaginations. Examples include "Indigenous

Futurisms," conceived by Anishinaabe scholar Grace Dillon in her introduction to the anthology, *Walking the Clouds* (2012); "Arabfuturism," Sulaïman Majali's "attempt to move towards a decolonial definition of the European-Arab (and beyond?)" in the article "Toward Arabfuturism/s" (2016); and the "Ricepunk Manifesto" of Yudhanjaya Wijeratne, which aims to center "South Asian styles of relationships," introspect on "structures of governance and community" and cherish "hybridity and hybrid cultures" (2022).

Afrofuturism

The term *Afrofuturism* was coined in 1994 by American cultural critic Mark Dery, who used it in his essay "Black to the Future" to describe the futurist works of African American writers such as Samuel Delany, Tricia Rose, and Greg Tate. Dery's appending of the prefix "Afro–" to "futurism" followed the imperial ethnographic practices that came before him, with the aim of describing the speculative work of Black storytellers of African descent—specifically those in the North American diaspora. Dery described Afrofuturists as employing "the images of technology" (1994: 180) to contribute to ongoing historical recovery projects by Black intellectuals of the time.

Afrofuturism later grew from a simple descriptive term into "both [an] aesthetic and [a mode of] critical thinking" (Lavender and Yaszek 2020: 4), and eventually rose to prominence in North America with the emergence of artists like science fiction authors Octavia Butler in the 1980s, and Nalo Hopkinson in the 1990s, and scholars like Alondra Nelson, Ytasha Womack, and Sheree Renee Thomas. It even expanded to encompass non-technology-driven imaginations, like those featuring mystic, spiritualist, and cosmological elements. Writers like Nisi Shawl believe this is necessary because "access to [the] scientific knowledge … has been denied to peoples of the African diaspora for much of history. And the classification of what is and not scientific knowledge … [is] frequently a matter of dispute" (Shawl 2018).

However, as more Black scholars and writers across the globe engaged with this term, it began to expand into a catch-all for all imaginative works created by Black artists or bearing sensibilities of the Black self, regardless of the geographical and identity loci of this "Black self." There is no greater embodiment of this than *Black Panther* (IMDb 2018), the titular comic-book hero based on an imagined African warrior-king of an imagined uncolonized African nation named Wakanda, which has grown powerful and technologically advanced by making the most of its rich resources. *Black Panther* was (and still is) meant to represent the power inherent in the independence and agency of the Black self and the Black nation. If decentered from the white gaze and from white supremacist pressures, the argument goes, and left to make the most of its own gifts and resources, the Black self will prosper.

Black Panther has been praised as a groundbreaking work of Afrofuturism— the globe-spanning cultural moment spawned by the 2018 film adaptation of the titular character, co-written by Ryan Coogler and Joe Robert Cole, and produced by Marvel Studios, is often pointed to as evidence of this. Black scholars and writers such as Jelani Cobb, an American journalism professor, have praised the film for giving Black people the world over the space to reimagine their own pasts and envision a future where not just their tongues, clothes, and technologies are decolonized, but their very beings are free of impressed colonial identities. "If the subordination of Africa had begun in the minds of white people," Cobb writes in *The New Yorker*, "its reclamation … would begin in the minds of black ones" (2018).

Buried within these accolades, however, is an unsavory truth: Wakanda and its warrior-king superhero were imagined and created by two white Americans in 1966—Stan Lee and Jack Kirby. Just like Afrofuturism as a descriptor was foisted upon artists of African heritage by the white gaze, the Black Panther and his Wakandan tale may center Africans, but remain productions of the white gaze. Therefore, at root, both Afrofuturism and its biggest global export, *Black Panther,* remain colonial projects.

For this reason, various Black artists and scholars have sought to distance themselves from the Afrofuturist label. This includes calls to do away with the label altogether because, as African-American author N. K. Jemisin puts it, there is no need to "segregate 'Africa' from 'futurism'" in the first place— futurism by Black and/or African artists is simply just futurism (Lavender and Yaszek 2020: 36). Others like Kenyan-Canadian author and journalist Minister Faust insist that, "We need a term of our own devising," and argues, in the same volume, that the term Afrofuturism, as it stands, offers no analytical value to the African self (Lavender and Yaszek 2020: 27–8).

Artists and scholars located on the African continent (or hailing from African countries), tend to agree. Ugandan-American professor Hope Wabuke and South-African author Mohale Mashigo have protested this ill-fitting expression and how it fails to capture the specific concerns of continental Africans. In an article titled "Afrofuturism, Africanfuturism, and the Language of Black Speculative Literature," published in the *Los Angeles Review of Books*, Wabuke wrote:

> "Dery's conception of Blackness … lacks room to conceive of Blackness outside of the Black American diaspora or a Blackness independent from any relationship to whiteness, erasing the long history of Blackness that existed before the centuries of violent oppression by whiteness."
>
> (2020)

Mashigo had similar concerns in her article in *The Johannesburg Review of Books*, where she states:

> "I believe Africans, living in Africa, need something entirely different from Afrofuturism. Our needs … are different from elsewhere on the globe; we actually live on this continent, as opposed to using it as a costume or a stage to play out our ideas."
>
> (2018)

No artist is more vocal about this discrepancy between continental and diasporic imaginations than Nigerian-American author and professor Nnedi Okorafor. Okorafor considered Afrofuturism so ill-fitting a descriptor that, in 2018, she coined a new term to describe her work as a diasporic African storyteller whose imaginations are driven by continental concerns.

Africanfuturism

In 2019, Okorafor published a manifesto of *Africanfuturism* on her website. "The term Afrofuturism had several definitions and some of the most prominent ones didn't describe what I was doing," she began. "I was being called this word [an Afrofuturist] whether I agreed or not … my work was therefore being read wrongly. I needed to regain control of how I was being defined" (Okorafor 2019).

Okorafor then goes on to define what sets Africanfuturism apart, positing that it

> is concerned with visions of the future, is interested in technology, leaves the earth, skews optimistic, is centered on and predominantly written by people of African descent (black people) and it is rooted first and foremost in Africa. It's less concerned with "what could have been" and more concerned with "what is and can/will be". It acknowledges, grapples with and carries "what has been.""

(2019)

Okorafor's main concern with Afrofuturism is the same raised by other scholars and artists: its uncomfortable orientation toward the West. To Okorafor, Africanfuturism's "default is non-western; its default/center is African." Despite this, though, Okorafor acknowledges that it is impossible to separate it completely from Afrofuturism or other similar descriptors. "Black [people] on the continent and in the Black Diaspora are all connected by blood, spirit, history and future," she says.

Africanfuturism, as a descriptor for stories centering the concerns of Africans on the continent, has begun to catch on. Scholars and artists of African speculative fiction have jumped at the opportunity to adopt this descriptor and carve out a niche for themselves. In 2020, Nigerian author Wole Talabi edited *Africanfuturism: An Anthology,* a collection of Africanfuturist stories featuring Nnedi Okorafor herself, as well as other contemporary African writers who have embraced this term, including Tendai Huchu, Dilman Dila, Tlotlo Tsamaase, Mazi Nwonwu, Rafeeat Aliyu, Mame Bougouma Diene, and Derek Lubangakene. This kind of embrace has especially grown since the formation of the African Speculative Fiction Society (ASFS 2020) in 2017, which has helped shuttle it into popular usage.

Alas, the divisive rather than inclusive approach of this term makes it an ill-fitting candidate for collectively discussing speculative stories centering Afrodescendant thought and selves. First, it relies heavily on a simplistic geographical locus of *continent versus diaspora*, which fails to encapsulate or reflect the complexity of geographical histories, connections, and identities of Afrodescendants. Secondly, it presents stories solely as projects of identity, rather than as passing through a complex formative pathway. The ancestry and/or nationality of an artist cannot be the singular determinant in defining their work—doing so reduces the work's complex engagement to a narrow dichotomy. Thirdly, in its attempt to decouple itself from Afrofuturism by employing geographical separation, Africanfuturism is forced to reckon with the concerns and thinking of the portion of the African population that has become African through means beyond traditional interpretations of origin and heritage. Employing a geographical locus raises questions about if such African voices may carry equal weight within this conversation. This is especially challenging when we consider the fraught histories of various non-Black settler populations in relation to indigenous Black African populations on the continent, including racist and segregationist concerns. Africanfuturism may de-privilege whiteness and the West, but how does it employ the same principles at home, is it capable of doing so, and should it do so at all?

These are the kinds of questions and complexities that drive my own research-creation, which exists in the spaces where these concerns overlap, especially between the cultural loci of geography/nationality, race/ethnicity, and other identity factors. It is within this work that I sought my own collective and inclusive term to describe stories that center and/or spring from Black and African speculative thought and selves, and how we may engage with them. In 2022, I settled upon *Afrocentric Futurisms*, the same expression now employed in and embodied by this collection.

The Case for "Afrocentric Futurisms"

It is undeniable that, to engage in artistic and scholarly study of speculative stories that center the Afrodescendant self, we require referential terminology. I began my search for such a term by first establishing my acceptance of the prefix *Afro-*, originating from the root word, *Āfer* (plural, *Āfrī*), the original classical Latin expression from which the contemporary terms used to describe Africa and its descendant peoples originates (*Oxford English Dictionary* 2023). The *Afro-* prefix, therefore, by any linguistic definition, denotes relation to the continent of Africa, including its descendants and their attendant concerns.

(This is not to be mistaken for the *Afro*, a non-prefix, which denotes a hairstyle produced by natural hair growth in Afrodescendant peoples.)

Based on our earlier analyses, it is agreed that the most desirable quality of an ideal umbrella term is a reference to its centering of the Afrodescendant self. "Centricity" here privileges the Afrodecendant gaze and concern. Putting that together with the "Afro-" prefix is how we land at the *Afrocentric* part of our proposed expression.

"Afrocentric" as a term of reference for the concerns of the Afrodescendant self is not a new term. American professor and philosopher Molefi Kete Asante began to use the expression as far back as 1988 in his seminal book, *Afrocentricity*, which attempted to situate the African-American self by first centering and situating the African roots within said self. Afrocentricity, as Asante defines it, is

> a frame of reference wherein phenomena are viewed from the perspective of the African person ... It centers on placing people of African origin in control of their lives and attitudes about the world.
>
> (1988: 2)

At its heart, this approach is much similar to the kind of argument authors and scholars like Okorafor, Wabuke, and Mashigo make about centering the African self in their own storytelling.

Critics of Afrocentricity as an epistemological theory have targeted its willingness to embrace the Afrodescendant self's roots on the African continent. Many have bound it with similar pre-existing and descendant expressions, especially *Afrocentrism*, a 1908s–90s school of thought that focused on extolling the Afrodescendant self by augmenting African history through a focus on its origins in ancient civilizations, and minimizing European input into the contemporary Afrodescendant self. (Levine 2008: 499–501). Patricia Hill Collins, a distinguished professor of sociology and one of such critics, maintains that through the 1970s and 1980s *Afrocentrism* focused on "African influences on African-American culture, consciousness, behavior, and social organization" (2009), a meaning which later shifted intellectually and politically in the 1990s after criticism from the US media and segments of higher education. Collins notes that "the main ideas of Afrocentrism, broadly defined, continue to have merit, but the term itself is too value laden to be useful" (2009: xii). Since then, other similar terms, including *Africentric* or *Africentrist*—a thought system and term employed by authors and scholars like Minister Faust (Lavender and Yaszek 2020: 31) to describe a continental-only focus and concern—have arisen, and have fallen to similar fates.

Like Collins, I believe that, despite the political and intellectual discord such a term generates, the concept of centering the Afrodescendant self, regardless of said self's geographical and identity loci, remains of value. It is in the very same broadness for which it is criticized that I find its appeal. As Kariamu Welsh writes in the foreword to Asante's book, "Afrocentricity leaves no one out" (1988: VII). This, I wholly, firmly, and truly believe. Employing this qualifier in good faith (i.e., with reference to the concepts of location, dislocation, and relocation inherent in adopting an Afrocentric consciousness within an increasingly global outlook) does not constitute a reduction of the term's worth, as Collins posits. Afrocentricity is not meant to be a catch-all for "speculative fiction written by Black people." Rather, "Afrocentric" as an umbrella term shines a spotlight on the specific concerns that plague Black and Afrodescendant selves and populations around the globe. It is most important that such umbrella terminology leaves room for drilling down to the specific loci within which we may analyze individual works contained, and "Afrocentric," as a qualifier, performs that role perfectly.

Now we turn to the choice of the term *Futurisms*, which is, first of all, a misnomer. My proposed iteration of futurism is one that decouples itself from Marinetti's and Dery's narrow colonial visions, and opens the term up to encompass all systems of Afrodescendant thought. This means that this *futurism* in this sense does not adhere singularly to Western ideas of scientific and technological furtherment, but opens it up to include cosmological, spiritual, and mystical elements. In the same vein, this *futurism* does not simply reference the chronological future, but engages with time and space as a conception of existence that is malleable and unbounded. This futurism posits that though these imaginations may exist in and/or be inspired by realist time that is chronologically in the past, present, or future, they do not have to reside in any of these times themselves. If anything, they may be considered timeless, engaging with both past, present, and future all at once.

The plurality of this term—*futurisms* rather than *futurism*—is also key. Accepting that there is no one way for the Afrodescendant self to imagine or re-imagine itself is important for this naming. As artists and scholars, we must understand that, though Afrodescendant populations share similar roots, their fruits will differ depending on their loci. A plural term mirrors the plurality of the Afrodescendant experience regardless of loci (and even within the same or similar loci). Therefore, any inclusive term worth its salt must make room for that diversity and complexity.

I therefore like to think of Afrocentric Futurisms as defined thus: imagined realities, alternate realities or alternative realities that center and privilege the Afrodescendant self. Its parameters, if we were to name them, would include:

- a decentering of the imperial/colonial gaze and a centering of the Afrodescendant self and its attendant concerns
- an investment in the timelessness and transspaciality inherent in Afrocentric storytelling forms, engaging location and spacetime without strict division
- a rejection of the dichotomy of science versus spiritual cosmology, embracing instead a cosmology-to-philosophy-to-science spectrum where speculation and imagination may exist within realms of science fiction, fantasy, fabulism, surrealism, etc. without strict division.

A cursory comparison of these parameters with the manifestos of the Afrodescendant-centered speculative storytelling terms and expressions we've previously mentioned and discussed (Afrofuturism, Africanfutirusm, Africanjujuism, Afrosurrealism, Afropantheology, etc.) demonstrates the Swiss Army knife nature of this proposed inclusive expression. Not only does it embrace the specific concerns of each pre-existing expression, its own parameters contain opportunities for the terms themselves to expand. Whether employed through the lens of storytelling form, approach to speculation, geography, and location, and other identity lenses—gender, spirituality, race, ethnicity, etc.—Afrocentric Futurisms is a truly inclusive expression that embraces all stakeholders without sacrificing the qualities that make each Afrocentric locus unique.

Afrocentric Futurist Consciousness in Action

The contributors to this volume have considered, carefully, the various terminology they employ for describing their own work and the work of others. The diversity of Afrocentric identities, thematic concerns, artistic and scholarly loci, and subjects of interest, is on full display in this volume, if nowhere else. Yet, all are bound together in their application of Afrocentric Futurisms as modes of thought.

Consider the shared fictional world of the *Sauútiverse* (officially the Sauúti Collective), a project created by various authors, artists, and purveyors of speculative art on the African continent and across its diasporas: Fabrice Guerrier, founder of production house-cum-publisher *Syllble*; Wole Talabi, the author and editor spearheading the collective; Ainehi Edoro, Founder and Editor-in-Chief of the online magazine *Brittle Paper*; and an array of artists all over the continent and the world, including a few who are contributors to this volume. Stephen Embleton, one such contributor to this volume, in his chapter "Cosmologies and Languages Building Africanfuturism," unpacks the Sauúti Collective's employment of various African languages and thought systems in its cosmologies and naming conventions. "The overarching aim was to create a secondary world (i.e., not of Earth and our own solar system) centered around African traditions, cultures and languages," Embleton says. "With around half of the collective leaning more towards 'past' and fantasy, the other half was interested in futures and science fiction worlds. African cosmologies gave us the ability to do both, without restrictions either way." This interpretation of non-linear time and employment of African-centered cosmological thought patterns of "timelessness" embodies the timelessness and transspaciality parameter of Afrocentric Futurisms as discussed above.

Though Embleton employs *Africanfuturism* in his chapter's title, his approach inadvertently embraces, as he puts it, the "vast array and differing worldviews" of the Afrodescendant self.

Eugen Bacon's chapter employs the expression *Afro-irreal* in an attempt to capture the eschewing of exactitude in her own works (specifically, short story collection *Chasing Whispers* and her novel *Mage of Fools*) and instead an investment in the outlandish-as-normal, in the reader being "okay with … that absurdity." The chapter insists on every authorial choice as an investment in establishing specificity, even though with an eye on eventual collectivity. Bacon drives home this point in her coda, stating: "It's less crucial to fiddle-fuddle with the chords and discordances of definitions … and more imperative to growing Afrocentric representation in the publishing industry that increasingly has a hungry readership ready to consume our kind of fiction that seeks to engage with difference."

Nuzo Onoh makes a similar case for the employment of African spiritualities in future stories of Africanfuturism, insisting that "Africa's ancient, pre-colonial spirituality has defined its people across continents and ages," and therefore deserves more representation in imagined future realities on the continent and in its diasporas, citing such manifestations in media (*Black Panther*) and literature (Octavia Butler's *Wild Seed*). "It is my opinion that African spirituality has never been completely lost despite the centuries of slavery and colonisation," Onoh states. "African spirituality is so rooted in African DNA that time, space and science are futile antagonists to its perpetuity." Yet again, both Onoh and Bacon engage in the consciousness of Afrocentric Futurisms by the very action of approaching these works through their specific critical lenses.

It may be said that every contributor to this volume continues in this pattern. Cheryl S. Ntumy's chapter discusses how faith and fantasy intertwine Afrodescendant speculative storytelling, and how she "borrowed heavily from this holistic worldview to develop a socio-spiritual system" within her novel series *Chronicles of the Countless Clans*, "where magic and mysticism are taken for granted." Tobi Ogundiran, similarly, discusses fabulist imaginings in his short story collection, *Jackal, Jackal*, centering his chapter on how he "weave(s) African (particularly Yoruba) folktakes with Western fairytales," while also interrogating "culture and cosmology centered on an imagined present or past."

Shingai Njeri Kagunda, in "Black Futurisms versus Systems of Domination," discusses mining for new language to express the nebulousness of her own Black-centered speculative storytelling, beginning with an embrace of a non-linear interpretation of time, and objective history, oral or written, as beholden to it. She posits, "any claim that a single narrative should and could be the dominant or sole valid narrative ... limits our ability to imagine other ways of being, not to mention our ability to empathize with experiences that fall outside of the dominant narrative." This gives way to her investment in Afrosurrealism in her own work (particularly in her award-winning debut novella *& This Is How to Stay Alive*), employing unbridled, Black-centered imagination as the first prong of a pitchfork of resistance against white-supremacist-helmed narratives of and about the Black body.

Other contributors have concerns that lean less metaphysical and engage more with socio-political concerns, while continuing to embody Afrocentric Futurist consciousness. Xan van Rooyen's chapter, for instance, brings narratives of queerness and queer-centeredness to the fore, drawing from historically documented narratives of gender and sexual fluidity on the African continent, and how they drew upon these histories to imagine, for their stories, an "Afrocentric futuristic world, Frayverse, a universe where abrasive and conflicting magics caused a rip between dimensions, allowing alien magic to bleed into the various interconnected worlds."

Aline-Mwezi Niyonsenga ponders "the future of one's cultural identity" in her chapter, peering through the lens of Afrofuturism to "function as a space for writers to explore the idea of cultural identity as a process of becoming." Stepping off Sofia Samatar's definition of Afrofuturism as "a philosophy of the remix," Niyonsenga goes on to "remix cultural references to Rwanda with a world of floating islands and a political climate similar to the Opium Wars" in her novelette *Fell Our Selves,* which "engages with themes of the return to one's roots, return home, and the possibility or impossibility of this."

Nerine Dorman's gaze at post-colonial themes in her work, "that re-envisions Africa," covers similar ground. She opens with a pertinent question, "What makes an African?" and attempts to acknowledge the multiplicity of

Africanness ("What my family's story teaches me is that my past is a tapestry … I have been birthed out of a cauldron of many stories and pasts") while interrogating what makes a piece of literature "recognizably African." Using examples from her work (short stories "Shame," "On the Other Side of the Sea," and "Arriving from Always"; novels *Sing Down the Stars* and *The Company of Birds*, etc.), she posits imagining the African self into realities "where diversity is the norm and is taken for granted, as it should be." With an eye on South Africa's history of apartheid, Dorman's chapter calls for imagined realities that center community, specifically those wherein its members embrace and acknowledge the historical actions that formed them, and envision new, reparative, and holistic ways to move forward.

Dilman Dila tackles democratic institutions in his chapter, dreaming up a model for "a country where things work, where every village has a high degree of self-sufficiency and every citizen has free and unlimited access to basic necessities of life … a true direct democracy where governance is by consensus, and it is communal." He announces that "I finally found a model for this world in the pre-colonial political systems of the Acholi," and unpacks the conceptualization of this imagined nation in his short story, "Yat Madit." "The world I dream about has grit and imperfections," Dilman finishes, "but it is a world of justice, where people govern themselves and share resources equitably, and power is not concentrated in the hands of a few."

Final Word

Now that we understand the origin and positionality of Afrocentric Futurisms, the discerning scholar may apply its active consciousness and open-armed framework—the privileging of the Afrodescendant self, an investment in timelessness, and an embrace of the spirituality-to-science spectrum—discover a connecting throughline between these works, and find an entry point into examining them. As the Afrodescendant self, in its various iterations across the world, finds new ways to define itself (and therefore shape its present and future), Afrocentric Futurisms offer a solid framework through which the

Afrodescendant self may perceive and seek their own imagined and alternate realities.

Employing this framework allows us push the boundaries of the known in order to access the unknown. For only within the unknown, can we find alternative ways of being ordinarily inaccessible within the confines of today's realities.

References

African Speculative Fiction Society (ASFS) (2020). [online] Available at <https://www.africansfs.com/> [Accessed August 24, 2023].

Asante, Molefi Kete (1988), *Afrocentricity (New Revised Edition)*, Trenton: Africa World Press, Inc.

Cobb, Jelani (2018), "'Black Panther' and the Invention of 'Africa'," *The New Yorker*. [online] Available at <https://newyorker.com/news/daily-comment/black-panther-and-the-invention-of-africa> [Accessed August 12, 2023].

Collins, Patricia (2009), *Black Feminist Thought: Knowledge, Consciousness, and the Politics of Empowerment*, Abingdon: Routledge.

Common Ground First Nations (2019), "Aboriginal, Indigenous or First Nations?," *CommonGround.org.au.* [online] Available at <https://www.commonground.org.au/learn/aboriginal-or-indigenous> Accessed via Internet Archive Wayback Machine <https://web.archive.org> [Accessed August 20, 2023].

Dery, Mark (1994), "Black to the Future: Interviews with Samuel R. Delany, Greg Tate, and Tricia Rose," in *Flame Wars: The Discourse of Cyberculture*, 179–222, Durham: Duke University Press. [online] Available at <https://doi-org.proxy.bib.uottawa.ca/10.1215/9780822396765-010> [Accessed August 12, 2023].

Dillon, Grace (2012), "Imagining Indigenous Futurisms," in *Walking the Clouds*, Tucson: The University of Arizona Press. [online] Available at <https://monoskop.org/images/0/0f/Dillon_Grace_L_ed_Walking_the_Clouds_An_Anthology_of_Indigenous_Science_Fiction_2012.pdf> [Accessed 12 August 2023].

IMDb (2018), *Black Panther*. [online] Available at <https://www.imdb.com/title/tt1825683> [Accessed August 12, 2023].

Lavender III, Isiah, and Lisa Yaszek (2020), *Literary Afrofuturism in the Twenty-First Century*, Columbus: Ohio State University Press.

Levine, Robert S. (2008), "Elegant Inconsistencies: Race, Nation, and Writing in Wilson Jeremiah Moses's *Afrotopia*," *American Literary History*, 20(3), 497–507.

Majali, Sulaïman (2016), "Toward Arabfuturism/s," *noveltymag.co.uk*. [online] Available at <https://noveltymag.co.uk/towards-arabfuturisms> [Accessed August 12, 2023].

Marinetti, Filippo (1909), *Manifesto of Futurism*, London: Sackville Gallery.

Mashigo, Mohale (2020), "Afrofuturism Is Not for Africans Living in Africa," *The Johannesburg Review of Books*. [online] Available at <https://johannesburgreviewofbooks.com/2018/10/01/afrofuturism-is-not-for-africans-living-in-africa-an-essay-by-mohale-mashigo-excerpted-from-her-new-collection-of-short-stories-intruders> [Accessed August 12, 2023].

Maurits, Peter J. (2019), "Futurism," in Paul Heike (ed.), *Critical Terms in Futures Studies*, 131–7, New York: Springer International Publishing.

Ngwena, Charles (2018), *What is Africanness? Contesting Nativism in Race, Culture and Sexualities*, Pretoria: Pretoria University Law Press.

Nwankwo, Chimalum Moses, and Louisa Uchum Egbunike (2021), "Speculative & Science Fiction: What is Past & Present … & What is Future?," in Chimalum Moses Nwankwo and Louisa Uchum Egbunike (eds.), *African Literature Today*, 1(39), 7–8.

Okorafor, Nnedi (2019), "Africanfuturism Defined," *Nnedi's Wahala Zone Blog*. [online] Available at <https://nnedi.blogspot.com/2019/10/africanfuturism-defined.html> [Accessed August 12, 2023].

Oxford English Dictionary (2023), "African, n. & adj., Etymology," Oxford: Oxford University Press. [online] Available at <https://doi.org/10.1093/OED/6867990429> [Accessed August 12, 2023].

Shawl, Nisi (2018), "A Crash Course in the History of Black Science Fiction," *NisiShawl.com*. [online] Available at <http://www.nisishawl.com/CCHBSF.html> [Accessed August 12, 2023].

Samatar, Sofia (2017), "Toward a Planetary History of Afrofuturism," *Research in African Literatures*, 48(4), 175–91.

Talabi, Wole (2020), *Africanfuturism: An Anthology*, Bristle Paper. [online] Available at <https://brittlepaper.com/2020/10/free-download-of-africanfuturism-an-anthology-stories-by-nnedi-okorafor-tl-huchu-dilman-dila-rafeeat-aliyu-tlotlo-tsamaase-mame-bougouma-diene-mazi-nwonwu-and-derek-lubangakene/> [Accessed August 12, 2023].

Wabuke, Hope (2020), "Afrofuturism, Africanfuturism, and the Language of Black Speculative Literature," *The Los Angeles Review of Books*. [online] Available at

<https://lareviewofbooks.org/article/afrofuturism-africanfuturism-and-the-language-of-black-speculative-literature/> [Accessed August 12, 2023].

Wijeratne, Yudhanjaya (2022), "The Ricepunk Manifesto," *Yudhanjaya.Notion.Site*, March. [online] Available at <https://yudhanjaya.notion.site/The-Ricepunk-Manifesto-b01fb0b12b8747e18467c3cbdd8edb89> [Accessed August 12, 2023].

Womack, Ytasha L. (2013), *Afrofuturism: The World of Black Sci-Fi and Fantasy Culture*, New York: Lawrence Hill Books.

2

Stephen Embleton: Cosmologies and Languages Building Africanfuturism, *South Africa/UK*

Bio

Stephen Embleton was born in KwaZulu-Natal, South Africa and is resident in Oxford, since being an Academic Visitor to the African Studies Centre, University of Oxford in 2022. His first short story was published in 2015 in *Imagine Africa 500* speculative fiction anthology, followed by the Beneath This Skin 2016 Edition of *Aké Review*, the debut edition of *Enkare Review* 2017 and more. He is a charter member of the African Speculative Fiction Society and its Nommo Awards initiative. His 2020 debut speculative fiction novel, *Soul Searching*, was shortlisted for the Nommo Award in 2021. His Young Adult (YA) fantasy novel, *Bones & Runes*, was a finalist in the 2021 James Currey Prize for African Literature, published in 2022. He was awarded the James Currey Fellowship, University of Oxford 2022. Stephen is editor of the 2023 edition of Flora Nwapa's posthumous final novel, *The Lake Goddess*, and is one of the eleven African writers in the Sauúti Collective shared-world.

In this chapter, I will talk about cosmologies and the use of languages in my novel Bones & Runes *(2022), and the world of Sauúti, a five-planet system in a world deeply rooted in African mythology, language, and culture, from a founding collective of African creators.*

Keywords: Africanfuturism, Folklore, Imagined Worlds, Linguistic Cosmologies, Sauúti

Creating Linguistic Cosmologies

You don't have to be Tolkien to create fictional languages, pantheons of gods, or cosmologies for fantasy worlds. But how people have told their stories, their histories, and, most importantly, their traditional beliefs through the ages—in the variety of ways—shows the depths of humans (condition/psyche) in developing their identities. Finding our place in the world coexists with the philosophical seeking and scientific evidence necessary to rationalize where we are in the inner and outer universe. This quest should be no different for fictional worlds.

It shouldn't only be left to the likes of Tolkien to create a cosmology for a fantasy world. You may not need the level of detail he and others have studiously dedicated (I cannot fault them for informing certain fascinating aspects of my own work, which I will later share here). But consider who your characters curse to, pray to, look up to the heavens to, and ask yourself this question: How will that change in 100 years, a millennia into the future?

Cosmologies are vital for any worldbuilding, as much as language, traditions, and histories, in telling stories set in specific times and places. Whether otherworldly, or real-world, belief systems are essential in plotting the past, present, and projecting forward into the future.

African writers have the unprecedented opportunity of creating worlds no one has ever seen before, representing existing languages or reforming new ones, incorporating the many writing and numerical systems from the continent, telling the stories of the array of gods and folk heroes comparable, if not wholly unique, on the world stage.

From my perspective, as an African, southern African cosmologies (along with the rest of the continent), myths, and folktales provide a wealth of insights into the storytelling, structure and oral traditions of the people. Language is therefore prime. For me, those worldviews play an integral part in anything I write, including my fictional, fantasy cultures—typically based on the people and cultures, and real-world systems (political, familial, and linguistic) around me.

My 2022 novel, *Bones & Runes*, specifically explores existing southern African mythology—from Zulu, Nguni, Namalaen, Hailom to the Hindu pantheon. I used the project as a means to investigate the structures, formats, and methods of African storytelling itself. By no means extensive, I looked across the continent at a variety of forms of oral traditions, their own hero/ine journeys in folklore and epics, and contrasted the portrayal of the very black-and-white Western trope of Good versus Evil.

In my view, there is no "good" or "evil"—a goddess can just as easily do something virtuous as wreak havoc. Much early research relegated certain deities and their deeds to the Christian devil, with little to no understanding of the cultural significance to the peoples concerned. For example, Èṣù—the deity in charge of law enforcement and orderliness in Yoruba cosmology—was described by the missionary bishop Samuel Ajayi Crowther, in an edition of his book *Vocabulary of the Yoruba Language*, as "devil; Satan" (1842 [1852]: 87).

My most recent project—an African-based shared world, the Sauúti Collective, spearheaded by award-winning author and editor Wole Talabi—looks to Africa for its worldbuilding. It offers an unprecedented opportunity for the ten writers (and expanding) to tap into our lived experiences from our lives in KwaZulu-Natal, Lagos, Ghana, Botswana, Tanzania, South Africa, and more.

African mythologies and beliefs, in their vast array and differing worldviews, have much to add to this project. The Afrocentric is something that many of us from the continent have been writing about for some time, but with little global visibility until recently, for example with the popularity of films like *Black Panther* (IMDb 2018). And, to a certain degree, I am speaking of the rise of African speculative fiction over the past two decades, but even more so those works from the past 100 years which have been overlooked, or require revisiting with fresh eyes on African fantasy and futurism.

In my research, and as part of my University of Oxford work, essay, and lectures, African literature—in its broad range of subject matter—is *all* encompassing and weaves traditional beliefs into stories and the societies they depict. Very few stories separate themselves from this cleavage to Mother Africa. Notably, forty-five of the first 101 works of the original African Writers Series, published by Heinemann and totalling 359 books between 1962 and the early 2000s, featuring the authors Chinua Achebe, Bessie Head, Wole Soyinka,

Ngũgĩ wa Thiong'o, Flora Nwapa, and more, are testament to this affinity with the continent. As examples, Achebe's use of folktales and proverbs; Head's application of magical realism, and elemental archetypes; and Soyinka's, wa Thiong'o's and Nwapa's traditional beliefs with the fantastical.

Recently, Nnedi Okorafor's coining of the words Africanfuturism and Africanjujuism has gone a long way in shining a light on the perspectives from the continent. If we don't create these Afrocentric frameworks, others less invested will do so, inaccurately.

I know more exciting discussions around this lively topic of Afrofuturism, Africanfuturism, Africanjujuism, cultural appropriation, and who is the best person to tell which story… are coming.

The Power of a Single Word

It all started for me with a single word featured in my 2020 speculative fiction novel, *Soul Searching* (2020a): Huriǁhao!nakhoena.

> Her thesis had focused on the world after the flood and in particular, the knowledge of southern Africa's autochthonous inhabitants, the Huriǁhao!nakhoena of legend. Everything pointed to the remains of a civilisation and their knowledge of the world before the inundation of the lands, passed on by the iHlengethwa, the ‡Gurubeb, to the peoples moving through the coastal domains of the south.
>
> (p. 218)

On a Monday morning in June 2020, at the height of COVID-19 lockdown in South Africa, I was researching African-based writing systems—both historical and modern—for my next novel, *Bones & Runes* (2022). *Soul Searching* (2020) was entering the final phase of its publication with edits and formatting, and there was a little uncertainty regarding the publishing landscape, but it was good to be motivated on the next novel.

Having studied typography and calligraphy for my thesis/dissertation in 1995, I have always had a passion for pictographs, alphabets, and lettering, from Cyrillic to Arabic script. Over the years I had researched many of the unique African forms, such as Geʿez (c.eigth–ninth century BCE), Nsibidi (from 400 to 1400 CE) frequently featured in Nnedi Okorafor's work, Tifinagh (third century BCE to the third century CE) descended from the Libyco-Berber script c.138 BCE, and many more. I came across a rather creative, functional, and unique writing system design referred to as isiBheqe soHlamvu or Ditema tsa Dinoko (Isibheqe 2023). This style of writing system's design—reminiscent of the iconic designs of the AmaNdebele, and drawing from the southern African region—offers a methodology and application that instantly caught my eye and interest. I immediately featured it in *Bones & Runes*.

I then reached out on the contact form on the isiBheqe soHlamvu website, to find out more, and to figure out how to interpret some of the concepts and phrases into the language for the novel. The next day I received an email from one of the creative minds behind it: Pule kaJanolintji. To say Pule is a linguist is an oversimplification—he is a creative philosopher and cosmologist (my description), and a viable person to collaborate with on things regarding culture, language, histories, and creative interpretations.

To this day, our conversations tend to begin academic and theoretical, but morph seamlessly into the creative and existential. The job of most writers and creators is to take mundane technical research and incorporate it creatively. You usually have to do that alone, and must assume a whole lot. Working with Pule is a productive collaboration. He has a naturally creative mind, making it a lot easier to brainstorm, have a back-and-forth with someone on the same wavelength and understanding of my objectives, while all in keeping with the "technical" nature of academic evidence and research.

Though my initial call with Pule started out about isiBheqe soHlamvu, an hour and twenty-two minutes later we had covered a dearth of topics centered around southern African cosmologies and traditions—everything I weaved into my work. Because *Soul Searching* was earmarked for final publication in August/September—two months later—I knew there were things I needed to reconsider. And one of them was small—one word, in fact, and it was not so small after all.

If ever I can reiterate the importance of language and linguistics in world building, and in creative works, it is in the single word Huriǁhao!nakhoena, which Pule and I came up with. In what would be a seemingly insignificant paragraph for a side character's backstory, I needed to come up with a name for a fictional lost civilization. A civilization which may have existed off the coast of southern Africa, eons ago, wiped out by the rising sea-levels after the last ice-age. After an initial long phone conversation with Pule, many WhatsApp conversations over days, finally after a week we had settled on the word or phrase: Huriǁhao!nakhoena.

Huriǁhao!nakhoena is both a word and a phrase—literally translated, it means "the people who built the settlements in the sea." To break it down:

- Huri (sea)
- ǁhao (shelter/settlement)
- !na (in/among)
- khoena (people/nation).

The work we put in, Pule's educating of me, and my clarity of the creative purpose and objectives, forever opened me up to the importance of the cosmology of a people, why and how they speak and believe the things they believe. This has created a fundamental shift in how I build my worlds in my writing—whether fictional or real-world people. Even more so with real-world people, it is imperative as a writer that I have some understanding of the people I am representing at a specific date and time. What has come before them? Why are they who they are at this moment?

Will this single word, Huriǁhao!nakhoena, have any impact on the average reader? Maybe not, but those from the region depicted, those who speak the language, will get it. To me that is significant.

Real-World Cosmologies—Folklore, Traditional Beliefs

In my Oxford lecture "There is Magic in African Literature," I speak about the importance of giving voice to African peoples, and approaching their cultures and traditions with respect:

> The AWS [African Writers Series] gave voice to writers on the Continent, in troubling times in the 1960s, through apartheid, and into the 90s. It gave those

writers a voice. It put those cultures on the map. It gave those cultures dignity. They were being written about by those people. And it was an opportunity for dispelling the notion of what the West perceived Africa to be. In that, from my perspective, traditional beliefs really came to the fore. Not just in nice cultural rites and rituals: it dispelled the myths of what those rituals might be. Words like superstition, witchcraft and black magic no longer had a place. That was how Africa and those cultures, rituals, belief systems, mythologies, folktales and oral traditions were perceived and portrayed by the West.

(2020b: 12)

I reiterate this in my keynote address titled "The African Writers Series and the Future of African Writing," also at Oxford:

In the broad theme of Traditional Beliefs, these were not just mentioning a culture's beliefs in day-to-day life, but actually going the step further and bringing the magic and fantasy into the narrative, like spells, spirit realms, afterlives; along with the speculative: alternate realities and fictional African countries. From my perspective as a science fiction and fantasy writer, these are all genres that are very much explicit, and not in the background of these 45 titles I picked out. They are weaved in and integral to the stories.

(14 February 2022)

I'd like to offer you two examples of my application of language and traditional beliefs in my fiction. The first is an excerpt that recites a premonition in isiZulu from the enigmatic water deity, Mamlambo, from my novel *Bones & Runes* (2022a). In traditional southern African folklore, Mamlambo is equivalent to, or similar to Mami Wata from other regions on the continent and beyond. While Mami Wata is usually depicted as a water spirit, Mamlambo is, in fact, the river herself. I use her words to serve as a forewarning that is translated, line-by-line later in the story, when her prediction becomes relevant to the other characters:

"What exactly was that poem Mamlambo recited?"
"*Kunengxabano.* There is a fight,' Mlilo added the translation."
"*Umhlobo uhlangana nomunye.* One friend meets another."
"*Abahlobo bayaxabana.* The friends are fighting."
"*Nabaphansi bona bayaxabana.* And the spirits below, they too are quarrelling."

"Abahlobo ababili bahlangana nomunye. Two friends meet another."
"Bese badelana bonke, omunye nomunye ahambe ngokwakhe,' he paused at
the thought and continued. 'Then they abandon each other, each one going
on their own."
"Ukuhamba wedwa ngukubona. To travel alone is to see."
"Omunye unikezwa umhwebo olingayo. Someone is given a tempting trade."
Uwela wedwa ukufika phesheya, omunye nomunye ngokwakhe. You cross
alone to that side, each one on their own.
Abahlobo ababili bahamba bayofuna umhlobo wabo. Two friends go to find
the third friend.
Abahlobo abathathu baphuma kude babonke. The three friends come from
a long way together. *Kube ukuthi babe munye.* Such that they became one.
"Bangene babonke empini. They entered all together into the war."

(p. 74)

In the second example, also in *Bones & Runes*, I apply inference. The
responses in English by one character to another's !Ora language infers
meaning to the reader without drowning them in translation or slowing down
the scene where character Dan represents the reader:

> "Last time I checked I don't speak !Orakobab, or ǀXam, or the
> Khoekhoegowab languages, bru." (p. 28)

And Mlilo sets about helping the reading:

> "I'll give you cues." (p. 28)

Haiseb proceeds to interrogate the two men:

> He looked back at the men. "ǀĀmas?'
> Mlilo nodded to Dan. "Mhm." Turning back to Haiseb he said, "The name
> of the boat is The Evening Reed Boat." He looked at Dan.
> "Uh, The Evening Reed Boat?" he said tentatively.
> Haiseb grunted his irritation and swung around towards the boat.
> "What did I say?"
> "Nothing," whispered Mlilo. "We have to watch this one. He wants us to
> slip up."
> "Hē !arib," Haiseb whispered, almost inaudible alongside the lapping
> waters, "Taeb ka?"

"This is The River of Hatred," said Mlilo, raising his voice to get the figure's attention, but rather causing Haiseb to slide up to Dan with his wide grin oozing a liquid stench.

"The R-River Hatred," repeated Dan taking a step back but not losing his grip.

(pp. 28–33)

And here we get to the most significant reason for this application of the !Ora language, and the need for inference. You may ask, *why is it important for a character like Haiseb to speak this language?* Because… cosmology! Haiseb is from southern African folklore. If he is the ancient being, creature or deity from lore, it would make sense that he would speak an older tongue from the region he emanates from—as one would imagine Odin or an ancient god speaking. It is therefore pertinent for Haiseb to speak !Ora. And certainly not Shakespearian English!

To give some context to the language, !Ora or !Orakobab was on the brink of dying out. It is the original language of Ngqosini people (!Ausin) and Cihoshe people (|Hõana). Not many speak it today but it is understood by many, much like English speakers understanding Shakespeare's English from 500 years ago.

Having lived in South Africa, in KwaZulu-Natal for 47 years, I am most excited to portray people with integrity, understanding the nuances of languages, belief systems. As a writer, even if you are bringing in your own fantasy—and in particular urban fantasy—you must infuse a degree of realism to it, in the real world. As Africans, we have multicultural influences from which to draw upon to create rich worlds.

I look forward to seeing many of the cultures which have not been widely or not at all represented, particularly in the science fiction and fantasy world, put on paper, on screen, by those who understand them and know them deep down.

Building Cosmologies for Imagined Worlds

As prefaced, cosmologies—belief systems—are essential in plotting the past, present, and projecting forward into the future. I apply this with Wole Talabi in "Our Mother, Creator: The Sauúti Creation Myth" for the Sauútiverse:

Our Mother stood alone in silence, radiant.
She was witness to nothing. Yet She knew of everything.
An eon passed, as if in a moment, and with an intake of cosmic breath, she
uttered the Word, releasing its power into existence.

(Embleton and Talabi 2023: 7)

It is my view that Africanfuturism and Africanjujuism are interlinked. If
anything, Africanjujuism—considered broadly to encompass real cosmologies
and traditional beliefs—comes first. Africanjujuism is a way of framing what
it is we take for granted and live with on a daily basis as reality rather than
fantasy. This might mean to speak with izangomas (shamans), to look at the
wider Zulu or Xhosa traditions, and then look to the western side of southern
Africa, to the |Xam, to the Namakhoen, in order to understand this kind of
jujuism. Africanjujuism is not something "other" we are making up; these
cosmologies have been around for centuries, millennia. Africanjujuism is a
lived experience that extends to the Caribbean, to Haiti, and to everything that
has gone out from the African continent to those regions through slave trade,
colonialism, and migrations. This transference is testament to the richness that
we, as Africans, have at our fingertips, our oral traditions that all come from
our cosmologies.

Africanfuturism has, or should have, roots in the magic of African cultures.
The one is not exclusive from the other—we can write both at the same time. The
Sauútiverse, an Afrocentric world by a collective of Africans, embodies this.

Understanding the Sauútiverse

Having worked, as most authors do, in isolation, the Sauúti project came
along with Wole Talabi's invitation. I was really interested, but daunted by
questioning how it would work with a diverse group from different parts of
the continent, now living in different parts of the world. Ten different life
experiences. Ten different world views. Ten different upbringings of varying
familial and cultural influences. Ten different languages and more!

Years on since inception of the Sauútiverse, I can now say it has been one of
the best experiences I have ever had—in terms of collaboration and support
… oh, and in worldbuilding. Those "ten differences" should have been an

indicator that we would have exciting dynamics to build upon and enrich our worlds, let alone expanding our own writing outside the collective.

The overarching aim was to create a secondary world (i.e., not of Earth and our own solar system) centered around African traditions, cultures, and languages. How we did this will forever form the basis for my future worldbuilding work, individually and collectively. One of the early discussions we had as a collective was regarding Time. With around half of the collective leaning more towards "past" and fantasy, the other half was interested in futures and science fiction worlds. African cosmologies gave us the ability to do both, without restrictions either way.

Hearkening back to the core aspects of African life, we knew oral traditions and chose sound to be our prime. Take spoken-word poetry—nothing but a single person speaking with conviction—and you will understand the power of performance, what sound does and how it goes beyond mere words and hearing sounds: it has a physical impact on your whole body. We chose the Sauútiverse to be a world of sound magic, sound as the cornerstone of the solar system. All life in this ecosystem emanates from sound—the Mother Sound—the creation sound. All beings, creatures, and people on the five planets within the twin-sun solar system, are finding or understanding their connection to that Mother Sound. Some find it through their ancestral roots, some through day-to-day living and more practical means of accessing it, others through journeys of self-discovery.

What is enthralling about the Sauútiverse is how it is based on our lived experiences as African writers, our own environments, our own languages, our own belief systems, our own namings, our own cultures. There is no singular influence which dominates this world, allowing for a truly collaborative creation.

A crucial thing that the Collective does is ease the lonesomeness of writers sitting in isolation: doing all the research by yourself—often research that is not necessarily what you want to be doing—and building your world by yourself. You have to put on various hats, now you're an engineer, now you're a quantum scientist, now you're a fashion designer, now you're a set dresser. Within the Sauúti Collective we wear different hats, carry different strengths, knowledge, and interests—our diversity allows everyone to pull together and build a massive universe in a matter of days, weeks, months.

I love to come to it as a linguist and a mythologist, thinking outside the box and with a wealth of histories to draw from, to root our worlds in a relatable reality. It is a clean slate, you can do anything, but it helps to look at those aspects of our own world, our own myth-building, our cosmologies to inform our fictional templates. In years prior, I had been researching myths that were not male-based, or male-centered. And, particularly in Northern parts of Africa, there are communities who centre themselves around a matriarch and goddess as the Creator goddess, for example the Ijaw people and their creator goddess Woyengi. I felt this was an interesting aspect to put to the group—as we threw around ideas and saw what people were connecting with. And the concept of a Mother Sound, the Mother Creator, really connected with the collective:

> The Word echoed outward, and She who had uttered the Word was witness to its power, as She beheld the creation of the heavens, stars, and a celestial body—the World—all from Her utterance. The World came from the Word. Our Mother became Creator. Our Mother, God.
>
> (Embleton and Talabi 2023: 7)

When discussing the creation of a universe—and by this I mean the very specific formation of stars and planets—you have those in the collective who are proficient in the science fact. They are the technical and analytical ones who can break down physics and give factual or sensible weight to everything we conceptualize on the fly. Then there are those artistic members of the group who take seriously but with a lot of playfulness other factors more in the creative vein—encouraging thinking outside the box—including the types of environments, landscapes or aspects of sound magic a writer would like to set a story in. We would then work backwards at times to explain, justify or sometimes leave it unexplainable for the purpose of a unique world, because there are, after all, many unexplainable phenomena in our own real world.

And while we are busy creating these "real" worlds, I envisage the cosmological, mythological point of view: how would one in this universe see the unfolding of their solar system in simple myth-building terms; how groups of early people develop their beliefs, when coming from a rudimentary state, attempting to explain the universe around them. The ancients didn't have the science, the telescopes, or evidence, and therefore associate certain aspects with elemental forces, cosmic events, or terrestrial phenomena.

Understanding the structure, language, and form of other creation myths, or epic poems, is fundamental to how the world forms in text. No one is reciting a scientific tome around the fire. They are reciting the drama, the characters and the wonder of a bygone time in the Sauútiverse.

As I neared the end of building the Creation Myth, working with Wole Talabi on the "real" timeline in space, the solar system and the planets, we associated each celestial body with a key god aspect or personality, as those elemental explanations from the ancient lost civilization within Sauúti. The number of times within our individual stories that each of us has mentioned or excerpted portions of the Creation Myth is a testament to the power of our worldbuilding as a collective, and the success of our Mother Sound origin:

"Our Mother Creator: The Sauúti Creation Myth" (Embleton, and Talabi 2023) and "The *Rakwa wa-Ya'yn*" ("The Song of Our Mother's Children") (Embleton, and Talabi 2023) in the Mahwé epic, where Mahwé is one of the five planets, exemplify the core essence of the Sauútiverse, and stand as the building blocks that everything comes from. In cosmological terms, charting the origins of our world helps us to individually and collectively understand the potential world view of our characters, the things that drive them, the beliefs they hold dear. And it sets the stage for all manner of possibilities for creating in a past or future world. At the same time, the Creation Myth is a broad origins story that must not be too prescriptive in that it hinders or limits an author's creativity later on. In a nutshell, as a Collective, we agreed that unless a concept serves a purpose in a story that impacts past and future stories in the Sauútiverse, it need not be embedded in the Sauúti Story Bible that's our reference guide.

Language, and Understanding the Five Planets in the Sauútiverse

Language, in this world and any other, can represent many things. To the Sauúti Collective, it formed the basis of an unknown prehistory, as well as a cultural phenomenon weaving through all parts of life in the world.

We did not want to use any one African language or dialect as our roadmap. Speaking with the linguist Pule kaJanolintji again, he gave us creative and practical insights into how we could develop an ancient, lost language. It did not have to be a fully developed language—it's been lost through time and circumstance—but we wanted something that permeated into the naming systems, locations, the planet names, the mythology, everything. Pule brought it all back to sound, "You've got sound, use that in your language, use the echoes, repeat words, repeat phrases."

We used this to our advantage and in the method of abstracting known words, and imagined words, away from any real-world root words or language. We are human, so we tend to work from the familiar—as we write and find naming, we take a word from our own languages or dialects, look at its meaning, and then play with its form.

Some African languages, particularly in West Africa, have implosives—where you're drawing in breath on a word—echoes, reduplication, reversal of words, all making for an exciting, creative layer to add. These were the tools and parameters we set up front, giving the Sauútiverse something unique in its sound building.

As examples of our experimentations with language and form, the key to the Sauúti world is the five-planet system which orbits a binary star. Beginning with our world, Sauúti—from the Swahili word "sauti" which means "voice" or "sound," and drawing out the "u" to create Sauúti, the Collective arrived at the following naming for our Afrocentric universe:

There are the two suns, Zuúv'ah and Juah-āju:

- *Zuuvah*—from the Shona word *zuva* meaning sun or day—drawn out pronunciation as emphasis on both the "Zuu" and "vah"
- *Juah-aju*—from the Swahili word *jua* meaning sun—spoken forwards and then split: ju-a/ a-ju.

There are five planets—each representing the theme of "song" from various African languages, and extrapolated and abstracted to varying degrees, to find unique and, at the same time, cohesive sounding names:

- *Zezépfeni*—from the Amharic word *zefeni* meaning song—using reduplication and emphasis on the second "ze"

- *Wiimb-ó*—from the Swahili word *wimbo* meaning song—a drawn out pronunciation with the emphasis on the "i," while the ó represents its Spirit Moon of legend
- *Órino-Rin*—from the Yoruba word *orin* meaning song—utilizing reduplication
- *Pinaa*—from the Setswana word *pina* meaning song—adding a drawn-out emphasis on the "aa"
- *Ekwukwe*—from the Igbo word *ukwe* meaning song or anthem—as the echo planet, u*kwe* is spoken backward then forward, but with an in-breath and then out-breath as the spoken form.

There is an uninhabited moon, Mahwé:

- *Mahwé*—from the Kirundi word "mawe" meaning mother—using a breathy "maah" and extrapolated with an extra "h," and an accent to distinguish it.

And regarding the sound magic of the world: at Aké Arts & Book Festival in Lagos, 2022, award-winning author Tendai Huchu pointed out that "having magic is all well and good"—you cannot just magically get your protagonist out of a bad situation. As a Collective, we took this into account and created reasonable parameters, where sound magic comes with its own set of restrictions, yet allowing us to push at those boundaries to see what we can and cannot do.

In Closing…

An African Proverb says it succinctly: "*If we stand tall it is because we stand on the shoulders of many ancestors.*"

As readers, we are humans who have made it this far because of our past, moulding our physical makeup, right down to our DNA and reflecting the outer world we build along the way. There are various aspects of our psyche which have developed over eons in a certain way. That is our story as a people on this planet. By looking to our own story and the building of our own world— its patterns of development and progress—and harnessing all that knowledge, we are able to tap into that storytelling as the archetypes of real or imagined worldbuilding. We all have a heartbeat. Musicians tap into that rhythm to connect with the listener. Our world is that heartbeat for the storytellers.

(Real) Worlds are built on a peoples' understanding of their environment, how they communicate among themselves, creating cohesive groups or conflicting groups, and surviving in that same environment. Where you position your story in both time and location, fiction or real, dictates many things: How people are speaking and socializing, their common day-to-day habits, and where they are technologically and politically. A character, historical or fictional, stepping off a ship in Cape Town harbour in 1980, will face experiences, technology and histories vastly different from someone in that same bay, known as ‖Hui!Gaeb, in a fictional age untouched by the arrival of any colonists.

Fictional worlds are no different. If these basic components are not considered, even if not featured explicitly in the narrative, then, like any society, reality (potentially) begins to fall apart. Sometimes a story will force a backstory on the writer; or an "out of date" word or out of place colloquialism can throw a reader out of the narrative. Other times a truism or proverb—a single sentence—can carry the weight of a history, real or imagined, of a people and their belief systems and traditions. The sparkling rainbow dust beneath your character's feet tell a story of those that came before, and what their future holds for them.

So here we are, creating the fables and folklore of our descendants.

References

Crowther, Samuel Ajayi (1852), *Vocabulary of the Yoruba Language*, London: Seeleys.

Embleton, Stephen (2020), *Soul Searching*, St. Andrews: Guardbridge Books.

Embleton, Stephen (2022a), *Bones & Runes*, London: Abibiman Publishing.

Embleton, Stephen (2022b), "There is Magic in African Literature," University of Oxford, African Studies Centre. [online] Available at <http://stephen.embleton.co.za/2022/02/there-is-magic-in-african-literature.html> [Accessed March 13, 2023].

Embleton, Stephen, and Wole Talabi (2023), *Mothersound: The Sauútiverse Anthology*, Eugene: Android Press.

Isibheqe (2023), "Ditema (Ditema tsa Dinoko/Isibheqe Sohlamvu)." [online] Available at <https://isibheqe.org.za/> [Accessed March 13, 2023].

IMDb (2018), *Black Panther*. [online] Available at <https://www.imdb.com/title/tt1825683/> [Accessed March 13, 2023].

3

Eugen Bacon: An Afrofuturistic Dystopia and the Afro-irreal, *Tanzania/Australia*

Bio

Eugen Bacon MA, MSc, PhD is an African Australian author of several novels and fiction collections. She's a British Fantasy Award winner, a Foreword Book of the Year silver award winner, a twice World Fantasy Award finalist, and a finalist in the British Science Fiction Association, Aurealis, Ditmar and Australian Shadow Awards. Eugen was announced in the honor list of the 2022 Otherwise Fellowships for "doing exciting work in gender and speculative fiction." *Danged Black Thing* by Transit Lounge Publishing made the Otherwise Award Honor List as a "sharp collection of Afro-Surrealist work," and was a 2024 Philip K. Dick Award finalist. Eugen's creative work has appeared worldwide, including in *Apex Magazine, Award Winning Australian Writing, Fantasy Magazine, Fantasy & Science Fiction*, and *Year's Best African Speculative Fiction*. Visit her website at eugenbacon.com.

In this chapter, I will talk about an Afrofuturistic dystopia and the Afro-irreal, with examples from my novel Mage of Fools *(2022), and collection of Black speculative short stories* Chasing Whispers *(2022).*

Keywords: Afrofuturism, Afro-Irreal, Afrosurrealism, Dystopia, Futurism

What's in a Name? Afrofuturism

it's too much so she stole her husband's
scissors—
as he huddled in her bed—
and snipped memories of belonging
thatched roofs that hum, the names of all those
people, a knock on a door to beg salt …
each snip is an altarpiece
a reminder of tragedy
from every eave

—"lost skin" (Bacon 2022c)

In the intrinsic African culture, a name means everything. You don't assign it randomly—you give thought to it. A name may tell you something about the clan, heritage, or protective animal spirit. If, for example, my name is Nyambuli, dichotomized into nya-mbuli, meaning "of" (nya) the "goat" (mbuli), then perhaps my people think I have a special affinity to the animal spirit of a goat. A name holds meaning, and knowing it is the beginning of knowing something intimate about the holder of the name. Where I come from, in the Swahili tradition, if I told you that my name is Kurwa, then you know that I am one of twins, and that I came out first, and my twin, Dotto, came second. If there is a Shija, then I am one of triplets, and Shija is the third born. If I tell you my name is Bahati—it means good luck in Swahili—then perhaps I was born to bring fortune, or at a time of fortune. In some traditional belief systems, a demon or spirit would withhold its name, because knowing the name gave you power over it—yes, a little like the Grimm brothers fairy tale "Rumpelstiltskin" (Project Gutenberg 2004).

And so this name, Afrofuturism, a borrowed name, is important—it matters what we call it, what we assign to it—and yet not. It is, after all, a borrowed name. There's much chord and discord on definitions surrounding what Afrofuturism is or isn't. Some writers are determined to avoid application of the word to their work, while others form closer alignment with other African-centered futurisms or Afrocentric terms such as Afropolitan—applied to diasporic African fiction written by authors like Chimamanda Ngozi Adichie and Nalo

Hopkinson; Ethno-gothic—coined by professor, author, and illustrator John Jennings to denote a subgenre of the fantastic depicting the black experience in the speculative arts; even Africanfuturism and Africanjujuism—Nnedi Okorafor's insistence on these terms to connect the works of black people on the continent and the diaspora by "blood, spirit, history and future" (Okorafor 2019; Edoro 2021).

I have written a few essays on Afrofuturism in my collection *An Earnest Blackness* (2022a), where I speak to my positioning on this complex debate. I share my experience from a WorldCon panel comprising Suyi Okungbowa, a renowned Nigerian author of fantasy, science fiction, and horror inspired by his West-African origins; Brandon O'Brien, a writer, performance poet, game designer, and then-editor of *Fiyah Magazine* from Trinidad and Tobago; Oghenechovwe Donald Ekpeki, a Hugo Award finalist and World Fantasy Award winning Nigerian writer:

> From the beginning, I was enthralled with what would become a hearty dialogue between my fellow panelists about the divergent views of Afrofuturism. Okungbowa did not believe what he wrote was Afrofuturism. He agreed that the term considered the possibilities existent in a person of African descent living anywhere in the future. But blackness, he said, exists in various ways across the globe and it's impossible to flatten into a single term; "Afrofuturism" is a projection of what blackness means today and what blackness might mean in the future. O'Brien suggested that acceptance or understanding of the term depended on one's relationship with the world. He found it problematic to attach a single word "given to us by a white man" to the diaspora. For him, Afrofuturism was a potential silo of black futuristic imagination, a way of seeing the value of known works, rather than a means of finding lesser-known works that may not thrive in a prefigured space or fit the lens that the publishing and film industries had already applied to the term. It would be interesting, he said, to see what the literary and cinematic elite planned to do with the term. Would they uplift or bludgeon the creative output of black people? Oghenechovwe saw limitations in the "us" (black people) within the "afro" where the reach of the term was not clearly defined or satisfactory, especially if it pertained to the broader diaspora and the exclusion of stories from within the African continent itself. He reminded the audience to be aware that there already existed lesser-known works by

writers and publishers like Milton Davis and Balogun Ojetade (who coined the term dieselfunk).

(pp. 53–4)

One way of interrogating Afrofuturism is to start by stating what it isn't.

Afrofuturism is not a white-people determination of what Afrocentric fiction is. Mark Dery—a white man—created the term in the 1990s, a term that is misconstrued because it's mostly applied to renowned writers with origins from Africa and the diaspora, who write stories that fall under the umbrella of what publishers and booksellers deem to be Afrofuturistic. In scope and context of Dery's introduction of the term in "Black to the Future: Interviews with Samuel R. Delany, Greg Tate, and Tricia Rose" (1994), Afrofuturism was historically relevant to the African-American experience and black people in the diaspora—which pertains to people whose ancestors migrated or were taken from the African continent, and includes anyone of African descent in Europe, North America, South America, Asia, the Antarctica, Australia, Oceania, and elsewhere.

Dery wrote: "The notion of Afrofuturism gives rise to a troubling antinomy: Can a community whose past has been deliberately rubbed out, and whose energies have subsequently been consumed by the search for legible traces of history, imagine possible futures? Furthermore, isn't the unreal estate of the future already owned by the technocrats, futurologists, streamliners, and set designers—white to man—who have engineered our collective fantasies?" (p. 180).

Whatever his lineage, Dery appeared to have a deep-rooted interest in Black people stories, and the power of futurism within and without the genre conventions of fiction. The term has since expanded to embrace art, literature, architecture, music, even style from within Africa and the diaspora, where Afrocentric creatives identify with it and some—like me—embrace it in association with our works.

Afrofuturism is not applying Africanism to any fiction by Googling African names (wa'Ng'ugi), hurling futuristic technology at it (wa'Ng'ugi and the Robot), and plonking the story somewhere on the African continent (wa'Ng'ugi and the Robot and the Witchdoctor of Lagos). Afrofuturistic stories call for diligent research, foresight, and understanding of the sociopolitical, and other slant of Africa—which is not a country. Deep-rooted knowledge or rigorous research will tell you that wa'Ng'ugi is not a communal name but is a unique reference that means "born of Ng'ugi," and it's a name specific to the Gikuyu people of East Africa, and they are a matriarchal society—you can't just apply that name to a patriarchal Lagosian and imagine that you've created something Afrofuturistic. Afrofuturism is not a story with a protagonist named Masai, in a story plot with some knowledge extracts from Wikipedia—the naming doesn't make it Afrocentric, and it's nothing to do with the fact that the protagonist is based in Atlanta, USA.

Afrofuturism need not be a term pertaining to the diaspora and not quite embracing people with lived experience in Africa, because that is simply a perception. I refuse to enter a spurious debate about where to posit my work (i.e. is it Afrofuturistic or some person's definition of an "other" futurism). If what I write is reimagining a future Africa, retelling her stories and those of her children, what does it matter that my work fits or doesn't fit someone else's definition of whichever-futurism?

I recall reading with righteous indignation the nonfiction book *Literary Afrofuturism in the Twenty-First Century* (Lavender III & Yaszek 2020), how I asked myself: where are the African writers? By this I meant the grassroot writers with lived experience, having been born on the continent and substantially lived there a long time, perhaps to adulthood. Looking at the selective representation in this critical discourse, I could see why other African writers might want to distance themselves from Afrofuturism, and perceive it as pertaining to the diaspora, because they are largely (still) not part of the conversation, as evident in this book published by Ohio State University Press.

Part I of the book's scholarly enquiry opens with an author roundtable on Afrofuturism, featuring Bill Campbell, Minister Faust, N. K. Jemisin, Nalo Hopkinson, Chinelo Onwualu, Nisi Shawl, and Nick Wood, in a smorgasbord of observation and thought surrounding recognition or unrecognition, acceptance or rejection, of the term "Afrofuturism," and its historical context. Sheree Renee Thomas generously speaks to "Dangerous Muses: Black Women Creating at the Forefront of Afrofuturism," where she highlights a renaissance of black female writers (for example, Nalo Hopkinson, Gloria Naylor, and Sofia Samatar) in a cultural hybridity of multi-voiced narratives, each empowering in its own right.

Part II of the book looks at the literary history of Afrofuturism, mostly from the African American (and some Afro Caribbean) context. Part III casts a gaze on Afrofuturism from a cultural prism, extending the conversation into Part IV that inevitably draws from the African roots and heritage that underpin the diverse perspectives of diasporic narratives. Broad in its coverage, there's a lingering sense of lacking in this volume—conspicuously missing is the inherent "African voice" of authors with a lived experience of Africa, and who intimately understand the continent and its traditions. Authors like Nuzo Onoh, Cheryl S. Ntumy, Dilman Dila, Tlotlo Tsamaase, Makene Onjerika, Shingai Njeri Kagunda, Wole Talabi, Ngũgĩ wa Thiong'o, and more, are glaringly absent. Yet they are intrinsic participants to this important conversation on the rise of Black speculative fiction that explores diversity and social (in)justice, that charts poignant stories with Black hero/ines who remake their worlds in a color zone of their own deep-rooted blood and bodily image.

What *Literary Afrofuturism in the Twenty-First Century* boldly achieves is to bring the Afro diaspora to life for new readers in a range of futurisms. It's a valuable book in critical thinking on stories that interrogate, muse on, and enliven culture, technology, and Black history, narratives that push genre boundaries and help resurrect "lost" or lesser-known artists while announcing new ones—mapping connections that increase the rise and visibility of new Pan-African literary speculative fiction.

There's more about Afrofuturism and its application in my novel *Mage of Fools* later in this chapter.

On the Afro-irreal

she walks with a gap across a city choked in smoke   each day disrupted as cynics protest pundits joke   theories fly about the cavernous hole in her torso   why tar-shined ravens and death-watch beetles soar through it   no one offers a mist blanket so she can fold her wings at midnight   she looks at herself mutters a prayer or a dream of rings
gives anyone who looks   an opus of her hollow

—"a mist blanket." (Bacon 2021a: 27)

What exactly is irreal fiction? That there already is a catch, as irreality promises no exactitude. One publisher of such fiction, The Café Irreal, describes it as "simply a story or piece of art where something non-realistic happens" (Evans 2008). As fantastical literature that demands the reader to trust and find immersion in the story's "impossibility," the irreal story stays unpredictable and believable in all its unbelievability. It's a viable story that "flows out of this absurdity" (Evans 2008) where there may be no motive in the protagonist for their action. It's almost a dreamlike sequence in a type of fiction that may be an allegory for somber themes in the real world. The reader finds immersion in the illusion, entranced in the satire or symbolism, cementing even while challenging realism. The irreal fiction writer is a "kind of illusionist," eliciting from the reader trust, even as solid brick walls bend, swirl, and soar. The reader of this kind of fiction has no "familiar mooring in the possible, or the conventionally (and ultimately unexplainable) impossible." They are alone, standing there, staring at, touching, even tasting the absurd in all its intensity. And they might be okay with it, that absurdity—as in my story "A Deep and Terrible Sadness, published in *Chasing Whispers* (2022b)":

> YOU'RE A TRAVELLER of the past, present, future. You arrive without land, without name. You have no mission, no affection. Yours is a goading that bares humanity's uncertainties, the kind of fear that breaks mirrors lined on walls. Your mercy is a blanking. The irreal.
>
> (p. 113)

In adopting the "you-narrative," in second person, this short story is already attempting to tease out fact versus fiction, employing metalepsis (figurative substitution) to disorient or reorient the reader's "frame of expectation" (Fludernik 2011: 101). The text encourages a writerly/readerly relationship that is not divorced but prosperous, a coexistence between the two roles and further hurling the reader into an abstractness already inherent in the story title:

> Deep is here, and here, and here again. An ocean without lines or axes to parallel dimensions. It's impossible to read how high or low the tide. Is it intertidal or littoral? And where in fog's sake is the continental shelf?
>
> Terrible is existential, an abyssal plane where it's relatively flat. You always have it, seek it, mind it, miss it. You are homeless from yourself, an inventory of ambitions you cannot replicate.

Sadness is irrational. It's a trench that shows no gate, just frozen lakes in a topography of salt, kilos and kilos of it. What use is excess saltiness if you're not marine?

There are no coordinates—you've known this all your life. It's a love of intricacies, a dislove of maps stitched like basilisks and manticores in monotone. Contours blur your eyes. But calligraphies pitch narratives of the past, present, future pregnant with the irreal.

Your location is terrible years old.

Your skin peels with sadness.

And no one you know is deep.

(pp. 115–16)

In his introduction to *Chasing Whispers*, author, editor, scholar, and publisher D. Harlan Wilson (2022) illuminates, in his words, what irrealism is:

Irrealism is a thing in itself, but it's also a methodology wherein authors might express themselves and explore motifs intimate to their purview and personal history. Kafka is the touchstone—the epitome of the form, as I see it. His variety of irreal fiction thematized the absurdity of bureaucracy and portrayed the many ways in which he felt trapped by institutional antagonists (ranging from his father and family to his job, the Culture Industry, and even his body). Bacon's variety is an exploration of her experience as a black woman in a volatile, often menacing world whose default stance is objectification, racism, misogyny, patriarchy, heteronormativity ...

(p. 10)

My short story collection *Chasing Whispers* casts a gaze at mostly women and children haunted by patriarchy, in stories packed with affection, dread, anguish, and hope. The connecting theme is a Black protagonist with a deep longing for someone, someplace, something ... and a recurring phrase in each story: "a deep and terrible sadness." The titular story "Chasing Whispers" opens the collection and immediately hurls the reader into the irreal of a personified house:

TODAY the house wore Zeda. She felt stretched. Necks and elbows tucked into her shawl. Fridges too. She was suffocating, and the house's monsters were responsible. Protrusions everywhere: belly buttons, kneecaps, pots, toilets. At her worst point she was a blindfold, an ill-fitting ski mask over the patio. That was before she turned into a clown costume full of circus in the garage. Worse: the house was shedding sawdust and it stank—no deodorant could fix it. Vacuuming was useless. It was as if the house was spiteful about something. She tried to cheer it up, smiled and twisted so it could fit better inside her shape. But the house grew more necks and corners. Bones, teeth and microwaves into her leotard. She knew it wasn't the house. It was him. Pepo.

(2022b: 13)

Pepo in Swahili means a haunting spirit. The story's protagonist, Zeda, has an infestation—she met Pepo online, now she's uncertain what's real or unreal, even as she recollects in a you-narrative, an omniscient narrator guiding the remembrance, of their meeting through online dating:

Touch is an open window and a door ajar. It's a familiar mall, the face of the future. Touch is fire, water, earth and air. It's a garden full of reflections and dreams. It's an archetype or a metaphor, or alchemy. It reminds you of a river or a beach, rain or sunshine. Touch is right here—you've arrived. The press of fingers tells you everything. Everything. And it's simultaneous, marvellous and not enough. You think of it again and again, ask what more you want and you cannot say. You don't linger on it because you're not crazy. Because touch may be an esplanade, but it's not insurance. She remembers his online profile: EpsomSalts.

(pp. 13–14)

Before the reader can settle, more blackness and the irreal appears in the second story "Memories of the Old Sun," where Mazu, a black queer man, is trying to shake off his mother's insistence on his marriage, while at the same time he's contemplating existential questions arising from his observations of the sentient AI, Jazz, that he has created, and sie's internalizing and questioning hir life and its meaning:

Jazz knows sie's a variable. Sie has an inbuilt scrapbook filled with memories, sometimes rushing, often rusting. They twirl inside hir head. File cards full of deserts and hungriness clipped away from hir heart. They are from names in a grammar sie doesn't remember, childhood friends or secrets: Bug, Dyn, Cyclone, Bash, Allon, Prim, Krema …

(p. 24)

Jazz's memories come and go, sie has longing for more, sie wants to be more:

> Sie remembers days of life and death when fate snatched sie away and sealed hir sorrow to an exact point. Days that were mistrials drowned in desire, studded with intersections where babies cried in syntax, never in melody, and lights pulsed but never turned red.
>
> (p. 25)

There's both a strangeness and familiarity with the text, with the characters in what Wilson explains: "The stories in this collection felt like they belonged in my head even as they escaped me. I remember texting the editor and saying: 'I like this book! It reminds me of … me?'" (2022: 7).

The Afro in my stories is in the Afrocentric protagonists like the queer man Mazu (his name a derivative of the word "mazuba," which means "sunshine" or "my love" in some African dialects), who is from Konakri and must now thwart off his mae (it means "mother" in some Bantu languages) in her efforts to find him a woman. Mae says: "The girls here are budding. I'll negotiate a wife with a good stomach. It shows in the clan—the ones who can make babies" (p. 23).

Now living overseas, Mazu misses the splendour of an African vista darker than tar, the starry nights and bush calls of the savanna, the moon's gaze on the regal height of baobab trees (p. 34).

Dabbling across genres, the stories in *Chasing Whispers* don't tell but show irrealism, sometimes in dreamlike sequences, conscious and subconscious episodes with potential to alienate or entrance the reader. The surrealism has firmer connection to reality than the reader might imagine, accomplishing much through less is more, and trusting the readers' intelligence to form their own conclusions, as Wilson did:

> At the same time, Bacon's voice is unique—these stories have something new and different to say, and they're deeply informed by her life as an African Australian outsider who has, among other things, clearly endured the entitled assholery of Little Men. The violence, suffering, and anguish that marks the history of civilization is an invariable product of this assholery, and Bacon illustrates it with as much beauty as truth. In so doing, she enacts

the title of this introduction, moving us towards an Afro-Irreality that calls attention to the haunted houses of the past, signals a better future, and accomplishes the increasingly rare feat of Making It New.

(pp. 10–11)

Dystopian Futurisms

there's an album full of digital pumpkins
balanced on pillared photographs
in past present dark rooms
reeled with future matter
loaded in night-time language
developed on monochrome clairvoyance
and a phosphorescence of leaders
who can't heliograph a quality fade
so they're not so great after all

—"Portable Longing" (Bacon 2022f: 168)

Dystopia is a subgenre of science fiction, and it is the antonym of utopia. A dystopian narrative feeds speculation on largely pessimistic narratives, potentially technologically or futuristically influenced, with adverse effects on the inhabitants of the dystopian world, whereas utopia dwells on fiction with "ideal" societies, but the idealism is potentially flawed and only benefiting a few rather than the majority—as in Ursula Le Guin's novel *The Dispossessed* (1974).

My dystopian novel, *Mage of Fools* (2022d) that's also Afrofuturistic, is set in a socialist country plagued by climate change. In the dystopian world of Mafinga, our protagonist Jasmin must contend with a dictator's sorcerer to cleanse the socialist state of its deadly pollution.

When I set out to write this story, I wanted it to be a novel with an urgent call to climate action, a strong female protagonist in a story of resilience, and locale to be in a made-up African country. It imagines a future Africa in the worst throes of climate collapse, culminating in a desolate world of oppressed people, where only few people benefit from "ujamaa"—African socialism.

Tanzania (the amalgamation of what was mainland Tanganyika and Zanzibar island) first gained independence in December 1961 from Britain, and became a British mandate after the First World War from the Germans (AAREG 1961). During the First World War, Britain captured the German holdings of German East Africa (Britannica 2022), that included present-day Rwanda, Burundi, mainland Tanganyika, and a part of Mozambique. Tanzania adopted ujamaa, a systemic approach to community and togetherness, an ideology theoretically sound but with potential for misuse.

Ujamaa in its purest form is the transcendence of equality, but protagonist Jasmin and her compatriots quickly learn that everyone is not equal—others are more equal than others. The story is imbued with ujamaa propaganda:

> "Together we are. Mafinga is equal, her people are free. We're good for each other, and we'll work as a unit to eradicate poverty. Individuality is barbaric, so we'll live together. The size of every person's effort will be the measure of the fullness of their stomach. I declare Ujamaa—together we are."
> (*King Magu's broadcast speech to the people of Mafinga*)
>
> (p. 18)

~

> A screen overhead replayed the king's monotone speech: "We will act swiftly and resolutely to eradicate revolutionaries who seek to pervade Mafinga with the poison of individualistic thinking. Our duty is to contribute to the whole, not to diminish it with selfish thought."
>
> (p. 22)

~

> "I thank the people of Mafinga—you're free from the burdens of individuality. Selfishness is toxic. The consensus of community demands that … "
>
> (p. 45)

But the citizens of Mafinga are not free. They live in tiny, controlled spaces, are forced into labor, and have no say in the indoctrination of their children:

> Jasmin watches as Omar navigates the space between the unpartitioned living area with its metal-like seats and spartan table, its kitchenette with

An Afrofuturistic Dystopia　　　　53

a tiny chiller and microwave, its multipurpose sink, the sleeping area with its floored mattress, its toilet—only a curtain for privacy. One wall is fitted with an automated screen that turns itself on, off at central command. You don't flick channels to choose the news, sports, documentaries, music or entertainment. Pzzz. Pzzz. The screen comes on at a whim with the propaganda of the moment: sometimes it's a choir of children in flowing pinafores and jester pantaloons singing slogans. Or the same children in sisal skirts and war paint doing a folk dance, chanting the Hau, Hau, Acha We song about decrying dissenters. Pzzz. Pzzz. The screen goes silent as it does now, momentarily asleep.

All units in Ujamaa Village are the same. They are metallic khaki in color. Everyone's within a kick, right there, next door. But you never hear anything—except the outside. And, mostly, as just then, the outside world brings the sound of dying.

Once a week you get a pass to use the Ujamaa Facility. It used to have gendered showers: hot sizzles and soap dispensers, a luxury despite the blandness of their products. But there are no more men in the village. Now the sizzler showers and their weekly extravagance are for everyone. There's no place for modesty.

Whoop. Whoop. The work siren goes.

(p. 10)

As doors open and doors close, the citizens of Mafinga must respond in unison to a siren, in an inverse world where night is day, people must sleep with the deadly sun is out, and night-time is for labour:

They file out, headed to labor in Central District. Preallocated duties at Ujamaa Factory, Ujamaa Tech, Ujamaa Medico, Ujamaa Yaya and many other Ujamaas await them. The lucky ones, specially favored for an aptitude toward loyalty to the king, serve as guards and supervisors, and return home to snug two-roomers. The skilled ones, Solo and her mates, are also lucky. They live and work in the king's mines—away from guards and supervisors, away from fear and indignity of day-by-day oppression. The skilled ones are entrusted with drilling mafinite, a gem equal in value to a diamond. But even they are not exempt from a major trait of the king's paranoia: freedom. They are bound by location and need special permits to leave the mines.

When did it come to this? wonders Jasmin as she and the children exit the room.

They join the sea of bodies, a human march at night-break. Only a fool would leave shelter by day. But you had to see who died, how they died, in the sick bays of Ujamaa Medico to know it wasn't a good idea to brave daylight.

(p. 12)

Paying attention to strength in the power of woman, characters in *Mage of Fools* (Bacon 2022d) look after each other and trust their elders like Mama Gambo—who has seen much in this militant world with its armed guards and supervisors with batons. When Jasmin discovers a truth about the "vitamin" supplements, how they are inhibiting and make people forget, Mama Gambo cautions her on who to tell:

Jasmin wonders whether she should share her knowledge with the women at the factory. But Mama Gambo's words last night when Jasmin asked about it reverberate in her head:

"It's foolishness to speak it to anyone."

"But why?" asked Jasmin.

"The heart of the wise woman lies quiet."

"But words may be the only foolishness we can afford," said Jasmin. "Shouldn't we look out for each other? You know as well as I do that the system doesn't care an inch about us."

Mama Gambo touched her arm. "Will you fight when you're carrying a basket full of eggs?" She nodded at Mia and Omar. "These children are your eggs. Never compromise them."

"It just appears that you've forgotten we have no husbands, Mama Gambo. We're all relatives of each other. There are workers in the factory—the Mama Apiyos and the Violets—who are close as family. And without family I am poor."

"Yes, we have no husbands. Atari thought that killing my husband was burying a library. But don't you see? He only released the text. Now it is many, and we must be wise with it."

"I didn't mean it that way … Baba Gambo … "

Mama Gambo shook her head firmly. "You can't unwind your words. If your only tool is a hammer, you'll treat everything as a nail. Much is wasted on useless words. All I am saying is the night has ears." She nodded at Omar, pretending not to listen, at Mia, purring in her sleep. "For them, remember. Always for them. They are our legacy."

"Is there anyone I can trust?"

"In Mafinga? No."

"Not even you?"

"Especially me."

It was then that Jasmin understood. She suddenly knew how Mama Gambo did it, how she woke up night by night, took other people's children despite her own pain. Hers was an inside bellow. And the cow that bellows does so for all the cows.

Baba Gambo's death was not in vain.

(pp. 50–1)

The Afro in my novel is in the Afrocentric characters like our protagonist Jasmin, and her children Mia (two years old, with twin cornrows that end in pigtails) and Omar (four years old, with a burst of curls on his head, pale chocolate skin soft like a baby's). Jasmin tells her children stories, keeping alive the power of literature handed across generations orally.

The Afrofuturistic dystopian world of *Mage of Fools* is a warning of how societies that benefit a few can go direly wrong, and how terrible things can get if we don't take climate action seriously. In a form of subversive activism, speculative fiction—including utopian and dystopian fiction—empowers a different kind of writing with a unique worldbuilding that can be a powerful conversation in itself, including in genre fiction. As I wrote in my prefatory essay, "Trends in Black Speculative Fiction" in *Fafnir—Nordic Journal of Science Fiction and Fantasy Research*:

> ... black speculative fiction continues to rise as a powerful conversation in genre fiction, and increasingly tackles precolonial, colonial, and postcolonial themes pertaining to identity and culture, as well as feminist and queer themes pertaining to engaging with difference.
>
> (2021b: 8)

Writers from Africa and the diaspora can leverage on this cautionary element of dystopian fiction and the ominous nature of its acumen to reinvent futuristic worlds that pay attention to current and extrapolated issues surrounding Mother Africa and her children globally.

Coda

Once upon a time guilt was a day when reason got nothing done and the silver sun refused to gleam. Dusk fell with the fervour of a night runner who launched at you with juju smelted in your dreams and transgressions without which you could have saved one person—yourself or Mother Africa. Your follies were precisely:

> *no comment*
> *an ineptitude for parables*
> *inexistence on the fence*
> *and maddening the hell*
> *out of poor people.*

—"mea culpa" (Bacon 2022e: 169)

In closing, it's less crucial to fiddle-fuddle with the chords and discordances of definitions (is it or is it not Afrofuturism?) and more imperative to grow Afrocentric representation in the publishing industry that increasingly has a hungry readership ready to consume our kind of fiction that seeks to engage with difference. It is vital that we do earnest research (not just from Wikipedia) to understand those things that are intrinsically African, so we can create convincing Afrocentric narratives. In my view, if Afrofuturism is to reimagine Africa in all its diversity, to expand and extrapolate it through literature, music, the visual arts, religion, even philosophy, anyhow that haunts imagination and transmutes a craving for revolution… how is this limiting?

Writers from Africa and the diaspora continue to interrogate and position the self and identity through story. Through text, we can replenish the skins of belonging, color in vivid hues what climate action/inaction might look like, endorse the profound role of girls and women in society, reconnect with our decolonized roots. In Afrocentric fiction, we can enact and perhaps realize the new dreams and destinies of Mother Africa.

As I stated in my collection of essays *An Earnest Blackness*:

There are many avenues of black-people narratives about social movement, technology, artistic expression, critical embodiment, and postmodernism that are bound to the marriage of "afro" and "futurism."

We can write about Africa, see it in a new light, tell stories of diversity and hope, stories of social justice, possibilities, probabilities, engaging with difference, dealing with the "other," hybridity, queering, origin tales about finding out who you are …

We can fight for freedom from discernible and concealed chains in different kinds of Afrofuturistic writings, as Octavia Butler did so effectively in her works on the black experience.

It's ultimately up to black writers to determine the semantics of Afrofuturism. The stories we tell will represent that determination. There's wealth in the diversity of our voices—we can sway power dynamics, illuminate hidden histories, give voice to those who cannot speak from the margins.

(2022a: 58)

As people of color with intrinsic heritage from the continent, we can increasingly leverage the inherent supremacy of storytelling, the richness of our traditions and the intensity of our African "soul" to contemplate somber or confronting themes and fundamental philosophical questions that insist, through Afrocentric fiction, on different future outcomes for Mother Africa and her peoples. I locate affinity with all Black-people stories that continue to write me in, and I can see myself in their protagonists and their quests towards truth or belonging, Afrofuturistic or otherwise.

References

AAREG (1961), "Tanzania Gains Independence from Britain." [online] Available at <https://aaregistry.org/story/tanzania-gains-independance-from-britain/> [Accessed December 31, 2022].

Britannica (2022), "Tanganyika: Historical State, Tanzania." [online] Available at <https://www.britannica.com/place/Tanganyika> [Accessed July 1, 2023].

Bacon, Eugen (2021a), "a mist blanket," in *Saving Shadows*, Alconbury Weston: NewCon Press, p. 27.

Bacon, Eugen (2021b), "Trends in Black Speculative Fiction," *Fafnir—Nordic Journal of Science Fiction and Fantasy Research*, 8(2), 7–13. [online] Available at <http://journal.finfar.org/articles/trends-in-black-speculative-fiction> [Accessed March 18, 2023].

Bacon, Eugen (2022a), *An Earnest Blackness*, Ohio: Anti-Oedipus Press.

Bacon, Eugen (2022b), *Chasing Whispers*, Ohio: Raw Dog Screaming Press.

Bacon, Eugen (2022c), "lost skin," in *Live Encounters*. [online] Available at <https://liveencounters.net/2022/10/28/live-encounters-poetry-writing-volume-four-nov-dec-2022/> [Accessed August 15, 2023].

Bacon, Eugen (2022d), *Mage of Fools*, Atlanta: Meerkat Press.

Bacon, Eugen (2022e), "mea culpa," in *African Literature Today 40: African Literature Comes of Age*, New York: James Currey.

Bacon, Eugen (2022f), "Portable Longing," in *African Literature Today 40: African Literature Comes of Age*, New York: James Currey.

Dery, Mark (1994), "Black to the Future: Interviews with Samuel R. Delany, Greg Tate, and Tricia Rose," in *Flame Wars: The Discourse of Cyberculture*, 179–222, Durham: Duke University Press. [online] Available at <https://doi-org.proxy.bib.uottawa.ca/10.1215/9780822396765-010> [Accessed August 12, 2023].

Edoro, Ainehi (2021), "What is Africanjujuism?," *Brittle Paper*. [online] Available at <https://brittlepaper.com/2021/07/what-is-africanjujuism/> [Accessed December 31, 2022].

Evans, G. S. (2008), "What is Irrealism?," *The Café Irreal*. [online] Available at <http://cafeirreal.alicewhittenburg.com/what_is_irr.htm> [Accessed December 31, 2022].

Fludernik, Monika (2011), "The Category of 'Person' in Fiction: You and We Narrative-multiplicity and Indeterminancy of Reference," in G. Olson (ed.), *Current Trends In Narratology*, 101–41, New York: De Gruyter.

Lavender III, Isiah, and Lisa Yaszek (2020), *Literary Afrofuturism in the Twenty-First Century*, Columbus: Ohio State University Press.

Le Guin, Ursula K. (1994), *The Dispossessed*, New York: Harper Voyager.

Okorafor, Nnedi (2019), "Africanfuturism Defined," *Nnedi Wahala's Zone*. [online] Available at <https://nnedi.blogspot.com/2019/10/africanfuturism-defined.html> [Accessed December 31, 2022].

Project Gutenberg (2004), "Rumpelstiltskin by Jacob Grimm and Wilhelm Grimm." [online] Available at <https://www.gutenberg.org/ebooks/12708> [Accessed August 17, 2023].

Wilson, D. Harlan (2022), "Towards an Afro-Irreality," in *Chasing Whispers*, 7–11, Maryland: Raw Dog Screaming Press.

4

Nuzo Onoh: The Power of African Spirituality in Africanfuturism, *Nigeria/UK*

Bio

Nuzo Onoh is a Nigerian-British writer of speculative fiction. She is a pioneer of the African horror literary subgenre. Hailed as the "Queen of African Horror," Nuzo's writing showcases both the beautiful and horrific in the African culture within fictitious narratives. Nuzo's works have featured in numerous magazines and anthologies. She has given talks and lectures about African Horror, including at the prestigious Miskatonic Institute of Horror Studies, London. Her works have also appeared in academic and feminist studies such as *Routledge Handbook of African Literature,* among others. Nuzo is the recipient of the 2022 Bram Stoker Lifetime Achievement Award.

Nuzo holds a Law degree and Master's Degree in Writing, both from Warwick University, England. She is a certified Civil Funeral Celebrant, licensed to conduct non-religious burial services. An avid musician, Nuzo plays the guitar and piano, and holds an NVQ in Digital Music Production. She lives in the West Midlands, United Kingdom.

In this chapter, I will talk about the power of African Spirituality in Africanfuturism, with examples from my novel A Dance for the Dead *(2022). It will cover paradoxes between the past and the future in Igbo philosophy and Africanfuturism, and application in my African horror novel.*

Keywords: African Spirituality, Africanfuturism, Ancestor Veneration, Igbo Religious Philosophy, Traditional Religions

Azuka versus Iruka: The paradox Between the Past and the Future in Igbo Philosophy and Africanfuturism

Amongst the Igbo ethnic group of Nigeria, West Africa, there are two popular names given to both males and females in the community—Azuka and Iruka. These two names represent the dualistic nature of the Igbo philosophy, culture, and cosmology. As a writer of Igbo ancestry, I have lived among the Igbos for a good part of my life and have grown up with a deep understanding of the dualistic nature of the Igbo philosophy. According to authors, Sohila Faghfori and Esmaeil Zohdi,

> … the principle of dualism and pairism, manifested in the Igbo concept of god, is deep-rooted in all aspects of Igbo life … in Igbo thought, even a person is a duality: a human being and a spirit being. The human being lives in the human world and the spirit being lives in the spirit world, all the time protecting its human "other." Igbo belief in chi bears testimony to the duality that pervades all things in Igbo life.
>
> (Faghfori and Zohdi 2012)

With this in mind, it is easy to appreciate the paradox of the two Igbo names, Azuka and Iruka. A literal and allegorical translation of Azuka is, "Past glory; the past is greater," while Iruka means, "Supreme future; the future is greater." And no; this Iruka is not from the Japanese language which is both a male name and the name for a dolphin, albeit, the Igbo "chi" shares the same meaning as the Japanese "chi." A deeper study of Igbo and Japanese linguistics reveals many shared words between the two cultures and Iruka happens to be one of them.

Azuka and Iruka at first glance would appear to contradict each other, and, perhaps, seem to be forcing a choice between one or the other; the past is either greater or less than the future. Therein lies the beauty of the Igbo culture, a culture that values equilibrium in all things. In the search for balance in all things, the Igbos see no complexity in the two extreme principles of Iruka and Azuka, thanks to their dualistic culture. Azuka and Iruka, therefore, represent my view of the dualism of Africanfuturism, the merging of the two worlds, the African past and the African reimagined future, to create a vibrant, unique, and holistic narrative that does justice to the African continent and its rich history in speculative works. The famous aphorism by the great Spanish philosopher, George Santayana, comes to mind—"Those who cannot remember the past are condemned to repeat it" (1905).

I would paraphrase this saying by stating that "Those who cannot remember the past are condemned to lose their future." While one cannot generalize this quote, since each past is unique to its own peoples and their circumstances, nonetheless, delving into the wisdoms and follies of the past is without doubt one of the crucial means for mankind to illuminate both their current and future histories. My personal belief, therefore, is that Africanfuturism is incomplete without reference to Africa's past, in particular Africa's ancient, pre-colonial spirituality that has defined its people across continents and ages.

The renowned writer, Chinua Achebe, reiterated the need for African writers to reject the negative Western stereotypes which caused them to turn away from their own cultures, values, and philosophies, to, instead, copy white civilizations they viewed as superior as a result of colonial indoctrinations (Achebe 1988).

According to Professor Paul Brians in a literary study guide:

> Achebe is trying not only to inform the outside world about Ibo traditions, but to remind his own people of their past and to assert that it had contained much value. All too many Africans in his time were ready to accept the European judgement that Africa had no history or culture worth considering.
>
> (2015)

Today, Chinua Achebe's teachings have come to spectacular fruition. Africanfuturism has loudly announced its arrival on the global creative stage. African writers, in particular, have taken their rightful place on the stage of speculative fiction. They are reclaiming their African past with pride and incorporating it into a future world once thought to be the sole domain of Western authors and creatives. Writers of African descent such as Nnedi Okorafor, Eugen Bacon, Mame Bougouma Diene, Tlotlo Tsamaase and Wole Talabi, to mention but a few, are becoming trailblazers in the field, winning awards and publishing acclaimed works of futurism steeped in African roots.

I am a writer of African horror, a narrative steeped predominantly in Africa's past, specifically, the old cultures, beliefs, practices, religions, lore, and cosmology of the Igbo community in modern-day Nigeria. My works are firmly rooted in Igbo spirituality and its impact on the people, both before, and post-colonialism. As such, I view myself as one of the custodians of an old civilization struggling to survive the crushing onslaught of what has been described as the "Three C's of Colonialism: Civilization, Christianity, and Commerce" (Scholarblogs.emory.au 2011).

I neither write science fiction nor dystopic and utopic works of Africanfuturism but I believe that my works, which embody African spirituality in all its fascinating complexities, will serve as a link between our glorious past and our supreme future—the Azuka and Iruka of Africanfuturism.

Afrofuturism and the African Voice

The evil of the holocaust led to the establishment of the new state of Israel; the harrowing tragedy of Hiroshima led to the Treaty on the Prohibition of Nuclear Weapons; the evils of slavery led to Abraham Lincoln's Emancipation Proclamation; while the harsh brutality and exploitation of colonialism led to the independence movement by African states. Today, in response to the explosion of Afrofuturism, Africanfuturism is the latest kid in the literary and creative fields.

There is this assumption that Afrofuturism belongs more to the African-American creatives and is relevant to their experiences in a Western world that has rejected and relegated them to inconsequential citizens of their own country. Consequently, writers and media discussing the phrase, tend to focus mainly on African-American advocates of Black futuristic works, with a paucity of African voices. An online article in the British art gallery site, Tate, describes Afrofuturism thus:

> The term afrofuturism has its origins in African-American science fiction. Today it is generally used to refer to literature, music and visual art that explores the African-American experience and in particular the role of slavery in that experience.
>
> (n.d.)

The Afrofuturism movement saw an exponential growth of new books, films, artwork, and music extoling the phrase and its themes. According to authors, Isiah Lavender III and Lisa Yaszek:

> Black people have finally wrestled control of their own future images, using the speculative art form known as Afrofuturism to reboot black identity, challenge white supremacy, and imagine a range of futures in full colour.
>
> (2020: 1)

But as author, reviewer, and editor Eugen Bacon wrote in her *Aurealis* magazine review of the book, *Literary Afrofuturism in the Twenty-First Century*:

> Broad in its coverage, there's a lingering sense of lacking in this volume— somewhat missing is the inherent 'African voice' of authors with a lived experience of Africa, and who intimately understand the continent and its traditions. Authors like Nuzo Onoh, Cheryl S. Ntumy, Dilman Dila, Tlotlo Tsamaase, Makene Onjerika, Shingai Njeri Kagunda, Wole Talabi, Ngũgĩ wa Thiong"o, and more, are conspicuously absent. Yet, they are intrinsic participants to this important conversation on the rise of black speculative fiction …
>
> (2022c: 156)

Africanfuturism is, therefore, Africa's response to Afrofuturism. It is our attempt to determine our reimagined futures, using our own voices to name our journeys and our creations. The highly innovative Sauútiverse futuristic world created by Wole Talabi et al. is a testament to how far Africanfuturism has come. The Sauútiverse is described as,

> … a fictional secondary world based on a blend of African cultural worldviews and inspirations. The name is inspired by the Swahili word for "voice". It is a five-planet system orbiting a binary star, where everything revolves around an intricate magic and technological system based on sound, oral traditions and music. It includes science-fiction elements of artificial intelligence and space flight, with both humanoid and non-humanoid creatures … You can think of it like Wakanda from Marvel's Black Panther by way of George RR Martin's Wild Cards, with all the rich interplanetary world-building of Frank Herbert's Dune. But make no mistake, the Sauútiverse is distinctly

African, being flexible enough to absorb and synthesize the multitude of its varied African cultural inspirations into something new.

(Afrocritik 2022)

These days, the terminologies Africanfuturism and Afrofuturism are so intertwined that both writers and readers, at times, use them indiscriminately to describe speculative works of Black futurism. The themes of Black survival and triumph into a future space drive both Afrofuturism and Africanfuturism. They both tend to feature some sort of fighting, protesting, and struggle, where Black people strive to reclaim something lost, something stolen from them, something denied them, something nostalgic and almost forgotten—their creativity, their power, their culture, their place in history, even their very names and lives within a futuristic space. It is, therefore, easy to see why the two phrases, Africanfuturism and Afrofuturism, have come to define futuristic works by Black writers, both in the motherland and diasporic spaces.

African Spirituality

Kenyan philosopher John S. Mbiti states that African spirituality is found in rituals, ceremonies and festivals of Africans, in shrines, sacred places and religious objects, in art and symbols, music and dance, proverbs, riddles and sayings, names of people and places, myths and legends, beliefs and customs—indeed in every aspect of life (1991: 20–30).

With Afrofuturism's focus on technology and the Black space in a reimagined future universe, it is easy to see why African spirituality, with its origins rooted firmly in the past, can at times seem a forgotten aspect of that futuristic journey. Thankfully, films like the *Black Panther* franchise have brought in a strong story and visual facets of African spirituality rooted in a futurist Black realm, while books like Octavia Butler's *Wild Seed* (1980), set in the twenty-seventh century, pays literary homage to African spirituality in a reimagined future world of magic, eugenics, and technology. As a writer of African horror stories steeped firmly in Africa's past, it is my belief that African spirituality is one of those elements of blackness that needs to be reclaimed and propelled into a glorious future world of Black utopia. However, I ask the question, how can you reclaim something that is already inside your genome, your blood and your very soul? The white American who coined the term "Afrofuturism" asked the question:

> Can a community whose past has been deliberately rubbed out, and whose energies have subsequently been consumed by the search for legible traces of its history, imagine possible futures?
>
> (Dery 1994)

The answer to this myopic question is a resounding "YES!" It is my opinion that African spirituality has never been completely lost despite the centuries of slavery and colonization. It had been denigrated, deemed pagan, barbaric, sinful, and unworthy of the white gaze and its destructive slavist/ colonist attention. Yet, by its very nature, African spirituality saved itself from annihilation and has survived everything thrown at it and its people through endless millennia and global consciousness expansions.

Our enslaved kin across the Atlantic had felt the loss of their motherland, the rootlessness, the alienation from their kin and culture, the evil and savage brutality of being trafficked away from everything they held dear. We Africans also experienced the loss of our freedoms, the destruction of colonialism and the near-annihilation of our culture, our history and almost everything we held dear. But one thing we share, one thing that could not be taken from us (Africans both in the motherland and across the Atlantic) is the healing power and wisdom of our spirituality. The African-American Spirituals, (formerly, Negro Spirituals), the Gullah-Geechee root-healing, the Cuban Regla de Ocha, the Brazilian Candomble, and the Haitian Vodou religion, to mention but a few, are all evidence of the survival of an ancient philosophy that transcends slavery, politics, religion, war, technology, and science. As I mentioned, African spirituality is so rooted in African DNA that time, space, and science are futile antagonists to its perpetuity. As Hope Wabuke states in the *Los Angeles Review of Books*:

> … Dery's operating question dismisses, firstly, the resilience, creativity, and imagination of the Black American diasporic imagination; secondly, it lacks

room to conceive of Blackness outside of the Black American diaspora or a Blackness independent from any relationship to whiteness, erasing the long history of Blackness that existed before the centuries of violent oppression by whiteness—and how that history creates the possibility of imagining the free Black futures that Dery deems impossible.

(2020)

Today, most works of Africanfuturism, Afrofuturism, and African speculative fiction include elements of African beliefs, practices, religions, and culture in a homage to African Spirituality, and my book, *A Dance for the Dead* (2022), follows in that vein. According to Professor Jacob Olupona, a noted scholar of indigenous African religions at the Harvard Divinity School, in his *Harvard Gazette* article:

African spiritual beliefs are not bound by a written text, like Judaism, Christianity, and Islam. Indigenous African religion is primarily an oral tradition and has never been fully codified …

(2015)

With over 4,000 different communities and counting, African cosmologies have a multiplicity of ways in which individual communities practice their spiritualties. As theology scholar Johannes J. Knoetze states:

Africa is a continent with a vast plethora of spiritualities … It needs to be stressed that there is not just one single African spirituality, although many of the characteristics of the African spiritualities are alike, but it may have different interpretations.

(2019)

In my community, the Igbo ethnic group of Nigeria, transmogrification and animalism are core aspects of our spiritualism, as well as communing with spirits, gods, and the ancestors. While some communities might worship their ancestors, the Igbos practice ancestor veneration as a central feature of our spirituality. Nigerian scholar Nwafor Matthew Ikechukwu writes:

Ancestor veneration is not the same as worship of a deity or deities … The veneration of ancestors is made manifest in the way the traditional Igbo pray. Because the ancestors are believed to be living even though they are physically dead, they are invoked in the prayers of the Igbo people.

(2017)

Other central elements of African spirituality found across most communities include traditional ceremonies, traditional healing methodologies, sacrificial rituals (including birth, death, cleansing, protection, healing rituals, age-grade initiations, etc.), oral storytelling, dance, and music. Battling malevolent entities like Christian exorcists do, and making blood sacrifices, just as in Judaism's old testament traditions, are other common features of African spirituality. These sacrifices to higher spirits and ancestors, and a belief in their ability to impact our past, current, and future lives is one of the strongest features of African spirituality, seen across most cultures across the vast continent. Knoetze reiterates this fact in the article "African Spiritual Phenomena and the Probable Influence on African Families":

> ... Africans make use of intermediaries in the form of ancestors during worship. Therefore, worship, which is described as prayers, sacrifices and offerings, and singing in dancing, is focussed on pleasing or making contact with the intermediaries or ancestors, or the invisible or spiritual world.
>
> (2019)

African Spirituality, *Black Panther* and *A Dance for the Dead*

In my book, *A Dance for the Dead*, I start the story with an Igbo proverb:

> When a man's penis grows too big for his loincloth, he shouldn't be shocked when a monkey mistakes it for its banana.
>
> (2022)

This saying encapsulates the importance of humility in Igbo culture, especially humility before one's ancestors and personal "chi" or guardian spirit. It also demonstrates a core element of Igbo spirituality, the use of proverbs and metaphors in everyday speech. The famed author, Chinua Achebe, demonstrated this peculiar cultural trait in his book, *Things Fall Apart* (2006). According to Chintya Winda N. et al.,

People in the Igbo Tribe use proverbs everyday as they are an important part of their culture and traditions, and the art of conversation is regarded very highly throughout the clan. The Igbo culture is a very oral language. "Proverbs are the palm oil with which words are eaten". This quote shows how important proverbs are in everyday life as they are referred to as "palm oil" which is a very important part of the tribe's life.

(2019)

In the famous futuristic film, *Black Panther* (IMDb 2018), the character T'Chaka makes use of African proverbs in his speech, something that enriches the film and authentically highlights its African roots:

"A man who has not prepared his children for his own death has failed as a father."

(2018)

Another core element of African spirituality, especially Igbo spirituality, is in the amalgamation of dance, masquerades, and music for rituals and celebrations, be it birth, death, marriage, war, farming, festivals, and divination rituals. From the title of the book, *A Dance for the Dead,* one can easily sense their importance in traditional Igbo spirituality. Like the oral storytelling traditions, they are also employed effectively in *Black Panther*:

One of the critical components of the film's music is the use of African-inspired themes ... from a variety of African musical styles and instruments, incorporating elements such as traditional African percussion, African choir singing, and the use of a xylophone-like instrument called the balafon. The musical fusion creates a sound that is both authentic and unique and reinforces the film's connection to its African roots.

(Chaudhry 2023)

In the first chapter of *A Dance for the Dead*, we witness the young Prince Ife dancing the famous Igede traditional dance, one of the most important dances in Igboland, in the village square in honor of the New Yam festival.

... he forced his mind to focus on the drums and the intoxicating pulse of the famous Igede dance beats. Softly, with tentative taps, the wooden

The Power of African Spirituality 69

gong joined the metal one, gently inviting the beaded and clay instruments into the undulating rhythm. Finally, the instruments were joined by their king, the leather-clad Igba drum with its throbbing, seductive beat. Ife's feet flew with the joy of the rhythm. The dust was a brown cloud underneath his hopping legs. His body gyrated and twisted as he allowed the magic of the Igede to transport him to breathless ecstasy.

(p. 5)

The Igede dance, which our hero Ife dances in spectacular fashion, demonstrates just how crucial dances are in every aspect of the Igbo culture and spirituality. This also explains why it had to be the greatest gift for the ancestors in the story. Only a freeborn person or their descendants can dance to the Igede during any event. That is why it is sometimes referred to as the Dance of Kings. Igbo people use their traditional music to pay homage to the ancestors and spirits, spread information, and voice criticisms, apart from entertainment and other purposes; and there are various dances for various events too. Certain masquerades are untouchable and feared, since they can be possessed by either the spirits of ancestors or the deities. So, when the masquerades dance, it is believed that they channel the spirit of the deities and ancestors. Like most cultural activities in African culture, colonialism, and Christianity have impacted the spiritual value of the masquerade and traditional dances in many societies although they are experiencing a strong resurgence in recent times (Ogbonna 2019).

Another element of African spirituality explored in both *A Dance for the Dead* and *Black Panther* is that of Ancestor veneration. The famous Ubuntu saying, "I am because you are" epitomizes the strong bonds Africans have with their ancestors. In Igbo spirituality, the dead who die at the right age and have been upstanding citizens, are deemed to become ancestors and earn the veneration of their descendants. According to author George Thomas Basden in his book *Among the Niger Ibos of Nigeria: 1912*:

Holding the most profound belief in the supernatural, the Ibo is deeply conscious of his relationship to the unseen world, and every precaution must be observed in order to keep the spirit of the departed in a state of peaceful contentment. The Ibo will endure everything demanded of him in this life. He will put up with hardships, the misbehaviour of his children, indeed anything, in order to insure [sic] that his burial will be properly performed. His whole future welfare depends upon this.

(1966)

This tells us just how important it is to have a good burial without which one can't be welcomed into the realm of the ancestors, and, hopefully, reincarnate back into their family. Professor Olupona states:

The role of ancestors in the African cosmology has always been significant. Ancestors can offer advice and bestow good fortune and honor to their living dependents, but they can also make demands, such as insisting that their shrines be properly maintained and propitiated.

(2015)

Ancestor veneration is not something observed formally, such as going to temples or specially designated places as some other cultures might do. Instead, some families might follow certain rituals like pouring down palmwine into the graves of their ancestors in libation or setting up shrines for them and visiting them on an ad hoc basis as need arises. But, on the whole, it is something done in the course of everyday life, including the names Igbos give their children, such as Nnamno or Nnamdi (my father lives), or Nna-ayọ (my father returns). In most Igbo villages, people belong to a clan usually named after a great ancestor. Toni Akose Ogobegwu explores this in the article "The Igbo Clan:"

Clans in the Igbo culture are traditional social groups that provide identity and community. They are often based on shared ancestry and are usually named after a common founding ancestor

(n.d.)

Many villages in Igboland are also named after a great ancestor, hence one finds a lot of villages and towns whose names start with the word "Umu," meaning "descendants or children of"—Umuozzi, Umuoji, Umunya, Umuechem, Umuitodo, and so forth. So, the ancestors play a vital role in Igbo spirituality and the living descendants try to do right by their ancestors to ensure they continue to remember and bless them (Ige 2006).

The Power of African Spirituality　　71

In my book, *A Dance for the Dead*, ancestor veneration is one of the key elements of the story and it culminates with a visit to the ancestral realm by the two protagonists.

> "What happens next after we fall into the death-sleep?" Dike asked.
> "Feather-Feet will go straight to the realm of the ancestors to embrace his destiny. It will be a painless and easy journey for him. As for you, the journey is different, tougher. You are now an Osu and will need cleansing to be granted entrance into the realm of The Old Ones. You will need to prove your worthiness by enduring the three deaths of Earth, water and fire."
>
> (pp. 206–7)

In the film, *Black Panther: Wakanda Forever* (IMDb 2022), released several years after I first wrote *A Dance for the Dead* (albeit, the book was published in November 2022, the same month the film was released), we observe the similarities in the use of the "black herb" to facilitate a mystic journey to the realm of the ancestors. In *Black Panther*, this is a futuristic affair; in *A Dance for the Dead*, it's an ancient affair. Yet, we see in this film how one can harness African spirituality into works of Africanfuturism/Afrofuturism, the perfect blending of the past and the future, the Azuka and Iruka of Igbo philosophy.

In *Black Panther: Wakanda Forever*, we also see the gathering of Queen Ramonda's family and the spiritual chiefs of Wakanda in the woodlands to carry out T'challa's funeral. They pour libations to the ancestors, just as is done in *A Dance for the Dead* (p. 27), once again applying another powerful aspect of African spirituality into a futuristic film. Again, making the woods the symbolic location of this ritual is another way *Black Panther* pays homage to African spirituality. Many African cultures, especially in eastern and western Nigeria, believe that trees and forests are mystical, with powers to bless, harm, or protect humans. In some East African communities, they bury their dead in specially designated forests, and the communities fiercely protect them from intrusion from outsiders. One is likely to find foodstuff and other forms of libation from relatives inside the forests (National Museums of Kenya 2008). The researcher, Omorovie Ikeke, writes:

> To many African peoples trees and forests had special significance … From several parts of Africa come accounts of trees which refused to be moved,

even by modern machinery designed for the task. These trees are believed to have magical power.

(2013)

In Igboland, trees and forest also play an important role in their spirituality. According to professor of African philosophy, Ikechukwu Anthony Kanu, in his article on Igbo sacred trees and plants,

> when the Igbo reverence sacred trees, it is not just because they have spiritual relevance but also because they symbolize life … Sacred forests were areas set aside by the Igbo ancestors as sacred sites and strictly protected by customary laws, beliefs and enforced taboos.

(2021)

So, for instance, there is a tree called the Ngwu tree, which features a lot in *A Dance for the Dead* (pp. 18, 35, 90). The Ngwu is said to be a mystical tree which is never planted. It grows by itself on lands destined for greatness, and, according to local lore, any blade that tries to cut it down instantly rusts. If an Ngwu suddenly falls, the Igbos believe that calamity or misfortune will befall the family. Its fall also signifies the impending death of a king or a famous person. And if one wakes up and find it growing in their compound, it means future greatness lies in the family. In *A Dance for the Dead*, we see the Ngwu tree both at the king's compound and growing in a circular formation inside the forbidden shrine, showing just how important this tree is in Igbo spirituality.

Another aspect of African spirituality that features in both *A Dance for the Dead* (pp. 6, 138, 246–8) and *Black Panther* is that of reincarnation. In Igbo spirituality, the dead can reincarnate back as many times as they like. The Igbos believe in the eternal spirit and life continuing after death and there are many burial rites to keep the dead in their own realm. This element of African spirituality is also explored in *Black Panther*:

> What is crucial is that the previous Black Panthers were imperfect … In effect, the conclusion of the movie is a statement of T'Challa exemplifying the true spirit of the first Black Panther … T'Challa is, in fact, three manifestations of the Black Panther.

(Eckstrand 2018)

African spirit men and women are another strong feature of African spirituality which feature in both *A Dance for the Dead* and *Black Panther*. Call them witchdoctors, bush-doctors, Juju-priests, or by any other name, the crucial role of medicine-men and -women in African spirituality is undeniable. These powerful individuals are found across almost all African cultures and their influence in the lives of the citizens is undeniable. In *A Dance for the Dead*, I demonstrated this absolute authority of the witchdoctor and how belief in his powers, real or fake, is enough to sustain his relevancy in the community:

> His full witchdoctor regalia, coupled with the terror-shrieks, were sufficient to get the girls to give in to his lust without threatening them with a *Juju* curse of infertility and early death. He'd never needed to exert much force to achieve his desires, not when his reputation served as his weapon.

(p. 3)

Black Panther also employs the use of spiritual chiefs similar to these powerful medicine-men and, in the film, we see them gathered together with Queen Ramonda and her family inside the sacred woods to carry out T'Challa's funeral rites. As Olupona states:

> If we were to lose Africa's diviners, we would also lose one of Africa's best keepers and sources of African history and culture.

(2015)

Concluding

The African-Australian writer, Eugen Bacon, one of the leading African writers of Afrofuturism, writes about the urgency in "deconstructing and reconstructing the written identities of people of color" in her article on Black speculative fiction (2022b). I believe that there can be no reimagining of Africa's future without reference to its spirituality and its ancient cultures and beliefs. To forget Africa's past is a betrayal of its people across the globe. By including African spirituality in its diverse totality into the worldbuilding of Africanfuturism and Afrofuturism, writers, publishers, and other creatives would add more authenticity and enrichment to their works. But as Bacon states in her chapter in this book on African voices, it has to be used authentically to be effective, just as it was ingeniously employed in the *Black Panther* franchise.

Many writers from the African continent are already employing this literary weapon of African spirituality in their works, demonstrating that perfection of Azuka and Iruka, as in Bacon's *Mage of Fools* (2022a). The end product is the amalgamation of the haunting past and beautiful future, weaved into a dazzling, literary gift for our present world. It is my hope that future literary works of Africanfuturism will get the respect and visibility they deserve by all the various branches of the publishing industry to ensure African writers take their rightful place in this trending futuristic worldbuilding genre.

References

Achebe, Chinua (1988), *Hopes and Impediments: Selected Essays 1965–87*, London: Pearson Education.

Achebe, Chinua (2006), *Things Fall Apart*, London: Penguin Classics.

Afrocritik (2022), "A First Look At The Sauútiverse." [online] Available at https://www.afrocritik.com/a-first-look-at-the-sauutiverse/ [Accessed May 4, 2023].

Bacon, Eugen (2022a), *Mage of Fools*, Atlanta: Meerkat Press.

Bacon, Eugen (2022b), "On Black Speculative Fiction," *Vector*. [online] Available at <https://vector-bsfa.com/2022/01/23/eugen-bacon-on-black-speculative-fiction/> [Accessed May 8, 2023].

Bacon, Eugen (2022c), "Review of *Literary Afrofuturism in the Twenty-First Century* by Lavender III, Isiah and Yaszek, Lisa," *Aurealis*, #156.

Basden, George T. (1966), *Among the Niger Ibos of Nigeria: 1912*, Abingdon: Routledge.

Brians, Paul (2015), "Chinua Achebe: Things Fall Apart Study Guide." [online] Available at<https://brians.wsu.edu/2016/10/19/chinua-achebe-things-fall-apart-study-guide/> [Accessed May 3, 2023].

Butler, Octavia (1980), *Wild Seed*, New York: Doubleday Books.

Chaudhry, Anubhav (2023), "The Rhythmic Heartbeat of Wakanda: Exploring the Music of *Black Panther*." [online] Available at <https://www.sportskeeda.com/

comics/the-rhythmic-heartbeat-wakanda-exploring-music-black-panther>
[Accessed May 6, 2023].

Chintya Winda N. et al. (2019), "Proverbs in Chinua Achebe's Novel *Things Fall Apart*," *KnowledgeE*. [online] Available at <https://knepublishing.com/index.php/Kne-Social/article/view/4841/9719> [Accessed May 6, 2023].

Dery, Mark (1994), "Black to the Future: Interviews with Samuel R. Delany, Greg Tate, and Tricia Rose," in *Flame Wars: The Discourse of Cyberculture*, 179–222, Durham: Duke University Press. [online] Available at <https://www.researchgate.net/publication/278667733_Black_to_the_Future_Interviews_with_Samuel_R_Delany_Greg_Tate_and_Tricia_Rose_FLAME_WARS_THE_DISCOURSE_OF_CYBERCULTURE> [Accessed May 5, 2023].

Eckstrand, Nathan (2018), "Black Issues in Philosophy: A Conversation on The Black Panther." [online] Available at <https://blog.apaonline.org/2018/02/20/black-issues-in-philosophy-a-conversation-on-the-black-panther/> [Accessed May 8, 2023].

Faghfori, Sohila, and Esmaeil Zohdi (2012), "Igbo Philosophy of Life and Psychological Parameters of Individual Wholeness," *PsyArt*. [online] Available at <https://psyartjournal.com/article/show/faghfori-igbo_philosophy_of_life_and_psychologica> [Accessed May 2, 2023].

Ige, Simeon Abiodun (2006), "The Cult of Ancestors in African Traditional Religion," *ResearchGate*. [online] Available at <https://www.researchgate.net/profile/Abiodun-Ige/publication/322486661_THE_CULT_OF_ANCESTORS_IN_AFRICAN_TRADITIONAL_RELIGION/links/5a5b050445851545027493c7/THE-CULT-OF-ANCESTORS-IN-AFRICAN-TRADITIONAL-RELIGION.pdf> [Accessed May 7, 2023].

Ikechukwu, Nwafor Matthew (2017), "The Living-Dead (Ancestors) Among the Igbo-African People: An Interpretation of Catholic Sainthood," *International Journal of Sociology and Anthropology*, 9(4), 35–42. [online] Available at <https://academicjournals.org/journal/IJSA/article-full-text-pdf/3A83D9563934> [Accessed May 6, 2023].

Ikeke, Mark Omorovie (2013), "The Forest in African Traditional Thought and Practice: An Ecophilosophical Discourse," *Open Journal of Philosophy*, 3(2), 345–50. [online] Available at <https://www.scirp.org/pdf/OJPP_2013052911080452.pdf> [Accessed May 7, 2023].

IMDb (2018), *Black Panther*. [online] Available at <https://www.imdb.com/title/tt1825683> [Accessed 4 June 2023].

IMDb (2022), *Black Panther: Wakanda Forever*. [online] Available at <https://www.imdb.com/title/tt9114286> [Accessed June 4, 2023].

Kanu, Ikechukwu Anthony (2021), "Sacred Trees/Plants: The Greening of Igbo-African Religion," *JASSD*. [online] Available at <https://acjol.org/index.php/jassd/article/view/1903> [Accessed May 8, 2023].

Knoetze, Johannes J. (2019), "African Spiritual Phenomena and the Probable Influence on African Families," *Scientific Electronic Library Online*. [online] Available at <http://www.scielo.org.za/scielo.php?script=sci_arttext&pid =S2305-08532019000400013> [Accessed May 6, 2023].

Lavender III, Isiah, and Lisa Yaszek (2020), *Literary Afrofuturism in the Twenty-First Century*, Columbus: Ohio State University Press.

Mbiti, John. S. (1991), *Introduction to African Religion*. Long Grove: Waveland Press.

National Museums of Kenya (2008). [online] Available at <https://museums.or.ke/sacred-mijikenda-kaya-forests> [Accessed June 4, 2023].

Ogbonna, Mazi (2019), "Igbo Masquerades and Their Importance to Society." [online] Available at <http://www.ekwendigbo.com/index.php/en/entertainment/item/29-igbo-masquerades-and-their-importance-to-society> [Accessed May 7, 2023].

Ogobegwu, Toni Akose (n.d.), "The Igbo Clan." [online] Available at <https://beingafrican.com/clans-totems-in-igbo-culture/> [Accessed May 7, 2023].

Olupona, Jacob (2015), "The Spirituality of Africa," *The Harvard Gazette*, October 6. [online] Available at <https://news.harvard.edu/gazette/story/2015/10/the-spirituality-of-africa/> [Accessed May 5, 2023].

Onoh, Nuzo (2022), *A Dance for the Dead*, Chicago: Dead Sky Publishing.

Santayana, George (1905), *The Life of Reason*, New York: Charles Scribner's Sons.

Scholarblogs.emory.au (2011), "The Philosophy of Colonialism: Civilization, Christianity, and Commerce." [online] Available at <https://scholarblogs.emory.edu/violenceinafrica/sample-page/the-philosophy-of-colonialism-civilization-christianity-and-commerce/> [Accessed May 3, 2023].

Tate (n.d.), "AFROFUTURISM". [online] Available at <https://www.tate.org.uk/art/art-terms/a/afrofuturism> [Accessed May 4, 2023].

Wabuke, Hope (2020), "Afrofuturism, Africanfuturism, and the Language of Black Speculative Literature," *Los Angeles Review of Books*. [online] Available at <https://lareviewofbooks.org/article/afrofuturism-africanfuturism-and-the-language-of-black-speculative-literature> [Accessed June 4, 2023].

5

Shingai Njeri Kagunda: Black-Futurisms Vs. Systems of Domination, *Kenya*

Bio

Shingai Njeri Kagunda is an Afrosurreal/futurist storyteller from Nairobi, Kenya with a Literary Arts MFA from Brown. Shingai's work has been featured in the *Best American Sci-fi and Fantasy 2020, Year's Best African Speculative Fiction 2021*, and *Year's Best Dark Fantasy and Horror 2020*. She has work in or upcoming in *Omenana Magazine, Fantasy Magazine*, FracturedLit, khōréō, *Africa Risen*, and *Uncanny Magazine*. Her debut novella *& This is How to Stay Alive* was published by Neon Hemlock Press in October 2021, and won the Ignyte Award for best novella in 2022. She is the co-editor of *Podcastle Magazine*, a Hugo nominated zine, and the co-founder of *Voodoonauts*, a Black speculative fiction summer workshop. Shingai is a creative writing teacher, an eternal student, and a lover of all things soft and Black.

In this chapter, I will talk about Black radical imagination, and the significance of Black futurisms as a revolt against throttling systems of domination. My discussion takes an intimate gaze at the Afrosurreal as a resistance to capitalism.

Keywords: Africanfuturism, Afrosurrealism, Afrofuturism, Black Futurism, Black Radical Imagination,

Is History Fact?

The story of my understanding of what Black-futurisms should center comes from a history of the Black Radical Imagination which I first encountered in Robin Kelley's *Freedom Dreams: The Black Radical Imagination* (2002). For the purpose of this text, I am using Black futurism in reference to Black speculative fiction at large, i.e., Afrofuturism, Afrosurrealism, Africanfuturism, Afrojujuism (also Africanjujuism), Afropantheology, etc.—the Black Radical Imagination is defined, according to the Studio Museum in Harlem, as "a revolutionary process of *thinking otherwise* using Black diasporic critique to articulate a vision for a different world" (2022).

I was working on my second book and first novel in progress, doing research on the Black Prophetic tradition, when Kelley offered me language and access to naming an imagining of the world that now comes as easy to me as breathing. This imagining is an exhale, a poet's comma, a breathless pause just before the next word, where the next word could be anything else, and the possibility of anything else is both exhilarating and terrifying in all the ways it has power to make sense of what came before.

But I am telling this story backward, from the end of the story, and by the end I mean the now of the story which is *this moment* of the story, because every story ends with what is happening in the final moment, and what happens after is left to the reader's imagination. So what came before and what is our now?

First, I must start with the philosophy of time I subscribe to, gifted to me by Black and Brown feminists, Pan-Africanists, Black anarchists, and disrupters of systems that normalize oppressive modes of production. What they have offered me is to think of time as non-linear, to think of the future as potential time that borrows heavily from the experience of the past and the present, and to view ourselves in the present as tomorrow's ancestors, while simultaneously doing the work of honoring our historical ancestors. This means that time cannot be linear, but in fact is always happening in the crevices of a past, present, and possible future.

This conceptualization of time is freeing for me, and allows me to see myself as part of a communal memory and a collective storytelling of the world that doesn't require me to be exceptional to be valid or *valued*.

The idea that I do not need to be exceptional to be valuable defies written history as taught to me for most of my early education. That particular history taught the value of Black bodies as wholly based off of our labor and ability to produce. It wasn't until university that I realized history was subjective, and it wasn't until a Black critique class I took in grad school that I fully understood how the history I learned most of my life was some colonizer's limited imagination of the world where I, and people who shared similar identities to me, would almost always only be tools to push the protagonists'—white men's—story forward. But again, I am jumping ahead of myself with this story, so let's go back.

Derek Walcott, a Saint Lucian poet, playwright, and Black liberation thinker, wrote an essay titled "The Muse of History" where he suggests that there are writers of "an old world" and writers of "a New World." The great divider between the two worlds being colonization. He says that, for writers of the New World—what I read in this context as post-colonial fiction—there is and has to be a rejection of the linear time of Old World history. He says,

> Yet, the method by which we are taught the past, the progress from motive to event is the same by which we read narrative fiction. In time every event becomes an exertion of memory and is thus subject to invention. The further the facts the more history petrifies into myth. Thus, as we grow older as a race, we grow aware that history is written. That it is a kind of literature without morality … and that everything depends on whether we write this fiction through the memory of hero or victim.
>
> (Walcott 1998: 37)

This particular quote reminds me of one of my favorite African proverbs, which I first encountered through Chinua Achebe's *Things Fall Apart* (2006): "Until the lion learns how to write, every story will glorify the hunter."

Later in Walcott's essay, he breaks apart the Old World's historical linearity that relies on a false "objective" history and emphasizes that "the vision of progress is the rational madness of history seen as sequential time of a dominated future" (1998: 41). He says that "an obsession with progress" (1998: 41) is not in the minds of the recently enslaved—which I also read generously as an extension to the ex-colonized.

While Walcott is saying that written history is not a reliable source of some sort of "objective" truth, he is also saying that the idea of history's "objectivity" benefits those in power who have had control over the narrative of history. The other side of this coin is that the subjectiveness of history is beneficial to those who are resisting structures and systems of domination. When Walcott calls the vision of progress a rational madness, I read it as him breaking apart the white supremacist, patriarchal constant need to move towards a future without sitting with the multiplicity of the past and present. The vision of progress is a vision of production and consumption. It is a refusal to take responsibility for the mass carnage a "dominated future" has cost the earth, colonized, and enslaved people everywhere. It is an aversion to sitting with the grief, and an aversion to paying attention to who doesn't fit into the linear progress-centered future envisioned by the white capital-centered narrative of history.

In my novella, *& This is How to Stay Alive* (2021), I play around with the subjectiveness of the narrative of time passing, which is what we call history. Time (personified) narrating the story says, "Some stories are part of every other story but only part, and therefore cannot speak for any other story" (2021: 13). Over and over again, throughout the characters Baraka, Kabi, and their family's story, there is an emphasis on each character's experience both being fully autonomous from and simultaneously in community with every other character's experience. It is important for me to avoid what Audre Lorde, an African American writer, womanist, radical feminist, professor, and civil rights activist, referred to as "the master's tools" which will never "dismantle the master's house" (Lorde 1984b: 110).

In this case the *tool* being any claim that a single narrative should and could be the dominant or sole valid narrative. Not only does this produce irrevocable damage in the ways it chooses to unsee people who share identities with specific characters, but who for a myriad of reasons have experienced the world very differently, it also limits our ability to imagine other ways of being, not to mention our ability to empathize with experiences that fall outside of the dominant narrative.

For the past couple of years, one of the ways I have sustained myself is by being a writing teacher. I have had the privilege—most of the time—of being able to create my own syllabus, and teach the type of experimental work that gives me joy. I have learned an incredible amount from the students I have gotten to share classroom spaces. They have healed me in their desire to create worlds that center the most marginalized of us. They have shared their exasperation with the world they have been born into. Recently, in a class I titled "Writing Revolution as Teenagers," we started by asking: Why write revolution?

We came to an acknowledgment that we are living in a time where we (me and the students) have all inherited the oppression of generations that came before us, and we are at a critical juncture where how we decide to face all the interlocking systems of oppression will deeply impact whether our world survives or not. We talked briefly about big societal narratives that are taken for granted as fact, and then talked about the counternarratives of resistance which have come up in response.

A revising of history that speaks to this resistance comes from both *Black Marxism* (1983) by Cedric Robinson, a book on race and the origins of capitalism, and *Caliban and the Witch* by Silvia Federici (2004), a book about gender and the origins of Capitalism. Robinson and Federici, in different ways, offer a politic of *intersectionality* which is a term coined by Kimberlé Crenshaw, an American civil rights advocate and leading scholar of critical race theory, and borrowed from a tradition of Womanists and Black feminists theories of Black womxn's lived experiences (Coaston 2019).

In part of *Black Marxism* (1983), Robinson traces the transition from feudalism to capitalism in fourteenth-century Europe. He makes the claim that racialization existed before capitalism, but the hierarchical domination of race was cemented, if not formed, by capitalism—an argument which illuminates capitalism's narrative that production is needed for progress. A capitalist mode of production has always demanded the most output in the least amount of time which necessitates the exploitation of human labor.

Robinson uses the term "racial capitalism" to describe the relationship between enslaved people's bodies and the production of capital for the white bourgeois. Explicitly, he states, "the Atlantic slave trade and the slavery of the New World were integral to the modern world economy" (Robinson 1983).

While tracing this history, Robinson says the formation of the,

Negro—whose precedents could be found in the racial fabrications concealing the Slavs (the slaves), the Irish and others—substantially eradicated in Western historical consciousness the necessity of remembering the significance of Nubia for Egypt's formation, of Egypt in the development of Greek civilization, of Africa for imperial Rome, and more pointedly of Islam's influence on Europe's economic, political, and intellectual history. From such a creature not even the suspicion of tradition needed to be entertained. In its stead there was the Black slave, a consequence masqueraded as an anthropology and a history.

(Robinson 1983: 4)

What Robinson is offering is the historical narrative that the Europeans had to convince themselves and African people of: that blackness was a category which was inherently subject to backwardness; that, for the African, any political, social, cultural, or economic history could not exist, and if it did it was conveniently forgotten and/or dismissed as irrelevant. Thus, Black people's value was dependent on their labor potential, a justification that was useful for the commodification of Black bodies everywhere. Regrettably, this is not merely historical thought but is happening in our current moment, for example as reported in the US NBC News on new Florida standards under Governor Ron DeSantis, aimed to teach students that "some Black people benefited from slavery because it taught useful skills" (Planas 2023).

Silvia Federici makes a similar argument to Robinson about women's bodies, correlating the history of technology to the history of women's bodies under capitalism. In her introduction to *Caliban and the Witch* (2004), Federici states,

From the beginning of the Women's Movement, feminist activists and theorists have seen the concept of the "body" as key to an understanding of the roots of male dominance and the construction of female social identity.

(p. 15)

Federici's idea that bodies were the first technology, which seems to be shared by Robinson's claims about race, challenges the historical narrative of the origins of capitalism being rooted in freedom. Bodies as technology is not only some wild sci-fi cow dung but also essential to any discussion around Black futurisms and speculative fiction.

Federici goes on to argue that women's bodies were relegated to the role of reproduction to create more labor for capitalist production. She says,

> Indeed, the political lesson that we can learn from *Caliban and the Witch* is that capitalism, as a social-economic system, is necessarily committed to racism and sexism. For capitalism must justify and mystify the contradictions built into its social relations—the promise of freedom vs. the reality of widespread coercion, and the promise of prosperity vs. the reality of widespread penury—by denigrating the "nature" of those it exploits: women, colonial subjects. the descendants of African slaves, the immigrants displaced by globalization.
>
> (Federici 2004: 17)

Hortense Spillers, a Black feminist critical thinker, pushes this argument further in a way that is a useful critique of Federici's history which assumes a type of universality, i.e., all women's bodies being subjected to the same type of domination. In *Mama's Baby, Papa's Maybe: An American Grammar Book* (1987), Spillers makes a distinction between the *body* and the *flesh*—the flesh being the unformed body stripped from ideologies of all identity including gender. In what she names as the "captive body," the female African was ungendered in the brutalization of slavery and colonization. She says, "it makes a good 'herstory' to want to 'forget', or to have failed to realize that the African female subject, under these historic conditions, is not only the target of rape ... but also the topic of specifically *externalized* acts of torture and prostration that we imagine as the peculiar province of *male* brutality and torture inflicted by other males." She then adds,

> This materialized scene of unprotected female flesh—of female flesh "ungendered"—offers a praxis and a theory, a text for living and for dying, and a method for reading both through their diverse mediations.
>
> (Spillers 1987: 68)

What I understand from Spillers' argument is that Black women's flesh was stripped of any potential to even become a body in the process of slavery and colonization. The flesh of the Black female, specifically then, was thoroughly negated of ANY sense of identity, safety, or personhood that could be found in race, class, or gender.

Is Representation Enough?

When my first African literature professor in an undergraduate classroom told me that we were going to study African writers, poets, leaders, and revolutionaries, instead of dead white men, it completely shifted my understanding of history, education, narrative, and my own place as a dark-skinned Kenyan perceived woman: everything about the way I saw the world changed.

And I dug into the alternative with a fury. I discovered the Negritude Movement (Tate 2023) that was built alongside the Harlem Renaissance (Britannica 2023) in the 1920s and 1930s. Both the Negritude Movement and Harlem Renaissance were cultural, political movements that came in response to African and African-descended people seeing through the veil of white supremacy.

If you search the archives, you will find in the Negritude movement stories and poetry and music and essays about Black love, joy, beauty, pleasure, dance, aesthetic. It was a moment of reclamation for a people who had been convinced that they had no right to access any of these things. And nearly a century later I, after a lifetime of colonized education, discovered the likes of David Diop, Leopold Senghor—the poet president of Senegal—, Aime Cesaire, Suzanne Cesaire, Langston Hughes, and other Black and African storytellers, poets, musicians, and artists who were reclaiming Blackness. In that moment I released a generational breath I did not even realize I had been holding, because it was evidence that there was also "a history" of resistance before me. A history of us telling our own stories in a way that reminded us of our personhood outside of whiteness: a history that categorically stated that we did not and never have existed for the white gaze, even though we had internalized a vision of ourselves through the narrative of whiteness and capitalism.

Negritude was where I first encountered Afrosurrealism, even though I did not have a name for it then. Craftwise, I see Afrosurrealism in Negritude as a poetics of play and imagination and experimentation that centers Black living. The contradiction here being that Black living can only exist with the ever-present history of Black dying. A theme that I and many other Afrosurrealists have explored in our works. Afrosurrealism loves juxtaposition and hates binaries. In that sense, Black dying and living together is not necessarily a contradiction but a dialectic.

For all these gifts of experimentation and exploration through the surreal, I am grateful to the Negritude movement, even as I see its flaws; flaws which I have seen repeated in some ideas of what Black futurisms should aspire to. Wole Soyinka, a Nigerian poet, playwright, and novelist, was among a couple of Black writers who critiqued Negritude for being insufficiently militant. Soyinka was famously known for saying something along the lines of, "A tiger does not proclaim its tigerness, it jumps on its prey."

The basis of this argument was that the politic of Blackness solely relying on reclaiming Black as beautiful, aesthetic, and valuable can only go so far in that it is still a response to white narratives of history as well as white determinants of value, and thus is still appealing to the white gaze. This is the trickiness of a politic of representation: that while African and African descended people are saying *I too can be beautiful or productive or useful* in the ways racial capitalism has only given whiteness access to, the system of capitalism is continuously finding new ways to reproduce violence and inequality.

As Sylvia Federici states in the last section of her introduction to *Caliban and the Witch*,

> It is impossible therefore to associate capitalism with any form of liberation or attribute the longevity of the system to its capacity to satisfy human needs. If capitalism has been able to reproduce itself, it is only because of the web of inequalities that it has built into the body of the world proletariat. And because of its capacity to globalize exploitation. This process is still unfolding under our eyes, as it has for the last 500 years.
>
> (Federici 2004: 17)

Under capitalism, Black and Brown bodies, global South bodies, women's bodies, and queer bodies will always be seen in terms of their value to the production of the market. One of my favorite interviews of all time is an interview of Julius Nyerere, the first president (also affectionately termed "the founding father") of Tanzania, posted on Afromarxist (2019) where, when asked what the values of Ujamaa (African socialism) were, Nyerere responds with,

... those values are values of justice, a respect for human beings, development which is people centred, development where you care about people, you can't say leave the development of the people to the market which has no heart at all since capitalism is completely ruthless.

He ends with the earnest plea,

"Who is going to help the poor? And the majority of people in our countries are poor. Who is going to stand for them? Not the market ..."

(AfroMarxist 2019)

The call here is not to just get a seat at the table, but to acknowledge that everything that was used to build the table was based on oppression, domination, and exploitation. And the only honest way to move towards Black futures is to burn down the table, scatter its ashes, and build something else.

What is the Role of Imagination?

It is fifty years from now, and you, a Black person, are here in this world, or some version of it, alive, breathing, and still. You are here and everything predicted that you would not be.

It is fifty years from now, and you a Black person are not here in this world, or some version of it, un-alive, breathless, and still. You are not here and the things that predicted you would not be, won.

A big dash in both these possible futures is dependent on whose imagination we allow to determine the rest of our lives and the future of our world. This is why we create, because everything that exists, does because someone imagined it was possible. In his book *Freedom Dreams: The Black Radical Imagination* (2002), Robin Kelley states, "My purpose in writing this book is simply to reopen a very old conversation about what kind of world we want to struggle for" (Kelley 2002: 7).

His is a statement I want to repurpose here and now—my purpose in writing this chapter is to reopen a very old conversation about what kind of world Afrofuturists, Africanfuturists, and other Black futurisms struggle for. And this work starts with unpacking whose imagination of the future we are living in.

This begins with acknowledging that the white colonial imagination determined the distribution of power in the world we live in, thus influencing who has access to resources and who doesn't, while also creating a society dependent on hierarchical structures of domination (see more on this discussion in Dilman Dila's chapter in this book on the hierarchies the colonizer imposed or assumed of the colonized). This replicates itself into the rest of society, its impacts felt in our sense of alienation from our labor, from each other, and from the earth that we are a part of.

The imagination of the white colonial subject was a speculation of separation, that valued the self as set apart from everything and everyone else. One of my favorite Audre Lorde quotes from her essay "Poetry is not a Luxury" (1984), first published in *Chrysalis* (1977), a feminist periodical of women's culture, then in her collection of essays, states,

> The white fathers told us, "I think, therefore I am." The Black mother within each of us—the poet—whispers in our dreams: "I feel, therefore I can be free.
>
> (Lorde 1984: 38)

I want to put this quote in conversation with Kelley's *Freedom Dreams* where he says,

> Progressive social movements do not simply produce statistics and narratives of oppression; rather, the best ones do what great poetry always does: transport us to another place, compel us to relive horrors and, more importantly, enable us to imagine a new society. We must remember that the conditions and the very existence of social movements enable participants to imagine something different, to realize that things need not always be this way. It is that imagination, that effort to see the future in the present, that I shall call "poetry" or "poetic knowledge."
>
> (Kelley 2002: 9)

Both of these statements are doing a myriad of different things simultaneously: first, acknowledging the limitations of the "white fathers'" imagination, which places value on a sort of intellect that leaves no room for the immaterial: speculative or imaginative. Second, the text aligns with Lorde's feminization of knowledge production through the prioritization of emotion. Lorde does this when she says, "The Black mother within each of us—the poet—whispers in our dreams: 'I feel, therefore I can be free.'" This is a deeply anticapitalist move because it centers feelings, and the expression of feelings (poetry) as a tool or a way of knowing that will get us free. Finally, interrupting linear movement of time by invoking the future into the present.

During my studies in graduate school, an idea I picked up and explored obsessively was that memory and imagination share space in the brain. I learned that the hippocampi comprise a pair of little seahorse-looking structures in the brain that make up the engine of memory in our thought structure. What has been realized in tandem with this is that imagination is also a fundamental function of the hippocampus, and for people whose hippocampus has been damaged, both their ability to remember and their ability to imagine are constricted (Wickelgren 2023).

When I was writing my novella *& This is How to Stay Alive*, I was thinking about the idea that, every time we remember something, our memory slightly changes it so the next time we remember, we are remembering our last memory instead of the actual event of the thing. Our minds then fill in the blanks of our memory, creating a historical fiction. I capture this in the following excerpt about protagonist Baraka:

> Memory is fiction but four years old and Mama used to call you her second girl. She said you would hold onto her skirt tighter than misty air holds onto water. Eight years old and Kabi fought a boy in the neighborhood for calling you a girl. That's when you learned you were wrong somehow. Twelve years old you liked a girl, she didn't like you back. Fourteen years old you had a best friend, his name was Vic; he taught you how to be a boy. Fourteen years old you liked a boy but you never said it out loud, you never even thought it in public. Fifteen years old boy moved away. Sixteen years old you prayed to be different and you prayed and you cried and you realized you were a problem. Seventeen years old you couldn't sleep and you smiled in public and you hurt in private and you asked God to make it all stop, this farce. Memory is fiction but you stayed alive. You did stay, you stayed alive you did, stay alive you stayed.

Until you couldn't anymore.

(Kagunda 2021: 40–1)

This section of my novella still makes the breath harder to reach when I read it because I carry how it feels in my bones. As much as the character Baraka is fictional, he is the culmination of people I have loved and lost, of people I have loved and thankfully not lost, and of myself. He is both a memory and a fiction, a work of my history and my imagination. And that is the legacy of his dying and his living together. Remember the juxtaposition of Afrosurrealism? We're getting there soon.

If our memory is tied to our imagination, and history is a type of fiction, then our imagination is also contingent on our history, and we imagine what we know is in some way possible. Black freedom dreams live in Black radical history. Our ancestors guide our descendants and we, in turn, imagine worlds that honor both those groups of people. I cannot help but think of Alexis Pauline Gumbs, a Black feminist writer, poet, and dreamer of other worlds whose short Afrofuturist story "Evidence" (2015) captures this so brilliantly. The story is divided into different exhibitions from different time periods. In one exhibition, Gumbs' descendant, twelve-year-old Alandrix, writes a letter back in time starting with "Dear ancestor Alexis." The segment below always takes my breath away because it is a statement of what is possible:

Dear Ancestor Alexis …

We are here five generations after you and a lot has happened. A lot of the things that used to exist when you were 12 and even when you were 28 don't exist anymore. People broke a lot of things other than silence during your lifetime. And people learned how to grow new things and in new ways. Now we are very good at growing. I'm growing a lot right now and everyone is supportive of growing time, which includes daydreams, deep breaths, and quiet walks. No one is impatient while anyone else is growing. It seems like people are growing all the time in different ways. It was great to learn about you and a time when whole communities decided to grow past silence. It is hard to read about the fact that sexual abuse, what we would now call the deepest violation of someone else's growing, used to happen all the time. It is hard to imagine what it felt like for people to walk around with all that hurt from harming and being harmed. But I can tell from the writing that people were afraid so much. History was so close. But the amazing thing is how people spoke and wrote and danced anyway. Imagine being afraid to speak. Anyway. I wanted to say thank you. Now in the 5th generation since the time of the silence breaking we are called hope holders and healers. There are still people doing a lot of healing, but it seems like generation after generation people got less and less afraid. People took those writings and started to recite them and then another generation hummed their melodies and then another generation clicked their rhythms and then another generation just walked them with their feet and now we just breathe it, what you were saying before about how love is the most powerful thing. how [sic] everything and everyone is sacred. I read a really old story where the character believed that time travel was dangerous because if you change one thing in the past the whole future changes and then you might never get born. I am still here writing this though so I think it's okay to tell you that everything works out. That it's okay. And it's not easy all the time, not even here, because so much has been broken, besides silence, but it is possible, it does feel possible. My friends and I feel possible all the time. So when you get afraid to speak, remember that you all were part of us all learning how to just do it. And most ... take it for granted. Except poets like me. I remember you. I feel it. Wow. Kapow.

love,

Alandrix (Gwwumbs 2015: 1–3)

In this excerpt, Alandrix is writing to our present moment which is her history.

But First We Must Destroy the World

Resistance to dominant power structures and systems has always been part and parcel to the history of speculative fiction, and, yet, there are ways that those systems of domination repeat themselves even within speculative fiction. So many of the comic book stories that a lot of us who find ourselves in this field loved while growing up were written by anarchists, and anti-institution creatives who would not settle for the *what is* and demanded through their creative praxis a *what if*. Obviously, like every other craft, speculative fiction is not a monolith and there were many different perspectives brought into the field, including deeply imperialist, American nationalist, conservative imaginations of the world. And these cannot be dismissed, neither can the tokenism offered to marginalized speculative futures attempting to keep us satiated when we demand space to tell our own stories.

If you get nothing else from this chapter, take this: Black capitalism is not and can never be the savior of Black futurisms. A future where Black people have access to every resource is a future where power and wealth are redistributed, hierarchy is turned on its head, and no one is left at the margins. This is the world Black futurisms must struggle for. I would even go so far as to say it is our duty, those of us who are invested in the work of liberation, to imagine the possibilities of these futures and then create them.

We must understand that if we do not completely overthrow systems that have equated our value to our labor, systems that remove us from our personhood and reduce us to our objective functions, then we are still resigning ourselves to the limited imagination of the white fathers of society, and, in essence, we will always be caught up in a game of responding to the white patriarchal capitalist desire.

If we agree that we must struggle for a new world, then part of that struggle is tearing down the old world. And this is possible because it has happened before. Because my ancestors broke apart the colonial world. Because Derek Walcott, and Aime Cesaire, and Suzanne Cesaire, and Frantz Fanon and Ngũgĩ wa Thiong'o, and Micere Mugo, and Chinua Achebe and Black and African poets and story tellers across the Pan-African diaspora tore apart the narratives of a white colonial world, and when you poke holes in a story, the story can no longer hold water.

So Black futurisms break this capitalist world's story apart. We break apart the narrative that it is the only way things can be. We offer new ways from our poetic knowledge, the Black mother inside each of us. We offer from our ancestors' ways of being that disrupt "productive time," that center grief and community, that redefine and rework what education is, and offer parenting and family as kinship instead of nuclear. And, in every facet of our society, we call out the legacy of whiteness and colonialism that has led to intersecting capitalist systems of domination.

One of my dear friends taught me to rethink my definition of the word violence. To think of how violence is only named violence when it is the working class in the streets protesting unfair conditions of labor and absurdly low qualities of life. Yet the state itself is never called violent for the ways it justifies its use of the military and police to take Black men and women's lives. Different African states are not called violent for the ways they redirect energy and resources to violence against queer people. Capitalism is not called violent for the way it forces competition, theft, and exploitation while alienating us from our work, ourselves, and each other.

And yet all these violations are felt every day. In the ways my characters in my novella *& This is How to Stay Alive* could not reconcile their value and personhood to the expectation to perform in order to fit into a societal construct of the world which, to reiterate, is subject to the limitation of the white capitalist imagination. In my character Baraka's death, I see the violence of the state. In Kabi and her family's struggle to grieve wholly, I see the violence of capitalism. I see violence in the way African spiritualities that do not neatly fall into the Abrahamic religions are equated to madness or evil. I have seen the violence of the capitalist state in the loss of people I have loved who didn't have to die, either because of lack of access to quality healthcare or because they believed the narrative that their Black life didn't matter. I have seen the violence of colonialism disseminated into neo-colonized societies with the unequal distribution of resources.

Kelley's description of the work facilitated by the Movement for Black Lives in his forward to Black Marxism is useful here,

> By calling for an end to the war on Black people—here and abroad—and the reinvestment in resources from the carceral and military state to education, health, and safety, creating a just, democratically controlled economy, the Movement for Black Lives effectively presents a plan to transform the entire nation, save the planet, and ultimately end racial capitalism. The political theorist Siddhant Issar makes the trenchant observation that the policy statement of the Movement for Black Lives explicitly names "racial capitalism" in order to expose and politicize the fact that the capitalist

economy is constituted by a racial logic. The need to politicize the line between capitalism and racial domination is itself a response to how this link has been depoliticized and concealed by liberal and influential left theorists of capitalism.

(Robinson 1983: 19)

After a bout of social media sharing of the brutalization of a Black man's body by the cops, Noname, who is a hip-hop artist, MC, and Black liberatory thinker posted on her Instagram stories something along the lines of, "we need more stories about resistance, more media that shows people burning down police precincts and 'eating' the rich, and overthrowing the state." A call that I resonate with and see beautifully done in *Bitter* (2022) by Akwaeke Emezi. *Bitter* is a book about a bunch of Black and Brown teenagers leading a revolution in a fictional city called Lucille. It tackles violence with an honesty and capaciousness that is necessary for the future of Black futurisms.

This type of work is what Toni Cade Bambara, the brilliant Black womanist writer, asked of us when she said, "the role of the artist is to make the revolution irresistible" (Momentom 2023).

Why Black Futurism?

This is where we have always lived: in the Black speculative. In the space that is held by both memory and imagination. In African folktales, Caribbean wives' tales, African diasporic spirituality … All of these have been part and parcel to our reality, the knowledge that the metaphysical was not separated from the physical. Instead, both are irrevocably interconnected. Pre-colonial African narratives of history had no distinct separation between the fantastical and the reality of the everyday. Stories about people were stories about ancestors, were stories about spirits, and stories about gods. Stories about trees were stories about soil, were stories about the tortoise and the hare, were stories about ogres, were stories about values that centered connectedness over alienation.

As a Black futurist writer, I place my work in the sub-category of Afrosurrealism because it holds all these truths while insisting on a material movement towards a future/possible time where we are returned to a large-scale value system based on connectedness. Suzanne Cesaire, who first called me into the fold of Afrosurrealism, was from Martinique: a writer, poet, and revolutionary often hidden behind her husband Aime Cesaire's work. She does not get half as much credit as is due her for her contribution to the field of Afrosurrealism.

When speaking of its revolutionary potential in *The Great Camouflage: Writings of Dissent* (2012), she said,

> Such is a surrealist activity, a total activity, the only one that can liberate humankind by revealing to it the unconscious. One of the activities that will aid in liberating people by illuminating the blind myths that have led them to this point.
>
> (Cesaire, Maximin, and Walker 2012: 37)

Later in the text she goes on to add,

> So, far from contradicting, diminishing, or diverting our revolutionary feeling for life, surrealism shored it up. It nourished in us an impatient strength, endlessly sustaining this massive army of negations. And then I think also to tomorrow. Millions of Black hands across the raging clouds of world war, will spread terror everywhere. Roused from a long benumbing torpor, this most deprived of all people will rise up, upon plains of ashes. Our surrealism will then supply them the leaven from their very depths. It will be time finally to transcend the sorted contemporary antinomies ...
>
> (p. 37)

In the work of Afrosurrealism there is an emphasis not to originate new ideas but to uncover what already exists but is hidden. "By illuminating the blind myths," Afrosurrealism strips white capitalist narratives of their believability. In contemporary times, more specifically, Afrosurrealist media has revealed the absurdity of race relations, illuminating the ways in which white capitalism benefits from our dessensitization to it. What we must ensure is that it does not slip into the neo-liberal trap of separating race from class hierarchy.

Suzanne Cesaire says that instead of "diverting our revolutionary feeling for life, surrealism shores it up." She is an ancestor and yet when she was writing this piece, she was thinking about us. We are the tomorrow she held onto, the millions of Black Hands across the raging clouds overthrowing the systems of hierarchical domination. Insisting on an imagination and a memory of a different world. A time collapsing, world breaking, life breathing insistence that honors those who came before us, those who will come after us, and those who are on the margins of the society we live in now.

References

Achebe, Chinua (2006), *Things Fall Apart*, London: Penguin Classics.

AfroMarxist (2019), "Julius Nyerere Interview (1996)," *YouTube*. [online] Available at: <https://www.youtube.com/watch?v=4rkrpFYBUEE> [Accessed 16 June 2021].

Britannica (2023), "Harlem Renaissance." [online]. Available at <https://www.britannica.com/event/Harlem-Renaissance-American-literature-and-art> [Accessed August 14, 2023].

Cesaire, Suzanne, Daniel Maximin, and Keith L. Walker (2012), *The Great Camouflage: Writings of Dissent (1941–1945)*, Middletown: Wesleyan University Press.

Coaston, Jane (2019), "The Intersectionality Wars." [online] Available at <https://www.vox.com/the-highlight/2019/5/20/18542843/intersectionality-conservatism-law-race-gender-discrimination> [Accessed August 14, 2023].

Emezi, Akwaeke (2022) *Bitter*, New York: Knopf Books for Young Readers.

Federici, Silvia (2004), *Caliban and the Witch: Women, the Body and Primitive Accumulation*, New York: Autonomedia.

Gumbs, Alexis Pauline (2015) "Evidence," in Adrienne Maree Brown and Walidah Imarisha (eds.), *Octavia's Brood*, 3–41, Chico: AK Press.

Kagunda, Shingai Njeri (2021), *&&& This Is How to Stay Alive*, Washington: Neon Hemlock.

Kelley, Robin D. G. (2002), *Freedom Dreams: The Black Radical Imagination*, Boston: Beacon Press.

Lorde, Audre (1977), "Poems Are Not Luxuries," *Chrysalis:* A Magazine of Women's Culture 3: 7.

Lorde, Audre (1984a), "Poetry is Not A Luxury," *Sister Outsider: Essays and Speeches*, Trumansburg: Crossing Press, 36–41.

Lorde, Audre (1984b), *The Master's Tools Will Never Dismantle the Master's House*, London: Penguin Books.

Momentom (2023), "Making the Revolution Irresistible." [online] Available at <https://www.momentomcollective.com/the-irresistible-revolution/> [Accessed August 14, 2023].

Planas, Antonio (2023), "New Florida Standards Teach Students That Some Black People Benefited from Slavery Because it Taught Useful Skills," *NBC News*. [online] Available at <https://www.nbcnews.com/news/us-news/new-florida-standards-teach-black-people-benefited-slavery-taught-usef-rcna95418> [Accessed August 14, 2023].

Robinson, Cedric J. (1983), *Black Marxism: The Making of the Black Radical Tradition*, Chapel Hill: University of North Carolina Press.

Spillers, Hortense J. (1987), "Mama's Baby, Papa's Maybe: An American Grammar Book," *Diacritics*, 17(2), 64–81. [online] Available at <doi:https://doi.org/10.2307/464747> [Accessed August 14, 2023].

Studio Museum in Harlem (2022), "Black Radical Imagination," The Studio Museum in Harlem. [online] Available at <https://studiomuseum.org/article/black-radical-imagination-3#:~:text=We%20define%20the%20Black%20Radical> [Accessed August 14, 2023].

Tate (2023), "Négritude." [online] Available at <https://www.tate.org.uk/art/art-terms/n/negritude#:~:text=N%C3%A9gritude%20was%20an%20anti%2Dcolonial,of%20blackness%20and%20African%20culture> [Accessed August 14, 2023].

Walcott, Derek (1998), "The Muse of History," *What the Twilight Says: Essays*, London: Faber & Faber, 36–41.

Wickelgren, Ingrid (2023), "Where Imagination Lives in Your Brain," *Scientific American*. [online] Available at <https://www.scientificamerican.com/article/where-imagination-lives-in-your-brain/> [Accessed August 14, 2023].

6

Cheryl S. Ntumy: Faith and Fantasy— Afrofuturist and Africanfuturist Spirituality, *Ghana*

Bio

Cheryl S. Ntumy is a Ghanaian writer of speculative fiction, young adult fiction, and romance. Her work has appeared in *FIYAH Magazine of Black Speculative Fiction*; *Apex Magazine*; *The Best of World SF Vol. 3*, and *Botswana Women Write*, among others. Her work has also been shortlisted for the Nommo Award for African Speculative Fiction, the Commonwealth Writers Short Story Prize and the Miles Morland Foundation Scholarship. She is a member of the Sauútiverse Collective, which created an Afrocentric shared universe for speculative fiction, and Petlo Literary Arts, an organization that develops and promotes creative writing in Botswana.

In this chapter, I will talk about faith and fantasy—Afrofuturist and Africanfuturist spirituality, by reflecting on my closer identification with Africanfuturism rather than Afrofuturism in my works. I explore aspects of my short story "Godmother" (2021a) and series The Chronicles of the Countless Clans.

Keywords: Africanfuturism, African Spirituality, Afrofuturism, Faith, Fantasy

The Difference Between Afrofuturism and Africanfuturism

The diverse and complex beliefs of the people of Africa have inspired fiction for generations. This inspiration takes many forms in the work of African writers, both on the continent and in the diaspora. In recent years, some authors, including Nnedi Okorafor, Mohale Mashigo, and Wole Talabi, have suggested there should be a distinction between Afrofuturism and Africanfuturism.

I support the need for this distinction for a few reasons. First, the term Afrofuturism was coined by Mark Dery (1994), a white American rather than an African, and speaks to an experience that is quite foreign to me. In this context, when I think of Afrofuturism I see it as a movement developed in and for the diaspora, with a global north-based audience as the focus. This view applies not just to Afrofuturism in terms of fiction, but also in terms of music, fine art, philosophy, and an overall aesthetic of Afrocentricity. It entails—or at least incorporates—the crafting of cultures and customs as a reimagining of history, and, by extension, a new, Afrocentric vision of the future.

Delan Bruce provides an apt characterization of Afrofuturism in the *UCLA Magazine*:

It's the story of musicians, artists, writers, philosophers, fashion icons, filmmakers, costume and set designers, actors, activists and academics who have believed in a better future for Black people—and for all people.

Afrofuturism, more concretely, can be understood as a wide-ranging social, political and artistic movement that dares to imagine a world where African-descended peoples and their cultures play a central role in the creation of that world …

Many of its aesthetic tropes—a rich color palette, African iconography and a fascination with technoculture—were laid down by cosmic philosopher and jazz giant Sun Ra, starting in the 1950s.

(2020)

The Afrofuturist philosophy and aesthetic are evident in films like *Black Panther* (IMDb 2018), which inspired different responses from Africans on the continent and African Americans. In reflecting on the film's significance to African-American audiences, Win Martin and Dr. Sarah Boyd stated in their essay:

Through his use of Afrofuturism, Coogler presents Wakanda as a wonderful mix of different African cultures and advanced technology as a place to be praised rather than pitied.

(2018)

Indeed, the costumes and architecture of the fictional African state, Wakanda, are glorious amalgamations of various African cultures, with a high-tech, haute couture edge. It pays homage to a pan-African dream and, therefore, despite its noble intentions, the amalgamation doesn't reflect the specificity of a genuine African people or country. It feels rootless. In the *Black Panther* universe, Wakanda is an insular state that hides from the world. When it does rear its head, it interacts mostly with non-African nations. The storyline is focused on the US, rather than on Africa, because Africans are not the target market.

I am inclined to agree with Uche Balogun's (2018) article "Black Panther: Wakanda is Not Africa," published in *The Kalahari Review*, which states that:

Black Panther is supposed to be a movie about Africa, but it really isn't. As much as we want positive representations of Africa in the media, Wakanda is not Africa, and it's ridiculous when people say, "Finally, a movie about us". What are Nigerian and Kenyan and Ghanaian movies about then?

(2018)

Balogun is saying that, as Africans, we had our own art, philosophies and aesthetics long before Afrofuturism emerged outside the continent, and therefore the movement does not—and cannot—speak for us. Others have drawn attention to Afrofuturism's inability to adequately express the African experience. In an online preface to her short story collection *Intruders* by Picador Africa, South African author Mohale Mashigo writes,

It would be disingenuous of me to take Afrofuturism wholesale and pretend that it is "my size". What I want for Africans living in Africa is to imagine a future in their storytelling that deals with issues that are unique to us.

(2018)

Mashigo, in my view, echoes Balogun's sentiment that Afrofuturism is simply not representative of the diverse experiences of Africans living on the continent. By contrast, I feel that Africanfuturists, who I would define as African writers living on the continent or African writers abroad who have a lived experience of the continent, write from the perspective of people who are in the racial and cultural majority in their society—stories that feel instinctively familiar to Africans on the continent, even as they are consumed by Westerners. I would say that these writers tend to ground their work in actual African cultures, traditions, and social norms—the experience of what it feels like to live on the continent, even when this experience is explored in an imaginary setting.

Nnedi Okorafor, who is credited with coining the term Africanfuturism, has a lot to say about it, including in her article "Africanfuturism Defined":

> The difference is that Africanfuturism is specifically and more directly rooted in African culture, history, mythology and point-of-view as it then branches into the Black Diaspora, and it does not privilege or center the West.
>
> (2019)

Wole Talabi expands on this perspective in his preface to Brittle Paper's *Africanfuturism Anthology*:

> Africanfuturist stories going as far back as the history of the genre can (and should) now be clearly seen and read through a lens that centres them and their viewpoints, encouraging readers around the work to actively engage with African traditions of thought, of science, of philosophy, of history, of dreams, of being. I believe there is value in this focus, in this clarity.
>
> While others in the many black speculative arts have been using similar terms including the distinct "African Futurism" (two words) to say similar things, by staking claim and giving definition to this term, Africanfuturism, there is now an anchor point, a clearer signpost for what many African authors are trying to do when they write certain kinds of science fiction—not just from Africa, or set in Africa, but about Africa.
>
> (2020)

By highlighting the ways in which Africanfuturism centers Africa, while Afrofuturism does not, Talabi shows that the two terms clarify distinct approaches to speculative fiction and serve an important purpose in understanding the work of African writers.

With this perspective in mind, this chapter will explore how my novel series *Chronicles of the Countless Clans*, an example of what I would call Africanfuturism or African fantasy, weaves elements of Ghanaian culture into an imaginary setting, religion, and magical system. I will contrast this with the way my science fiction short story "Godmother," a work that leans more towards Afrofuturism, reimagines contemporary Ghanaian views on community and spiritual devotion.

The differences in tone, focus, and approach will illustrate the distinctions between the two subgenres and reflect on how African experiences of spirituality and community, whether specific and rooted in reality or broadly reimagined, influence the way we tell our stories.

Fact and Fantasy in *Chronicles of the Countless Clans*

Religion is an integral part of life in African society. In my experience, there is rarely a distinction between matters of the flesh and those of the spirit in the African world, where there's also a strong emphasis on the community rather than on the individual, a topic Fulata Moyo discusses in her exploration of gender constructs and religion in Africa, stating "To be human in Africa is to be a community" (2004: 72).

Stephen Zvawanda posits that African traditional religions differ from others in several distinct ways. He states:

> Unlike other world faiths, African traditional religions have no predominant doctrinal teachings. Rather, they have certain vital elements that function as core beliefs. Among these beliefs are origin myths, the presence of deities, ancestor veneration, and divination. African cosmology (explanation of the nature of the universe) tends to assert that there is a Supreme God who is helped by a number of lesser deities. Spirits are the connection between the living and the invisible worlds. Anyone can communicate with the spirits, but priests, priestesses, prophets, and diviners have more direct access to invisible arenas of the world.
>
> (2004: 4)

These core beliefs of origin mythology, deities, divination, and ancestor veneration permeate a lot of African speculative fiction. Stories like Lesley

Nneka Arimah's "Who Will Greet You at Home?" (2015), about a child made of hair, or Mbaeze Nnedimma's "Ihekanwa" (2022), about a goddess who devours men, reflect the reality of African religion in ways that feel grounded despite the fictional elements of the stories. I would call both these works—and others like them—Africanfuturism. In the worlds they depict, the spiritual realm exists as a matter of course, rather than something debatable. Africanfuturism stories might tackle universal themes—love, work, family troubles—but the mystical thread that is ubiquitous in African culture runs through them. Scholars Onah Gregory Ajima and Eyong Usang Ubana (2018) discuss the concept of health and wholeness in traditional African religion and social medicine. They state:

> For the Africans, the entire world is one fluid, coherent unit in which spirits, plants, animals, the elements, the dead and human beings interact. There is a thin line between any two sections of reality … man strives all times to maintain a harmonious relationship with all the forces that impinge on his life and being … wooing of benevolent forces and keeping in check of malevolent ones.
>
> (2018: 3)

Ajima and Ubana express the way in which the spirit realm and the physical realm operate in concert in African cultures. That is, the mundane aspects of life inform the supernatural and vice versa. I borrowed heavily from this holistic worldview to develop a socio-spiritual system in the novels within my series *Chronicles of the Countless Clans*, where magic and mysticism are taken for granted. It was important to me that the story felt genuinely African, despite its more outlandish elements. As such, I based the Countless Clans on my own native country, Ghana. There is a marked distinction between the culture, topography and environment of the clans of the North and South in the story, as is the case in modern-day Ghana. The fictional languages in the story, Ikan and Ve, are based on the languages of the Akan and Ewe peoples. The names are real Ghanaian names, many selected for their meanings, which reflect aspects of the characters' personalities and path in life. Bestowing names in this fashion is a common practice in Ghana and other African countries, where naming has significance. I applied the same approach to naming places, in some cases using human names for places if the names felt apt.

In creating the deities in the first novel of the series, *They Made Us Blood and Fury*, I drew from figures in Ghanaian traditional beliefs, especially those of my own people, the Ewes.

> Figures of the three gods appeared. Avlega, hunter, warrior, protector, goddess of fire and flame, with her lifeblood bow. Yame, god of the skies, of the sun and stars, with his akrafena made of lightning. Mawata, goddess of the earth, of mountains and rivers and fertility, with floods gushing from her lips.
>
> (2021b: 378)

Mawata is based on the mermaid figure Mami Wata, who appears in myths and legends from countries across Africa and the Diaspora. Yame came from Nyame, traditionally the Akan Creator God, whose name has since been repurposed to refer to the God of the Christian Bible. Avlega was inspired by the Anlo-Ewe goddess Avle, who likes to impersonate men. I incorporated this androgyny into my description of Avlega. The religion of the Countless Clans takes some inspiration from the Tro beliefs of the Anlo-Ewe, including elements such as divination, possession, and even the existence of a sacred forest.

Most African religions include a belief in a Supreme Being, with lesser gods that intercede on behalf of human beings. Among the Anlo-Ewe, this Being is Mawu-Lisa. In the *Chronicles of the Countless Clans* series, I replace the Supreme Being with a vague, ultimately unknowable force that people simply refer to as "life." This unknowable force bears some resemblance to the concept of fate and manifests through both natural and supernatural phenomena. Sometimes the nomadic clans in the story use the terms "life" and "magic" interchangeably, as seen in my novel *They Made Us Blood and Fury*:

> The High Priestess shook her head. "Magic is not mine to hoard. It longs to be shared, to be celebrated. But magic is life and there can be no life without death."
>
> (2021b: 9)

And in *They Gave Us Stealth and Cunning*:

"Life governs everything," Mawt said. "And magic is life."

"Magic is life," Aseye repeated, nodding. She understood. "And will is the vessel by which magic is transformed from pure energy into action. Matter."

(2022: 198)

Divination makes many appearances in the series—folk respect seers and take their visions and advice seriously. Divination and healing are both seen as gifts from the gods.

Possession is a central theme in the series as well. The protagonist carries a vengeful spirit within her that periodically takes control of her body. Possession is a common facet of African religions and can be both negative (i.e., possession by an evil spirit or the spirit of one who wishes to harm others) and positive (i.e., possession by a revered ancestor or a deity). One way in which such possession occurs is through trance, which often involves music and dance. It is believed that those performing these rituals enter a state of trance in which they come to embody their deities, or particular spirits, and exhibit their characteristics (The Patriot 2018).

This is reflected in *They Made Us Blood and Fury* in the sacred dance of the nomads, which the protagonist Aseye witnesses firsthand:

Around the flames people were dancing, a mix of nomads she recognized and gods she did not. The gods were tall, some towering over the nomads, or small as cats, voluptuous and sensual or slender and graceful as reeds. They were male and female and neither and both, with halos of hair and braids that dragged in the dust and shorn heads and crowns of stars and fire and stone.

As Aseye watched, entranced, some of the gods bent double and emitted sparks from their curved spines, and others opened their mouths wide enough to swallow camels and roared the roars of lions, or called out like birds, or whistled haunting melodies of the wind. And then she saw one of the small roaring lion gods spin away from the fire and grow a little, and become the mute little girl that Beda had healed. She realized then that the gods *were* the nomads. They danced and changed and changed back.

(2021b: 261–2)

In this scene Aseye observes the transformation that occurs when the nomads drink their sacred wine—they don't just embody gods. Rather, their innate magical abilities manifest in physical form to reflect how they would look in the spirit realm. In essence, they are already gods, but it's only when they drink the sacred wine and participate in the ritual dance that their divine forms are visible. Drums play a major role in African spirituality—in musical rituals they are often the focal point. They are used as a means of communication with both the material world and the spirit realm, with different types of drums serving different ceremonial purposes. Franklin Ugobude notes this relevance of drums in African spirituality in his article in *The Guardian*:

> Traditionally, these drums represent the soul of the community they're found in. They are used for celebrating ceremonial events and rituals within the community.
>
> (2020)

In *Chronicles of the Countless Clans*, talking drums pass on news, a practice common across West African cultures in the past and still used in modern times, to a certain extent (Marfo 2023).

However, drums are far more important ritualistically. In my novels, the Elders of Anyi play the sacred drum to wake the dormant warrior spirit that possesses the protagonist, Aseye. The same drum allowed the spirit to inhabit Aseye's body in the first place and will eventually unleash the full power of the spirit, giving it complete control of its host and effectively destroying Aseye's soul. As soon as the spirit wakes, it seeks out a ceremonial drum so it can be free to do its work. Anyi soldiers, human or spirit, must perform a drum ceremony to obtain permission to take life. This ritual is inspired by the Atrikpui dance-drumming of the Anlo-Ewe people. C. L. Ladzekpo describes this real-life ritual in his article "Introduction to Anlo-Ewe Culture and History":

> In the military culture, the dance-drumming repertoire, among other things, assumes the responsibility for the emotional and spiritual preparedness of the population for battle. For example, the repertoire of Atrikpui dance-drumming is replete with centuries of valued Anlo-Ewe war-fighting tactics and military codes of honor. Through the text, texture and choreography of Atrikpui, the military valor and skill (prowess) of ancestral heroes are invoked in exhorting their descendants to emulate.

Sanctity of human life is the most cherished moral value among the Anlo-Ewe. Taking human life is a taboo. This value is enshrined as an essential component of a normal state of mental health …

… Through the text, texture and choreography of Atrikpui dance-drumming, the warriors are also provided with the training and skill of reconciling themselves with breaking the sacred taboo before going into battle.

(1995)

In the second novel of my series, I describe the drum ceremony:

Adevu began to play a rapid rhythm. Aseye mimicked it. He played another. She repeated it as well. The avlevi expanded inside her like fetid air. Adevu played one more beat. Aseye repeated it.

And then her hands took up a song of their own and her feet began to move and the darkness came over her shoulder the way it had done before. Her consciousness dropped, making way for the avlevi as her body played and danced her closer and closer to oblivion. With each step she fell a little lower. Pieces of her peeled away as she fell. Down, down, down …

(2022: 151–2)

Ghana is not the only country that served as inspiration for the series. I drew from several African nations, for example Senegal and Ancient Egypt, in developing the world beyond the borders of the Countless Clans. All these customs, beliefs, and languages, while forming a backdrop for the series and informing the way the world operates, were not taken wholesale. They provided a platform from which I could develop a world that felt at once familiar and foreign. For instance, rather than tapping into the prevailing concepts of so-called African tradition relating to gender and sexuality, which reflect a Judeo-Christian, colonial perspective instead of a genuinely indigenous one, I looked back to pre-colonial Africa in reimagining gender and sexuality in the series.

Scholars argue that gender roles were not as regimented in those days as conservative Africans of today would like to believe. Mohammed Elnaiem (2021) writes of the Chibados or Quimbanda from Angola. These male diviners participated in ritualistic anal sex and were believed to transfer powerful female spirits to each other in this way. Homosexual activities and relationships did not arrive with Europeans. They had always occurred in our cultures and African languages have long had the terminology for them. In some cultures people who were born biologically male lived their lives as women, marrying men, and there was even a tradition of marriage between heterosexual women. In "The Deviant African Genders That Colonialism Condemned," Elnaiem states:

> This practice of same-sex marriage was documented in more than 40 precolonial African societies: a woman could marry one or more women if she could secure the bridewealth necessary or was expected to uphold and augment kinship ties …
>
> It would be anachronistic to call these ways of being "transgender." That would be to retrofit them into gender categories that we use in the twenty-first century.
>
> (2021)

In the imaginary world of the Countless Clans, therefore, gender and sexuality fall on a spectrum. Women and men can and do engage in the same kind of work. Various gender expressions and sexualities exist, and these identities are neither labeled nor questioned but rather taken for granted. There is no head of the house, at least not in a culturally determined sense. A person's occupation, lifestyle, and sexual relationships are determined by their abilities, environment, and desires. Their influence in the community is determined by their position or role. People fall in love, marry, and reproduce as they please. Sexuality is fluid and there is no stigma attached to same-sex relationships or, for that matter, asexuality (except for royalty, who are obligated to marry and produce heirs in one way or the other). I explore transgender identity in the series through an African lens, in the sense that it is inexorably attached to magic. The character Diop's transition in my novel *They Made Us Blood and Fury* is, in this lens, not a medical one but rather a supernatural one:

> "It's not a secret," Beda said with a small smile. "Diop is a man, we all knew it from early on, but his body said differently. Because of this, his natural magic was locked inside him. It took many years, many rituals before his body could speak the truth."
>
> (2021b: 299–300)

I have always felt that the most interesting thing about stories is not what they reveal through portrayals of things we already know and understand, but what they reveal by transcending the known and venturing into the realm of improbability—or impossibility. With this focus, I used the real African religious and social paradigms to explore in my novels what could be.

For example, the Anyi clan, the most important clan in the series and the setting of many of the major events, combines elements of Ewe culture and practices with a loose reference to the behavior of bees. Anyi has a political leader, a religious leader, and a Queen, a mystical, almost extraterrestrial creature that doesn't speak or think but exists only to produce lifeblood. The Queen is modeled on an extreme version of the queen bee and the lifeblood approximates honey—a magical substance that powers everything from rituals and basic tools to medicine and weapons. The people of Anyi have this same substance in their blood. They are the only people in the world with this biological trait. I knew that to make such an outlandish idea even remotely plausible, outside a science-fiction novel, I would need to ground the story in a cultural context that felt authentic.

Using my own culture as a reference point gave me more freedom to let my imagination roam. This, I think, is the magic of Africanfuturism and any other speculative fiction genre grounded in existing cultures. The fantasy can soar to greater heights and venture into deeper waters without losing the sense of familiarity that allows stories to ring true. It never struck me as implausible, while reading Arimah's "Who Will Greet You at Home?" that someone would make a child out of hair and the women around her would sing that child to life. I have no idea whether there is a real-life inspiration for the story, but, because the other cultural elements were in place, it felt seamless.

Kylie Kiunguyu writes about writerly perspective in her article "Afrofuturism or Africanfuturism: Is the Difference Important?":

> … living on a continent where blackness is the norm, not the exception, and intricate ancestry and tradition dictate daily life, provides a unique point of view that varies from Africans in the diaspora.
>
> This point of view when channelled into literature and cinematography births worlds that transcend time, suspend belief, and go beyond established frameworks but are still rooted in African tradition, religion, mysticism, folklore, and mythology.

(2022)

The Future of African Spirituality as Imagined in "Godmother"

In my short story "Godmother," I chose to focus on African (specifically Ghanaian) expressions of Christianity rather than African Traditional Religions. The fictional story is set in the near future, where the government has clamped down on the evangelical megachurches popularized by real-world "spiritual leaders" such as Prophet Shepherd Bushiri of the Enlightened Christian Gathering International Church and the charismatic Nigerian pastor, televangelist, and philanthropist, the late Temitope Balogun Joshua. In real life, that type of government clamping down is unlikely in a country in which Christianity is so deeply ingrained that the common response to the question "How are you?" is "By His grace," as in "We are well, by the grace of God."

Pastorpreneurs, a term to refer the likes of Bushiri and Joshua, set up churches as businesses. There are many of them in West Africa; upon returning to Ghana after spending most of my life in Botswana, the sheer number of churches in Accra was my biggest culture shock. Pastorpreneurs inspire devotion in their followers and disdain in their detractors. A pastorpreneur, according to Nweke's analysis of the current state of churchmanship in Nigeria "is at best a Capitalist, a disciple of money and a deceiver of humanity" (2017). They are proponents of the so-called "prosperity gospel," which preaches that material wealth and good health are the fruits of faith (Donovan 2023), and they earn vast sums of money through the support (or at the expense) of their congregants.

In the short story "Godmother," pastorpreneurs are no more. Public preaching—or more accurately, public proclamations that cannot be proven—have been outlawed. An entire government department, the Department of Authentication, exists to ensure all information released to the public is accurate and verifiable. This has the desired effect of protecting vulnerable citizens from being victimized by charlatans, but it has also sucked all the magic out of life, a tragedy for a people who possess a deep, fundamental relationship with the mystical, a relationship that informs every aspect of their lives.

"Godmother" leans toward Afrofuturism, but could also fall into the places where Afrofuturism and Africanfuturism overlap. Though set in Accra, it features few cultural elements that would seem familiar and typical to Ghanaian readers—not much authentic Ghanaian culture comes through. Instead it is a vision of a carefully curated future, an Afrocentric one, certainly, but not a particularly positive one. I envisioned a world in which our very own leaders had severed our spiritual tether with cold precision. In my view, such a world might look like the contained Accra that this excerpt depicts:

> The denizens of Accra … walk quickly, many of them with buds in their ears, listening to whatever gets them through the day. There is no tedious small talk, no gossip between neighbors. Everyone is focused. Hawkers weave through the streets, making efficient transactions with minimal discussion.
>
> "Toothpaste."
>
> "5 cedi."
>
> Phones are whipped out, credit changes hands, and hawker and customer part ways with a curt word of thanks. No needless chatter, no dawdling. No public preaching (the steep fine for disseminating unsubstantiated information put a stop to that). Order prevails.
>
> (2021a: 8–9)

An Accra this sanitized might be all but impossible for us to recognize nowadays, but the protagonist Attah, who knows no other way to live, believes this is how things ought to be. His devotion to the government overrides his internal compass. However, this devotion offers no satisfaction because, even at work, Attah doesn't belong. Furthermore, spirituality in one form or another is integral to the African way of life. By shutting that side of himself down, Attah not only severs his connection to his wider community, but also his connection to himself. Zvawanda expresses this disconnection succinctly when he says:

> Because religion permeates all aspects of a traditional African culture, if an individual rejects the culture's religion, he or she may become isolated from family, friends, and the community.
>
> (2004: 4–5)

Africans have a powerful need for community. Attah is desperate for acknowledgment and recognition. He longs to be seen and valued by those

Afrofuturist/Africanfuturist Spirituality

around him, as we all do. Christopher Agulanna acknowledges this in his article "Community and Wellbeing in an African Culture":

> Africans believe that it is only in the community where the life of the individual acquires true meaning. In other words, it is not in living as an isolated being but in mutually interacting with other members of community that the individual can ever hope to realize his social aspirations in life.
>
> (2010: 288)

As such, it is my belief that, were we to be institutionally cut off from our established sources of spiritual nourishment and community, we would suffer. Furthermore, we would rebel. We would invariably seek out substitutes and find ways to circumvent the rules. In the short story, people have indeed found another way to connect—through a medical AI nicknamed Godmother. Godmother provides basic medical services to Accra's residents, both in person and virtually, through an app. The AI becomes so popular that her cultural significance starts to resemble that of the religious leaders of the past. The public adores her. In true African fashion, her name reflects her character— she is indeed a godmother to the people.

The Department of Authentication (DoA) responds to this with dismay, putting out public announcements that only reinforce their alienation from the public:

> "Alerting all passengers: This a public notice from the Department of Authentication."
>
> My attention shifts the moment I see the announcement onscreen. I sit up tall, chest puffed out to display the badge emblazoned with my name and rank. I adjust my collar. Clear my throat. If a glance were directed at me I would smile and nod, as if to say, "Yes, I am a DoA officer. Please don't be intimidated. I'm at your service."
>
> But no one looks my way, not even the baby strapped to his mother's back a few seats ahead, and babies look at everything. This is a well-documented fact. Yet I'm not surprised. No one is looking at anyone else.
>
> "Please be advised that the Zolamed AI, ZolaMX3, commonly known as Godmother, is a manmade entity and does not possess any supernatural abilities," the announcement goes on. "Godmother is a medical robot,

not a god, prophet, or magician. Please visit the DoA portal for further information. Thank you for your attention."

That's when it happens. The man beside me glances at me. I'm so stunned that I forget my manners and stare into his scowling face.

"You people," he mutters. "Always missing the point."

(Ntumy 2021a: 1–2)

The protagonist, Attah, is assigned to investigate Godmother in the hopes of uncovering something that can be used against her. The DoA's concerns are further clarified in the words of Attah's boss:

"Eh, look, a real estate mogul has donated a church to the Godmother cult." She shares this tidbit without raising her head from the virtual documents she's perusing. "They call it a fellowship hall or some such nonsense, a place where misguided citizens will gather to worship a machine." She kisses her teeth. "The public needs to be protected from this blatant distortion of facts. Godmother is a collection of circuits, not a divine representative."

I chew my lower lip. This is a serious matter, indeed, but shouldn't she be discussing it with the DoA executives?

Captain Dzidzor sighs. "Unfortunately, Godmother's popularity makes it difficult to intervene without aggravating her followers. We have chosen a subtler approach. Informal, routine KYC, performed by you."

(Ntumy 2021a: 2–3)

As the story progresses, it becomes clear that the DoA is, indeed, missing the point. In its desperate efforts to control information and dispel misinformation, it has eroded the very fabric of society and the connection we all need to not only survive, but also to thrive. Buari, the last of the pastorpreneurs, now serving time for his mass deceptions, attempts to explain this to Attah:

"People need to feed off others," Buari explains. "That's how we're built." His smile turns sly. "Why do you think people hate DoA so much?"

I bristle at the words. "Eh, look here … "

"You deprive us of the thing we need most. Each other."

"That is inaccurate."

"With your Citizen's Guide and your Offenders List, you remind us that we can't trust each other, that each of us is alone in the world, and no one wants to be reminded." He shrugs again. "I gave people what they wanted.

Afrofuturist/Africanfuturist Spirituality 113

You take it away. I might be a criminal, but they'll always hate you more than they hate me."

(Ntumy 2021a: 12)

Our relationship to religion has always intrigued me. Africans are a deeply spiritual people, and devotion seems to come naturally, so I am not at all surprised by the influence of pastorpreneurs and megachurches on the continent—or the spread of religious fundamentalism. In crafting my story I wondered whether that fervor could be transferred from a cause or particular individuals to a technological entity. Considering rising concerns about the effect of technology on our mental health and wellbeing, especially social media, I wanted to explore the link between devotion and technology in a positive light, rather than a question of people being manipulated or controlled.

In the character of Godmother, I wanted to create a machine that is programed to behave like a human being—but not the human beings of the story's current circumstances. Rather, she was modelled on the traditional understanding of a healer—someone wise and kind, who has the technical knowledge required to heal individuals, but whose priority is the wellbeing of the community as a whole. When Attah finally allows himself to recognize this, he trades his unrequited devotion to the DoA for devotion that offers him something in return. Risking his career, he attends a gathering of Godmother's followers and experiences a sense of belonging and joy for the first time:

"Welcome, my brother," they say. "Pleased to meet you." My throat constricts and I feel an unfamiliar swell of emotion.

Are they really pleased to meet me? How can they mean it? And yet *I* am so pleased to meet *them* that my face aches from smiling.

Godmother sits quietly in a corner, talking to a group of people, their heads huddled together like old friends. Someone approaches her. She raises her head and smiles. The energy is palpable, the hall reverberating with the force of all of us experiencing this together. Fire, like the Last Charlatan said. I can feel it in my marrow, hot and dangerous and delicious. Someone puts an arm around my shoulder. I stiffen, and then laugh, giddy with belonging.

(Ntumy 2021a: 20)

It is this optimistic reimagining of the future through a broadly African lens that, in my view, makes this an Afrofuturist work, with Africanfuturist elements. The technology is inherently Afrocentric, developed from the ground up by Africans. The setting is a world created by and for Black people—a world over which no colonial shadows hang, all mistakes are exclusively ours and the purest form of spirituality is built around technology that rehabilitates humanity. The story ends with Attah embracing his true self—that is to say, his African self, acknowledging his need for community and rediscovering his innate connection to others.

Coda

I have discussed in this chapter how the diverse and complex beliefs of African peoples inspire Afrocentric fiction both on the continent and in the diaspora. While I agree with the need for the distinction between Afrofuturism and Africanfuturism, in the interests of accuracy and academic classification, I also think that authors should determine these labels for themselves. When I began writing this chapter I saw myself as an Africanfuturist.

But I love Afrofuturism as a consumer, and appreciate it for its significance as a movement. It is from the roots of Afrofuturism that discussions about Africanfuturism took sprout. Each new term generates dialogue and inspires a wealth of stories. As the feature article published on AfrikaIsWoke.com on the difference between Africanfuturism and Afrofuturism states:

> Both the African Futurism of Native African experience and the Afrofuturism of the Black Diaspora experience are equally important to the development of Black Futurist works, and perhaps the most critical aspect of the difference between African Futurism and Afrofuturism is not to focus on the distinction, but rather to be aware that Black Futurism is a tool to expand on both the Native African and Black Diaspora experience ...
>
> (2022)

I find this take refreshing. After some introspection and a deeper analysis of my work, I am not sure I fit into either camp. My work dips into Afrofuturism or Africanfuturism, or neither—it may simply be Black speculative fiction: a highly imaginative narrative that heroes Black people stories. I enjoy having the freedom to dabble, and believe we all write from our own worldview, to some extent, regardless of genre. As an African who has always lived among Africans, I do not see myself as part of a minority that must carve out a place in the world, and so my stories will never be about that. I feel that the world is as much mine as anyone else's. I want my readers to feel that way, too.

My interest is not in exploring, to use Mohale Mashigo's words, issues unique to Africans. I want to explore issues that affect humanity at large—through African settings, because I am African, but also because I believe our stories are universal. We love, we dream, we grieve, we celebrate, we worship, we doubt and despair. We follow non-African religions as well as our own, and balance cerebral European education with the visceral, instinctive knowledge that some things are beyond our understanding. To paraphrase Walt Whitman's words in "Song of Myself" (1855)—Africans are large and contain multitudes. If the African experience, with its holistic worldview, is not universal, what is?

The future I envision for African writers of all stripes is one in which we write ourselves out of our boxes. I hope we can navigate genres and terms and make them serve us when we need them to, without becoming encumbered by them. I see Afrofuturism, Africanfuturism, Black Futurism and other emerging futurisms as a sign that we are moving in the right direction.

References

Afrika Is Woke (2022), "The Difference Between African Futurism and Afrofuturism." [online] Available at <https://www.afrikaiswoke.com/afrifuturism-v-afrofuturism/> [Accessed March 26, 2023].

Agulanna, Christopher (2010), "Community and Wellbeing in an African Culture," University of Ibadan. [online] Available at <https://www.kirj.ee/public/trames_pdf/2010/issue_3/trames-2010-3-282-297.pdf> [Accessed March 23, 2023].

Ajima, Onah Gregory, and Eyong Usang Ubana (2018), "The Concept of Health and Wholeness in Traditional African Religion and Social Medicine," *ResearchGate*. [online] Available at <https://www.researchgate.net/publication/327675390_The_Concept_of_Health_and_Wholeness_in_Traditional_African_Religion_and_Social_Medicine> [Accessed March 23, 2023].

Arimah, Lesly Nneka (2015), "Who Will Greet You at Home?," *The New Yorker*. [online] Available at <https://www.newyorker.com/magazine/2015/10/26/who-will-greet-you-at-home> [Accessed March 24, 2023].

Balogun, Uche (2018), "*Black Panther: Wakanda* Is Not Africa," *The Kalahari Review*. [online] Available at <https://kalaharireview.com/black-panther-wakanda-is-not-africa-de1f6699300f> [Accessed March 25, 2023].

Bruce, Delan (2020), "Afrofuturism: From the Past to the Living Present," *UCLA Magazine* [online] Available at <https://newsroom.ucla.edu/magazine/afrofuturism> [Accessed March 25, 2023].

Dery, Mark (1994), *Flame Wars: The Discourse of Cyberculture*, Durham: Duke University Press.

Donovan, Bryn (2023), "Prosperity Gospel," *Encyclopedia Britannica*. [online] Available at <https://www.britannica.com/topic/prosperity-gospel> [Accessed March 25, 2023].

Elnaiem, Mohammed (2021), "The Deviant African Genders That Colonialism Condemned," *JSTOR Daily*. [online] Available at <https://daily.jstor.org/the-deviant-african-genders-that-colonialism-condemned/> [Accessed March 24, 2023].

IMDb (2018), *Black Panther*. [online] Available at <https://www.imdb.com/title/tt1825683/> [Accessed April 8, 2023].

Kiunguyu, Kylie (2022), "Afrofuturism or Africanfuturism: Is the Difference Important?," *This Is Africa*. [online] Available at <https://thisisafrica.me/arts-and-culture/afrofuturism-or-africanfuturism-is-the-difference-important/> [Accessed March 24, 2023].

Ladzekpo, C. L. (1995), "Introduction to Anlo-Ewe Culture and History." [online] Available at <http://richardhodges.com/ladzekpo/Intro.html> [Accessed March 23, 2023].

Marfo, Eric Apah (2023), "Talking Drums in Contemporary Ghana: The Atumpan in Focus," *Ghana News Agency*. [online] Available at <https://gna.org.gh/2023/03/talking-drums-in-contemporary-ghana-the-atumpan-in-focus/> [Accessed March 26, 2023].

Martin, Win, and Sarah Boyd (2018), "The Significance of Black Panther to African American Society." [online] Available at <https://apercu.web.unc.edu/2018/04/the-black-panther-to-african-american-society/> [Accessed March 24, 2023].

Mashigo, Mohale (2018), "Afrofuturism is Not for Africans Living in Africa," *The Johannesburg Review of Books*. [online] Available at <https://johannesburgreviewofbooks.com/2018/10/01/afrofuturism-is-not-for-africans-living-in-africa-an-essay-by-mohale-mashigo-excerpted-from-her-new-collection-of-short-stories-intruders/> [Accessed January 2, 2023].

Moyo, Fulata Lusungu (2004), "Religion, Spirituality and Being a Woman in Africa: Gender Construction within the African Religio-Cultural Experiences," [online] *Agenda: Empowering Women for Gender Equity* 61: 72–8. [online] http://www.jstor.org/stable/4066604> [Accessed March 23, 2023].

Nnedimma, Mbaeze (2022), "Ihekanwa," in Stephen Embleton (ed.) *The James Currey Anthology*, London: Abibiman Publishing, 3–15.

Ntumy, Cheryl S. (2021), "Godmother," *Apex Magazine: International Futurists Issue*. [online] Available at <https://apex-magazine.com/short-fiction/godmother/> [Accessed March 25, 2023].

Ntumy, Cheryl S. (2021), *They Made Us Blood and Fury: Chronicles of the Countless Clans Book 1*, Independent: Amazon KDP.

Ntumy, Cheryl S. (2022), *They Gave Us Stealth and Cunning: Chronicles of the Countless Clans Book 2*, Independent: Amazon KDP.

Nweke, Victor C.A. (2017), "Professional Philosophizers and the Challenge of Churchpreneurship in Contemporary Nigeria," *ResearchGate*. [online] Available at <https://www.researchgate.net/publication/323987728_PROFESSIONAL_PHILOSOPHIZERS_AND_THE_CHALLENGE_OF_CHURCHMANSHIP_IN_CONTEMPORARY_NIGERIA_A_LOGICAL_ANALYSIS> [Accessed March 25, 2023].

Okorafor, Nnedi (2019), "Africanfuturism Defined", *Nnedi's Wahala Zone Blog*. [online] Available at <https://nnedi.blogspot.com/2019/10/africanfuturism-defined.html> [Accessed January 2, 2023].

Talabi, Wole (2020), "Africanfuturism: An Anchor Point for Science Fiction that Centers Africa," *Brittle Paper*. [online] Available at <https://brittlepaper.com/2020/10/africanfuturism-an-anchor-point-for-science-fiction-that-centers-africa/> [Accessed March 24, 2023].

The Patriot (2018), "Music and Dance in Spiritual Possession." [online] Available at <https://www.thepatriot.co.zw/old_posts/music-and-dance-in-spiritual-possession/> [Accessed March 23, 2023].

Ugobude, Franklin (2020), "The Importance of Drums in African Tradition," *The Guardian*. [online] Available at <https://guardian.ng/life/the-importance-of-drums-in-african-tradition/> [Accessed March 23, 2023].

Whitman, Walt (1855), "Song of Myself," in *Leaves of Grass*, Brooklyn: Independent.

Zvawanda, Stephen (2004), "African Traditional Religions," Worldmark Encyclopaedia of Religious Practices, *Academia*. [online] Available at <https://www.academia.edu/31737727/African_Traditional_Religions> [Accessed March 23, 2023].

7

Xan van Rooyen: Queer Imaginings in Africanfuturism Inspired by African History, *South Africa/Finland*

Bio

Climber, tattoo collector, and peanut-butter connoisseur, **Xan van Rooyen** is an autistic, non-binary storyteller from South Africa, living in Finland. Xan has a Master's degree in music, and—when not teaching—enjoys conjuring strange worlds and creating quirky characters. You can find Xan's stories in the likes of *Three-Lobed Burning Eye*, *Daily Science Fiction*, and *Galaxy's Edge* among others. They have also written several novels including YA fantasy *My Name is Magic*, and adult aetherpunk novel *Silver Helix*. Xan is also a founding member of the Sauútiverse, an African writer's collective with their first anthology published by Android Press. Feel free to say hi on socials @xan_writer.

In this chapter, I will talk about queerness, queer theory, and the application of queer imaginings in Africanfuturism, inspired by African history. This chapter is a brief exploration of how to resurrect the ancient and traditional queerness present across the African continent, eroded and erased by Western hegemony as we move toward an African-inspired post-gender society.

Keywords: Africanfuturism, African History, Decolonizing Queerness, Postgenderism, Queer Imaginings

On the Word "Queer"

Coming into use sometime in the early sixteenth century to mean odd, peculiar, or eccentric, "queer" was often used derogatorily, primarily to describe gay men by the late ninteenth century. As professor in history and cultural historian, Timothy W. Jones, argues in his article "Reviled, Reclaimed and Respected: The History of the Word 'Queer,'" the word queer has subsequently been reclaimed by many within the LGBTQIA+ community, and has become an all-inclusive umbrella term denoting a variety of genders and sexualities as a critical and even political identity to challenge heteronormativity. In the same article, Jones (2023) states that,

> Queer theory drew on social constructionism—the theory that people develop knowledge of the world in a social context—to critique the idea any sexuality or gender identity was normal or natural. This showed how particular norms of sexuality and gender were historically contingent.

This is important when trying to understand indigenous queer identities in pre-colonial Africa, and how they may have evolved without Western interference.

In this text, I use "queer" as a way of including all identities beyond cisgender, which describes those whose gender identity aligns with the sex they were assigned at birth, and heterosexual, which refers to those who are sexually attracted to people of the opposite sex. I personally prefer the word "queer" as it allows for a certain fluidity of identity, and also implies acceptance of those who either don't yet know which specific label best fits who they are or who eschew the rigidity of labels altogether.

Queer Beginnings

Despite the modern rhetoric used by far too many African politicians blaming colonizers for bringing queerness to Africa, who call queerness "un-African" to justify draconian anti-LGBT+ legislation, there is historical and anthropological evidence that suggests otherwise. Numerous and specific

Queer Imaginings in Africanfuturism

examples are evidenced in *Boy-Wives and Female-Husbands: Studies in African Homosexualities* (2001), compiled and edited by scholar and historian, Stephen O. Murray, along with scholar and activist Will Roscoe. Their book is arguably one of the most extensive resources on queer identities across the African continent, showcasing exemplars from every quarter of pre-colonial Africa.

More examples appear in *The Guardian* article "Homosexuality Un-African? The Claim is an Historical Embarrassment," written by Eusebius McKaiser, a South African author, journalist and political analyst (2012). A similarly titled article, "Homosexuality is Not Un-African," by accomplished Ugandan scholar, author, and human rights activist Sylvia Tamale provides the example of ancient cave paintings, estimated to be over 2,000 years old, by the San people near Guruve in Zimbabwe, which illustrate two men engaged in a homoerotic form of ritual sex (2014). One has only to look at the ancient Egyptian pantheon to see myriad queer identities, including intersex and transgender deities, where even Mut—the goddess of Motherhood—is often depicted as having an erect penis, says Nigerian scholar and poet, Bright Alozie, in their article "Did Europe Bring Homophobia to Africa?" (2021). During precolonial times and before Abrahamic religions came to the continent, there were examples of queer identities and relationships either existing with the full acceptance of their community, or, at very least, without condemnation. As former high-ranking government minister and current member of the Botswana parliament, Unity Dow, said during a panel discussion named "Resisting Homophobia: The Colonial Origins of Anti-Gay Laws" (Milotshwa, and Smith 2023): "The response to difference (in pre-colonial Africa) was never punishment."

Such examples include the Shangaan of southern Africa who referred to same-sex male relations as inkotshane (male-wife); the gor-digen or men-women of Wolof-speakers in Senegal; the mudoko dako or effeminate males among the Langi of northern Uganda who were treated as women and allowed to marry men, and the motsoalle or "special friends," a term still used to this day by Basotho women to describe socially acceptable lesbian relationships (Tamale 2014). According to Chan Tov McNamarah (2018), a scholar who focuses on anti-discrimination law particularly for gender and sexual minorities, in their article on the role of law in the construction of the post-colonial queerphobic state, the Zulu rebel Nongoloza Mathebula ordered his troops to forego sex with women in favor of taking younger male initiates as izinkotchane or boy wives. This was common practice in precolonial northern Congo too, where Azande warrior-men routinely married boys, even paying a bride price to the boys' parents (Alozie 2021).

Bridget Boakye, a data scientist and writer, discusses in her article "King Mwanga II of Buganda, the 19th century Ugandan King Who Was Gay" (2018) how homosexuality has also been well documented in the Buganda royal court, where it was an open secret that King Mwanga ll, the last monarch of Buganda who ruled from 1884 to 1888, and from 1889 to 1897 before the British take-over, was homosexual. He was known to be relentless in his attacks against the British and Christian missionaries, who threatened not only his rule, but also his society's values and beliefs.

It would, however, be inaccurate to portray precolonial Africa as a queer utopia. Even among indigenous cultures, queerness wasn't tolerated everywhere, specifically in Nigeria and, perhaps, ironically, in Uganda. The one major exception to this was woman-to-woman relationships, particularly common among the Igbo people, which allowed an infertile woman to legally marry another woman who would bear children by the first woman's husband as heirs (McNamarah 2018). In fact, argues Tamale, woman-to-woman marriages exist to this day among the Igbo, as well as among the Nandi and Kisii of Kenya, the Nuer of Sudan, and the Kuria of Tanzania, granting women the right to marry each other for economic, diplomatic, and reproductive reasons.

But such practices are not always viewed positively, as Kenyan journalist Mercy Adhiambo writes in her article "Where Scary Traditions Allow Women to 'Marry' Women" (2018), by those within the community. One could argue they should not even be viewed as truly queer when the relationships tend to be of a non-sexual nature between the women, with asexual affection for one another seemingly not the primary consideration. When reviewing the statements and anecdotal evidence provided by the women involved in such arrangements (Adhiambo 2018), it raises issues of women's rights, body autonomy, and consent, which makes me hesitant to consider such family arrangements, though certainly different from the Western heterosexual monogamous norm, as examples of queerness.

A problem remains, however, in that queerness in precolonial Africa is often scrutinized through a Western lens, defined and identified according to queerness as understood by Western standards. Queer experiences in Africa do not always reflect nor neatly align with the West's idea of queer sexuality or gender identity. Queerness among many Afrocentric cultures is imbricated with spirituality. The Ndebele and Shona in Zimbabwe, the Azande in Sudan and Congo, the Nupe in Nigeria, and the Tutsi in Rwanda and Burundi all engaged in same-sex acts for various spiritual reasons in precolonial times. In indigenous African societies, being homosexual was believed to endow the individual with magical powers. The zvibanda, chibados, or quimbanda of the Ndonga people of Angola were considered to be of a third-gender similar to the gangas and kibambaa of Namibia, a caste of male diviners said to contain powerful female spirits, that could be shared with other men through intercourse (Tamale 2014).

According to Nwando Achebe—a Nigerian-American scholar and award-winning historian, and based on her survey of female political and spiritual authority in *Female Monarchs and Merchant Queens in Africa* (2020)—such evidence shows the interconnected nature of the universe, which allows biological men and women to become female-gendered males and male-gendered females. This interconnectedness further suggests that, even in ancient times, there was an awareness of the difference between biological sex and gender identity, an idea already well documented by Murray and Roscoe in their extensive research into African queerness (2021).

One famous example of gender fluidity is Queen Njinga Mbanda, ruler of the Mbundu people in present-day Angola. Rising to power in 1624 to vehemently resist Portuguese dominion, Queen Njinga Mbanda challenged notions of the gender binary by assuming multiple sexual and gender roles, which could perhaps be understood rather as gender identities from a modern queer lens. Not only did she answer to "King" during battle, but she frequently dressed as a man, married other women, and even had a harem of men whom she dressed as women (Alozie 2021). Her mere existence could be seen as radical.

Freelance mental health and human rights journalist Lydia Smith argues in her harrowing 2015 article "Corrective Rape: The Homophobic Fallout of

Post-Apartheid South Africa" that this perception of radicality tends to happen any time a woman shows she doesn't need a man—for physical protection, economic security, sexual pleasure, etc. Smith describes in her article how some men believe they can cure women (almost always Black women) of lesbianism by raping them—an example not only of egregious entitlement predicated on the belief that women exist only to satisfy the needs of men, but one that is rooted in a long-standing tradition of violence against women, especially when they behave in a way that threatens the deeply entrenched patriarchal values hardly unique to African society.

While this list of queerness in precolonial Africa is by no means exhaustive, it certainly shows the prevalence and diversity of queer identities and practices in precolonial times, and raises the question Kenyan lawyer and writer Aileen Waitaaga Kimuhu expressed during a Resistance Bureau discussion:

> Why (do) we as a society, as individuals, as our leaders, why (do) we continue to hold onto this idea that queer sexualities and Africanness are antithetical?
> (Mlotshwa and Smith 2023)

Kimuhu goes on to answer her own question, stating that this notion that queer sexualities and Africanness are antithetical is, in part, because our histories were written to deliberately exclude queer sexualities—in the same way that history has been white-washed, it has also been straight-washed. Kimuhu (2023) stresses the importance of decolonization and how it goes well beyond geographical redistribution:

> Independence is not just territorial, it is intellectual, it is psychological, it is emotional. We did not fully reclaim our histories or our cultures, we just merely colored within the lines that they (colonists) had provided.

As McKaiser argues in his *Guardian* article, it wasn't queerness that colonists brought to the continent, but rather violent and oppressive homophobia and transphobia, as seen in the South African examples of corrective rape. It was only in the wake of Abrahmic religions and colonization that African countries began to institute anti-LGBT+ legislation.

Sadly, the statistics speak for themselves. Of the thirty-three African countries where homosexuality is criminalized, eighteen inherited the colonial "sodomy law" from their British colonists. French colonies fared no better—although France decriminalized same-sex relationships in 1791, it still imposed its own sodomy laws upon its African colonies as a means of oppression. German and Dutch colonies inherited similar anti-gay laws, further proving a strong connection between modern anti-LGBT+ rhetoric and European colonialism (McNamarah 2018).

An exception might exist in the aggressive queerphobia in modern-day Uganda and Nigeria, which Nigerian scholar and journalist Chiké Frankie Edozien argues—in the preface of *Queer Africa: Selected Stories* (Makhosazana, and Martin 2018)—could more accurately be attributed to the work of evangelical Christians from the US. Nigerian human rights activist and storyteller, Olumide Makanjuola, reiterated this fact during the Resistance Bureau discussion (Mlotshwa, and Smith 2023), bringing up numerous examples of how politicians base their policies on Christian fundamentalism, not out of any true belief in the tenets of the faith, but rather because they are "in bed with" fundamentalist groups—such as Family Watch International— who fund their political campaigns. This, indeed, shows continued meddling by the West in African affairs. Suffice to say, most anti-queer sentiment now rife on the African continent can trace its origins to colonization and the attempts of Western hegemony to oppress and negate indigenous cultures and practices. While territory might have been reclaimed, Africans still have much work to do to untangle their African identity—queer or otherwise—from their former colonists'.

Decolonizing Queerness and Postgenderism in my Stories

I have always been drawn to science fiction and fantasy for its potential to question—if not outright rebel against—the "real-world" status quo, and manifest the pondered "what if?." The what ifs that have become an integral part of my writing process include what if queerness were a non-issue? What if society could exist where being queer was the norm and there was no need to ever come out? What if the default pronoun upon meeting someone new was gender neutral, if no one assumed or much cared about a person's gender unless it was personally relevant? What if all this normalized queerness could exist in an otherwise African-inspired story world? To achieve such a world, one would need to eschew Western hegemony, decolonize current views of queerness within African societies, and consider a postgender future.

Postgenderism is a term first used by American professor Donna Haraway in her essay "A Cyborg Manifesto" (2016) first published in 1985, and it posits a view of the future where differences in human sexuality and gender identity might be overcome using advanced biotech. This is an idea award-winning scholar and philosopher of posthumanism Francesca Ferrando further explores in their article "Is the Post-Human a Post-Woman? Cyborgs, Robots, Artificial Intelligence and the Futures of Gender: A Case Study":

> In the future, gender will most likely evolve into something different, and thus create a "post," which does not imply obliterations, assimilations or neutralizations. Such an evolution might as well provide a multiplication of genders, not necessarily related to the feminine and masculine archetypes.
>
> (2014)

My view of the future aligns with both Haraway and Ferrando in that I believe advances in biotechnology and increased understanding of human psychology will cause a social paradigm shift further challenging existing binary notions of gender. This will force us to finally accept, if not embrace and celebrate, that gender identity has never been solely based on, nor defined by, biological sex, but exists rather as a constellation of fluid possibilities defying even the notion of a spectrum with "man" on one end and "woman" on the other.

Canadian bioethicist, transhumanist, and futurist George Dvorsky seems to share this idea of the future, and suggests in his essay "Postgenderism: Beyond the Gender Binary" that technological advancements will erode the notion of binary gender and that this will be liberatory:

> Postgenderists argue that gender is an arbitrary and unnecessary limitation on human potential, and foresee the elimination of involuntary biological and psychological gendering in the human species through the application of neurotechnology, biotechnology and reproductive technologies.

Postgenderists contend that dyadic gender roles and sexual dimorphisms are generally to the detriment of individuals and society. Assisted reproduction will make it possible for individuals of any sex to reproduce in any combinations they choose, with or without "mothers" and "fathers," and artificial wombs will make biological wombs unnecessary for reproduction. Greater biological fluidity and psychological androgyny will allow future persons to explore both masculine and feminine aspects of personality. Postgenderists do not call for the end of all gender traits, or universal androgyny, but rather that those traits become a matter of choice. Bodies and personalities in our postgender future will no longer be constrained and circumscribed by gendered traits, but enriched by their use in the palette of diverse self-expression.

(2008)

How then to revive indigenous understandings of queerness, and meld ancient practice within a sci-fi or fantasy milieu? Postgenderism is not only the purview of science fiction. The philosophical paradigm can be applied to fantasy worldbuilding as well.

Between 2020 and 2022, I wrote and had published several stories set in my Afrocentric futuristic world, Frayverse, a universe where abrasive and conflicting magics caused a rip between dimensions, allowing alien magic to bleed into the various interconnected worlds. These worlds often featured African-inspired settings, drawing simultaneously from African culture and my own lived experiences in South Africa. The stories are also all unapologetically queer. In fact, I make a point to always include queer characters in my stories, especially trans and non-binary ones. My stories are not loud proclamations of rebellion, but rather quietly subversive in their attempts to normalize what is sadly and, too often, barely tolerated in the real world.

Sometimes these gestures are as simple as banal introductions, normalizing the use of pronouns, as in my short story "Of Feathers and Flowers":

The music danced between them in firefly flickers and the kermis gave a hypnogogic jerk. The space between them folded in on itself until they breathed each other's breath, knees touching, hair tangling.

"I'm Ara. She and her," she said.

"Renier. He and him." He offered her his hand and she shook it.

(2021a: 136)

Similarly, I endeavor to maintain a non-binary gaze when my protagonist encounters someone new. In my short story "Shatterling," my character, Sam, meets a stranger while on the hunt for pieces of his missing soul:

> A person, shorter and darker skinned, blocked his path. Arms folded, brows furrowed, mouth a thin twist. They spoke, repeating themselves in several languages before Sam nodded in understanding.
>
> "I can hear it," they said.
>
> "One of yours?" he replied in the same tongue, the syllables thick and awkward against his lips.
>
> "Obviously." They didn't look like a Shatterling but Sam knew better than to judge. The worst damage was usually where you couldn't see it.
>
> (2022: 44)

Here Sam uses a gender-neutral pronoun (they) showing that not only does he avoid assuming a person's gender, but that gender has no impact on the interaction. When Sam notes "They didn't look like a Shatterling ... " the fact this refers to not judging someone based on what one can immediately see is not a coincidence, and it's my own subtle reminder to those who might wish to know this stranger's gender, albeit completely irrelevant to the story. In my book *By the Blood of Rowans* (2021b), though admittedly in no way inspired by or an extension of African culture, I take this a step further with my non-binary main character Ash, whose anatomy is never mentioned in the book. This led to consternation from some cishet (cisgender and heterosexual) beta readers who questioned if Ash was "really" a boy or a girl so that they, the reader, could better relate to them and picture them in their head. Not only did these readers completely miss the point of Ash being *non-binary* in my book, but they also illustrated the need many non-queer and cisgender queer people have to know about a person's body parts in order to know how to relate and interact with them. While I dream of a postgender future, this proves we have a long way to get there.

Too often in stories, particularly those written by cisgender authors, the trans characters are subjected to something known as a "shock reveal" where, having passed as someone cis, they are revealed to be trans, usually in a way that is humiliating for the trans character while evoking anger in the other, usually cis, character/s witnessing the reveal. This is an incredibly damaging trope given the number of trans people, especially trans women, who are murdered under similar circumstances with the murderer able to excuse their violent behavior with the "trans panic defense" as detailed in the comprehensive article titled "Transgender Rights and Issues" published by Georgetown University (Adams et al. 2020). In my short story "Of Feathers and Flowers" I deliberately challenge this trope, creating a scene with a reveal that features feelings of shame and anger but subverts expectations:

> She pulled off his shirt expecting a chest slabbed with the muscle promised by the breadth of his shoulders.
>
> His chest was bound, muscle and more, constrained by eyelets and bow-tied strings.
>
> A tidal wave of his humiliation crashed through her, leaving a bitter riptide as she fingered the bindings. Her own anger gnashed serrated teeth within her. Who had made him feel shame for this? Her anger simmered in the air between them, rank and acid.
>
> This is nothing to be ashamed of.
>
> "It's not what you think." He caught her fingers. Ara pulled back, letting Renier loose the knots.
>
> He set the binder on the straw-stuffed mattress beside them, the inside stained black and red. Ara traced a finger along the sharp outline of his collarbone and slowly down his chest to the feather embroidered above his heart. The stitches were taut, dragging at the bruised skin. Scabs cracked and oozed.
>
> Her fingers tingled with the spell-work woven through his flesh. Magic, though none like she knew.
>
> "What is this?" She asked. "What does it make you?"
>
> "A soldier," he said, exhaling a dying gasp of pride "At least, I used to be."
>
> (2021a: 139–40)

This excerpt also engages with difference, challenging yet another real-world discriminatory view that queer people, especially trans people, should not serve in the military, a view that former US President Donald Trump wrote into legislation, banning trans people from serving in the US military, effective 2019. Although his successor Joe Biden subsequently reversed this ban and while twenty-one countries—mostly Western European—allow trans people to serve openly in the military, according to a study surveying trans US military personnel, almost all participants reported having had stigmatizing experiences and experiencing discrimination while serving (Schvey et al. 2020).

As African history has shown us, gender identity was no challenge for the warrior Queen Njinga Mbanda nor for the Agojie women who earned such a ferocious reputation as soldiers serving the ninteenth-century kingdom of Dahomey—that even Hollywood took note and made a movie about these incredible warriors in *The Woman King* (IMDb 2022), starring Viola Davis. Neither was it a challenge for my trans character Renier.

But while my Frayverse stories may take inspiration from Africa with their settings, naming conventions, and imagery, I never wrote them to be true reflections of African philosophy or culture and never would have considered labeling my work Africanfuturism—until I became a founding member of the Sauúti Collective.

I was nervous when I joined what was then simply a group of African writers who'd come together to create the Afrocentric Sauútiverse (Sauúti 2023) founded on and inspired by African philosophy, mythology, and culture. I had never been part of a writers' collective before and was a little intimidated by some names involved in the project. I felt entirely out of my depth, unsure of my worldbuilding skills, and even more unsure of how the collective might receive my own queerness.

After introductions and initial discussions about what it meant to collectively create a story-verse, it became apparent we were all on the same page and the Sauútiverse was born: a binary star system created by the Mother where sound and music have magical power in keeping with the oral traditions of African cultures. Here was an entire universe predicated on African understandings, deliberately shunning Western sentiment in favor of an African perspective. Here was my opportunity to explore queerness in a science fantasy world that directly connected with indigenous views.

In the original version of my story "The Heretic Harmonic" (2024)—the first story I wrote set in the Sauútiverse—my main character is Aziiwa, a menigari who possesses the rare and special ability to see spirits and commune with the ancestors all the time. Aziiwa is also non-binary, a fact shown by the use of gender-neutral pronouns, an identity never questioned by members of their community because, in this world, gender identity is a non-issue. Not only is Aziiwa non-binary and blessed with the gift of being a menigari, they are also chosen by the village Elder to inherit her memories of magic and eventually take up her mantle leading the island community.

> As Elder-to-be, Aziiwa led the musical procession, and the islanders followed. They stamped their feet, the cocoons threaded around their ankles jingling syncopations as everyone beat their heels into the dust. Aziiwa plucked melodies from their valiha and sang in counterpoint to the refrain belted by the rest of the islanders.
>
> (van Rooyen 2024: 7)

And from a few paragraphs later …

> The islanders waited for Aziiwa to commence the final farewell, a song-spell meant to sever Jevuuwaje's umbilical to the realm of the living, setting her free to join the ancestors. A song with magic contained in each utterance preserved from the primal tongue inherited from the Mother herself.
>
> (van Rooyen 2024: 10)

Aziiwa is a leader, beloved and trusted by their community. They are valued and held in high regard, all in keeping with how many indigenous African cultures viewed people who transcended the gender binary.

Similarly, in my story "Lost in the Echoes," in the first Sauúti anthology by Android Press in November 2023, I again have a trans protagonist. In this story, Ruk also has a unique ability—he is a Taq'qerara, someone capable of altering a person's sound aura for better or worse—for which his community venerates him. However, Ruk finds his near god-like status suffocating.

> When he'd first been named Taq'qerara and placed upon a skewering pedestal, his people had come to him in supplication, their adoration like sonic caresses soothing his aching flesh. *You must search, must find, release, heal, you must fulfill the prophecy.* Their adulation became like nails, leaving him bloodied and suffocating beneath the weight of their expectation.
>
> Perhaps he could indeed use his power one last time.
>
> He would remake himself. He would un-become what he'd never wanted to be—a scar to finally seal the hurt, numbing his senses to the world.
>
> The Mother had made a mistake before and Ruk had had to correct his anatomy.

It had been another mistake to make him Taq'qerara. But no more.

(2023: 19–20)

When writing Ruk, I was very aware of how he might transition in this world that has both magic and advanced technology, though magic is certainly favored within most Sauúti communities. I didn't want Ruk to be magically rendered according to what others might consider necessary in order to pass as a cis male. I wanted his trans identity to be an integral part of who he is and his journey, but to also show how trans people are treated in the Sauútiverse, at least within this particular culture on one of the five planets. Just as Africa is not a country with a monolithic culture, neither is the Sauútiverse.

> At fifteen, when the tribal healer had cut and sung his breasts to thin lines of keloid, the scars marking Ruk's face had been altered and she became he. If only the uroh-ogi could've also excised the Mother-sliver embedded in his soul; if only the healer could've sung away the power he didn't deserve.
>
> (2023: 8)

This is the only time Ruk being trans is explicitly mentioned, but it's vital to the story, not only in terms of his journey but also in showing the worldbuilding. Within this tribal community, Ruk being trans is fully accepted and has no bearing on his revered status. He does not need to escape his own community for being queer, nor does he need to seek out some big city healer (uro-ogi) with more progressive views and more advanced understandings of medicine to receive gender affirming care—it's his own tribal healer, with a role like both the isangoma and nyanga of South Africa, who unquestionably provides necessary medical care. Ruk's internal conflict and struggles with identity throughout the story have nothing to do with his queerness, illustrating that while being trans (or queer or neurodivergent or disabled) is inextricably part of a person's identity, this does not need to be the central *issue* of the character's story arc.

The Future Is Queer

As stated in the African LGBTI Manifesto/Declaration written in April 2010 at a roundtable discussion in Nairobi, Kenya,

As long as African LGBTI people are oppressed, the whole of Africa is oppressed (Editors, *Black Agenda Review* 2021)

This echoes a sentiment shared by Nelson Mandela in the preface for Richard Stengel's book *Mandela's Way: Fifteen Lessons on Life, Love, and Courage,*

In Africa there is a concept known as "ubuntu"—the profound sense that we are human only through the humanity of others; if we are to accomplish anything in this life it will in equal measure be due to the work and achievements of others.

(2010: xi)

Or as Sylvia Tamale puts it,

The homosexuality-is-un-African mantra negates everything that African history and tradition has transmitted to posterity. A tenet of African philosophy holds that "I am because you are." In short, it matters little about the differences that each one of us displays but much about the essence of humanity that binds us together. What really matters is the respect for human dignity and diversity.

(2014)

In this conversation on gender and sexuality as a critical and political identity to challenge heteronormativity, I haven't considered the "futurism" labels, especially as they may or may not apply to my own work as a white South African. Now, as a founding member of the Sauútiverse, I feel more at ease with an Africanfuturism label applied to my Sauúti stories according to the definition Nnedi Okarafur provides:

Africanfuturism: Wakanda builds its first outpost in a neighboring African country.

(2019)

But I am someone who has eschewed labels in general and only use them to help others' understanding of my identity, rather than the mechanism by which I understand myself: am I non-binary or genderqueer? Am I bisexual or pansexual, and can I be those while also being asexual? Am I better understood as specifically autistic or more broadly neurodivergent? Since I exist as I am with or without those labels, I will leave defining my stories to readers and critics, and focus instead on exploring the next what if.

That said, I do feel the weight of responsibility upon my shoulders as I continue to conjure queer imaginings in futuristic fantastical realms and consider the many *what ifs* to be answered by my sci-fi futures. I feel too, the presence of the unhappy ghosts of those ancestors who knew better and shake their heads at all we have forgotten about love and acceptance, about community and humanity. But what if we could resurrect ancient, indigenous perspectives of queerness? What if we could decolonize our minds and be rid of the oppression left in the wake of colonizers? What if we could imagine a future no longer tainted by queerphobia, where people were free to live as their authentic selves without fear or shame? This is the future I long for, and one I continue to write toward.

References

Achebe, Nwando (2020), *Female Monarchs and Merchant Queens in Africa*, Athens: Ohio University Press.

Adams, Judson, Halle Edwards, Rachel Guy, Maya Springhawk Robnett, Rachel Scholz-Bright, and Breanna Weber (2020), "Transgender Rights and Issues," *The Georgetown Journal of Gender and the Law*, 21(2): 479–539. [online] Available at <https://www.law.georgetown.edu/gender-journal/wp-content/uploads/sites/20/2021/01/GT-GJGL200007.pdf> [Accessed on 16 April 2023].

Adhiambo, Mercy (2018), "Where Scary Traditions Allow Women to 'Marry' Women," *The Sunday Standard*. [online] Available at <https://www.standardmedia.co.ke/kenya/article/2001257316/where-scary-traditions-allow-women-to-marry-women> [Accessed on April 16, 2023].

Alozie, Bright (2021), "Did Europe Bring Homophobia to Africa?," *AAIHS: Black Perspectives*. [online] Available at <https://www.aaihs.org/did-europe-bring-homophobia-to-africa/> [Accessed on April 7, 2023].

Boakye, Bridget (2018), "King Mwanga II of Buganda, the 19th Century Ugandan King Who Was Gay," *Face2Face Africa*. [online] Available at <https://face2faceafrica.com/article/king-mwanga-ii-of-buganda-the-19th-century-ugandan-king-who-was-gay> [Accessed on April 7, 2023].

Dvorsky, George (2008), "Postgenderism: Beyond the Gender Binary," *Sentient Developments*. [online] Available at <http://www.sentientdevelopments.com/2008/03/postgenderism-beyond-gender-binary.html> [Accessed on April 9, 2023].

Editors, *The Black Agenda Review* (2020), "MANIFESTO: African LGBTI Manifesto/Declaration, April 18, 2010," *Black Agenda Report*. [online] Available at <https://www.blackagendareport.com/manifesto-african-lgbti-manifestodeclaration-april-18-2010> [Accessed on April 7, 2023].

Ferrando, Francesca (2014), "Is the Post-Human a Post-Woman? Cyborgs, Robots, Artificial Intelligence and the Futures of Gender: A Case Study," *European Journal of Futures Research*, 2(43). [online] Available at https://link.springer.com/article/10.1007/s40309-014-0043-8 [Accessed on April 9, 2023].

Haraway, Donna J. (2016), *A Cyborg Manifesto: Science, Technology, and Socialist-Feminism in the Late Twentieth Century*, Minneapolis: University of Minnesota Press. [online] Available at <https://warwick.ac.uk/fac/arts/english/currentstudents/undergraduate/modules/fictionnownarrativemediaandtheoryinthe21stcentury/manifestly_haraway_—-_a_cyborg_manifesto_science_technology_and_socialist-feminism_in_the_pdf> [Accessed on April 9, 2023].

IMDb (2022), *The Woman King*. [online] Available at <https://www.imdb.com/title/tt8093700/> [Accessed April 15, 2023].

Jones, Timothy W. (2023), "Reviled, Reclaimed and Respected: The History of the Word 'Queer,'" *The Conversation*. [online] Available at <https://theconversation.com/reviled-reclaimed-and-respected-the-history-of-the-word-queer-197533> [Accessed April 5, 2023].

Makhosazana, Xaba, and Karen Martin (eds.) (2018), *Queer Africa: Selected Stories*, Oxford: New Internationalist.

McKaiser, Eusebius (2012), "Homosexuality Un-African? The Claim is an Historical Embarrassment," *The Guardian*. [online] Available at <https://www.theguardian.com/world/2012/oct/02/homosexuality-unafrican-claim-historical-embarrassment> [Accessed April 7, 2023].

McNamarah, Chan Tov (2018), "Silent, Spoken, Written, and Enforced: The Role of Law in the Construction of the Post-Colonial Queerphobic State," *Cornell International Law Journal*. [online] Available at <https://ww3.lawschool.cornell.edu/research/ILJ/upload/McNamarah-note-final.pdf> [Accessed April 7, 2023].

Mlotshwa, Mantate, and Jeffrey Smith (2023), "Resisting Homophobia: The Colonial Origins of Anti-Gay Laws." [online] Available at <https://www.youtube.com/watch?v=WJavs887cLU> [Accessed April 30, 2023].

Murray, S. O., W. Roscoe, and M. Epprecht (2021), *Boy-Wives and Female Husbands: Studies in African Homosexualities*, Albany: State University of New York Press.

Okorafor, Nnedi (2019), "Africanfuturism Defined," *Nnedi Wahala's Zone Blog.* [online] Available at <https://nnedi.blogspot.com/2019/10/africanfuturism-defined.html> [Accessed April 19, 2023].

Sauúti (2023). [online] Available at <https://syllble.com/sauuti/ [Accessed April 15, 2023].

Schvey, N. A., D. A. Klein, A. T. Pearlman, R. I. Kraff, and D. S. Riggs (2020), "Stigma, Health, and Psychosocial Functioning Among Transgender Active Duty Service Members in the U.S. Military," *Stigma and Health*, 5(2), 188–98. [online] Available at <https://doi.org/10.1037/sah0000190> [Accessed on April 16, 2023].

Smith, Lydia (2015), "Corrective Rape: The Homophobic Fallout of Post-Apartheid South Africa," *American Renaissance*. [online] Available at <https://www.amren.com/news/2015/06/corrective-rape-the-homophobic-fallout-of-post-apartheid-south-africa/> [Accessed on April 7, 2023].

Stengel, Richard (2010), *Mandela's Way: Fifteen Lessons on Life, Love, and Courage*, New York: Crown Archteype.

Tamale, Sylvia (2014), "Homosexuality is Not Un-African," *Aljazeera America*. [online] Available at <http://america.aljazeera.com/opinions/2014/4/homosexuality-africamuseveniugandanigeriaethiopia.html> [Accessed on April 7, 2023].

van Rooyen, Xan (2021a), "Of Feathers and Flowers," in Rowan Rook (ed.), *All Worlds Wayfarer*, Issue VIII, 132–44.

van Rooyen, Xan (2021b), *By the Blood of Rowans*, Cape Town: Skolion

van Rooyen, Xan (2022), "Shatterling," *Bards & Sages Quarterly*, January, 46–53.

van Rooyen, Xan (2023), "Lost in the Echoes," *Mothersound: The Sauútiverse Anthology*, Oregon: Android Press, 338–58.

van Rooyen, Xan (2024), "The Heretic Harmonic," *Andromeda Spaceways Magazine*, 94, 41–52.

8

Aline-Mwezi Niyonsenga: Afrofuturism and Exploring Cultural Identity as a Process of Becoming, *Rwanda/Australia*

Bio

Aline-Mwezi Niyonsenga's name is short for "moonlight" in Kinyarwanda. She writes Black speculative fiction. Her work has reflected on migrant experiences with the help of a lion goddess, tornado auntie, magical fish, and the occasional ghost. Her short stories have been published in *GigaNotoSaurus, Augur Magazine, Fantasy Magazine, FIYAH Magazine of Black Speculative Fiction, demos journal, Selene Quarterly Magazine, Apparition Lit, Djed Press, Underground Writers,* and *Jalada Africa*, among others. They have also appeared in anthologies such as *Africa Risen* and *super/natural: art and fiction for the future.* You can find links to her works on her website: aline-mweziniyonsenga.com.

In this chapter, I will consider Afrofuturism and exploring cultural identity as a process of becoming through fiction. I pay attention to the self and morphing identities through the application of futurism, with examples from my novelette "Fell Our Selves" (2023).

Keywords: Afrofuturism, African Diaspora, Becoming, Cultural Identity, Migratory Subjectivities

What Afrofuturism Might Be

Broadly defined, Afrofuturism is a subgenre where writers can imagine alternate futures for people of African descent. It is "an intersection of imagination, technology, the future, and liberation" that combines "elements of science fiction, historical fiction, speculative fiction, fantasy, Afrocentricity, and magic realism with non-Western beliefs" (Womack 2013: 9; Edugyan 2022: 147). In this genre, writers can imagine pessimistic or hopeful futures with systems and technology that either liberate or continue to oppress Black people. By speculating on these futures, they can challenge white supremacy or redefine what it means to be "Black." They can also imagine futures that accept non-Western ways of knowing, by introducing African cosmologies. Writers can use this subgenre to reflect on the experiences of people of African descent situated in the West or elsewhere. They can also reflect on the experiences of African people rooted in the continent.

Samuel R. Delany, in the essay "The Mirror of Afrofuturism" (2020), claims that any Black writer who is writing in science fiction is writing Afrofuturist works. It can be a catch-all term that's "pretty much anything you want it to be and not a rigorous category at all," writes Delany (2020: 184), and that raises more questions than answers, concludes author and editor Sheree Renée Thomas in her essay "And So Shaped the World" (2016: 4). In this flexible way, the possibilities for Afrofuturism are as endless as its imagined futures.

Some claim Afrofuturism is simply one strand of black speculative fiction, and that it is under this wider umbrella that writers imagine African futures (Burnett 2019: 124). Grounding Afrofuturism in speculative fiction allows the freedom to use it as a catch-all term to explore all speculations of African realities, whether they are positive or negative. Afrofuturism can be an organizing subgenre term rather than a set literary category.

How I Define Afrofuturism

The way I would like to define Afrofuturism is as a "story of dislocation" (Edugyan 2022: 155). As Esi Edugyan elaborates in her essay "Africa and the Art of the Future," I would like to define Afrofuturism as a "story of recovery, of finding new anchors" (2022: 155). Through Afrofuturism, Black writers recover lost paths and establish new origins. They redefine their identity by remixing its pieces into something new. Slave trade and colonialism both introduced schisms in cultural memory, erasing pre-colonial cultures in a European agenda of genocide. Afrofuturism as a subgenre is a space to imagine what could have been and what could be based on the fragments of the past.

I would also like to set Afrofuturism as a strand of Black speculative fiction. Speculative fiction is a genre through which writers can reflect on migratory subjectivities (Feracho 2017: 35), or what it is like to be a migrant. It is within this genre that I set my novelette "Fell Our Selves" (2023). I use it to explore migratory subjectivities through the physical and inner journeys of its characters, Dustin and Akeza.

My work especially resonates with the idea that Afrofuturism attracts what is new to its fold, and "what is new is a fluid, shapeshifting concept for those who speculate, extrapolate, innovate" (Thomas 2016: 4). The concept of shapeshifting applies neatly to discussions about hybrid cultural identities, or cultural identity as a constant process of becoming (Glissant 1989, 1997; Hall and du Gay 1996; Willey 2013; Bradley and Marassa 2014; Afful 2016; Holgado 2017). Migratory subjectivities constantly shift and remix depending on their relation to cultural contexts. This is why I deliberately use shapeshifting as a central device in "Fell Our Selves."

Who Afrofuturism Is For

When Afrofuturism was originally coined by the white cultural critic Mark Dery, it referred to science fiction that imagined people of African descent in the future. This definition didn't immediately include people from the African continent (Samatar 2017: 175; Delany 2020: 173; Dixon 2021: 121–2). As such, there are those who think "Afrofuturism" is a limiting term that only refers to those African descendants in the Americas, rather than extending to include Africans based in the continent (Samatar 2017; Okorafor 2019; Edoro 2021).

Africans and recent African migrants are often left out of discussions about black identity and the African diaspora. In literary studies, there is an assumption that the African diaspora only refers to people directly affected by the transatlantic slave trade (Bradley and Marassa 2014; Afful 2016; Carrera-Suárez 2017; Holgado 2017; Cobo-Piñero 2018), and that Afrofuturist works only refer to those subjects (Byrd 2021: 47). Nowadays, the African diaspora is broader than that, with authors like Nnedi Okorafor placing African migrants at the centre of narratives in works like *Binti* (2015) and *Akata Witch* (2011).

In the essay, "Toward a Planetary History of Afrofuturism" (2017), author Sofia Samatar attempts to define Afrofuturism in a way that considers the influence of African literary predecessors and artists. Samatar observes that formations of the subgenre's history describe Africa as "being late to the game" (2017: 176), and while author Ytasha L. Womack, in the book *Afrofuturism: The World of Black Sci-Fi and Fantasy Culture* (2013), brings African artists into the discussion, she does so without discussing their position or relation to the African continent (Samatar 2017: 176). Samatar considers a planetary history of Afrofuturism that centers Africa as its place of origin and, in doing so, identifies common patterns within the subgenre, such as bricolage and remixology. She also calls out areas that writers can explore further, such as the relationship between Afrofuturistic blends of folklore, fantasy, and technology, and the genre of magic realism. Through Samatar's exploration, Afrofuturism becomes a subgenre that can apply to the experiences of every Black person whose place of origin is Africa.

Positionality and Afrofuturism

I am a cis-gendered, able-bodied, heterosexual woman of African descent, born in Quebec, Canada to parents who immigrated from Rwanda. I am also a migrant who has lived in the United States of America, and a first-generation immigrant to Australia.

In discussions on how Afrofuturism compares to Africanfuturism or Africanjujuism, there seems to always be a distinction between who the subjects of these genres are. Either we are talking about the African diaspora from the forced migration of the transatlantic slave trade (Byrd 2021: 47) or Africans positioned in the continent (Okorafor 2019; Edoro 2021). You are either coming straight from the continent or you are not. Where do the children of recent African migrants fit in the exploration of Black futures?

Is it Afrofuturist to consider the future of one's cultural identity?

My cultural identity occupies an in-between space of all and none of these: Quebecois, Canadian, Rwandan, and Australian. When you occupy a liminal space, is your identity collective or individual? Is it worth exploring the self-determination of this identity through fiction?

In a review of "Literary Afrofuturism in the Twenty-First Century" (2021), Frederick Douglass Dixon asserts that to "define one's identity remains a prerequisite for self-determination" (Dixon 2021: 121). Knowing who you are and where you have come from can help you determine where you are going. This theme can be explored at both an individual and collective level under the umbrella of Afrofuturism.

Remixing Cultural Identity in Afrofuturist literature

In *Literary Afrofuturism in the Twenty-First Century*, Isiah Lavender III and Lisa Yaszek introduce Afrofuturism as a call for Black authors to "reboot the black identity, challenge white supremacy, and imagine a range of futures in full color" (2020: 1). In this way, Afrofuturism as a genre provides an opportunity to imagine an organized Black people reckoning with the past to determine how they'll define their future.

According to Samatar, "Afrofuturism can be read as a philosophy of the remix" (2017: 179). In Afrofuturist works, suggests Samatar, fragments of the past are combined in new ways to imagine different futures. Afrofuturist works demonstrate "a poetics of the fragment. Here the fragment holds possibility: the sign of becoming rather than dissolution" (p.179) Fragments become something new when put together, and this can refer to imagining new concepts of identity through literature. The idea of "becoming" is prevalent in discussions of hybridity in cultural identity, especially in relation to subjects of the African diaspora (Glissant 1989, 1997; Hall and du Gay 1996; Willey 2013; Bradley and Marassa 2014; Afful 2016; Holgado 2017). As writers remix fragments to imagine futures in Afrofuturist works, they can also remix these fragments to explore what it means to be of African descent.

Afrofuturism can function as a space for writers to explore the idea of cultural identity as a process of becoming: "Afrofuturism seeks to return, to reclaim history as a necessary part of becoming" (Samatar 2017: 189). By examining the legacy of the past, writers can carve the future of one's cultural identity. This is especially interesting in the case of recent migrants from Africa or children of African migrants, like me.

In this way, a philosophy of the remix can be used in "the formation of African and African diasporic subjectivities" (Samatar 2017: 180), or as ways to explore how cultural identity can be constructed in the African diaspora. In "Fell Our Selves," I remix cultural references to Rwanda with a world of floating islands and a political climate similar to the Opium Wars. I use this setting to explore the inner journeys of two characters as they reflect on their displacement from their ancestral land and how this affects their cultural identity.

"Fell Our Selves" engages with themes of the return to one's roots, return home, and the possibility or impossibility of this. Writers have room to explore these ideas further through African diasporic science fiction.

Blending Science Fiction and Fantasy in Afrofuturist Literature

Though Afrofuturism is rooted in science fiction, some think it should include elements of fantasy in its definition because it aligns with African ways of knowing. The Black Speculative Arts Movement (BSAM), for example, asserts that between fantasy and exact knowledge, there is magic, and magic leads to exact knowledge (Anderson 2016: 229–30). Integrating other ways of knowing in science fiction is a way to acknowledge that these ways of knowing are just as valid as Western ones. This results in a blend of science fiction and fantasy genres that both serve to speculate African futures.

Combining folklore and science fiction is possible through Samatar's exploration of Afrofuturism: "In the philosophy of the remix, the combination of folklore and science fiction is perfectly possible; in the poetics of mythmaking, which draws on the past in order to imagine the future, it is necessary" (Samatar 2017: 182–3). Afrofuturist works use the past to inform the future and myth to inform worldbuilding.

"Fell Our Selves" is a good example of such a combination. In the story, Dustin's country of origin is called Ngunda—the name of a folkloric figure that built the land of Rwanda. I apply it in my novelette to the name of a floating island. The main characters, Akeza and Dustin, both reflect on the folkloric story of Kamegeri's rock to inform how they define their cultural identity. Their clash in opinions on the story helps them assert their cultural identities: Akeza as "Ngundan," and Dustin as "Majestian."

This is not the first story that integrates folklore in speculative settings. Indeed, "The use of folk beliefs and stories is a distinguishing characteristic of African diasporic science fiction" (Samatar 2017: 183). One of these is Jamaican-Canadian author Nalo Hopkinson's *Brown Girl in the Ring* (1998), a novel with a post-apocalyptic setting and a possession by duppy (malevolent spirit or ghost in Caribbean folklore) story at its core. "Fell Our Selves" has a similar fantastical setting with a culture rooted in folk stories that blends with the advanced technology of shapeshifting ships.

In Samatar's words, I believe that examining "Afrofuturistic blends of folklore, fantasy, and technology in a global context would make significant contributions to the study of both magical realism and science fiction" (2017: 184). Through fiction, replacing Western ways of knowing for African ones will allow writers to explore decolonized futures. This could expose readerships to alternate ways of seeing the world and different ways to conceptualize future technology.

Shapeshifting and Diaspora Subjectivity in "Fell Our Selves"

In my novelette "Fell Our Selves," I attempt to convey what Emma Pérez, an American author and scholar renowned for queer Chicana feminist studies, calls a "diaspora subjectivity" that "is always in movement, disrupting, recreating and mobile in its representation, converging the past with the present for a new future" (Pérez 1999: 79; Feracho 2017: 42). I do this through the pilgrimage-like journey of Dustin and Akeza. Theirs is a physical journey that is linear: from one part of the floating island of Majestia to another. Their emotional journey is less so, as they struggle to come to terms with their shifting sense of cultural identity. They reckon with the past in their consideration of folktale and personal history. They also reckon with the present and future as they gain a greater understanding of themselves and what they want to become.

The central mystery of the story is linked to the ship they travel in: the notorious Shapeshifter. Shapeshifters use a mysterious technology that allows them to take on the form of any known vehicle in the story's world. How they do this is a secret closely guarded by Ngundans, so that even Dustin, the ship's mechanic, does not fully know the ship's inner workings. Akeza, his mysterious client, instructs him to treat the ship as he would the model it looks like. The Shapeshifter acts as a device to highlight the cultural differences between Akeza and Dustin. Dustin feels like he is a clueless Majestian that looks ethnically Ngundan, and Akeza acts as a "typical" Ngundan.

Dustin struggles with his self-identification in regard to his cultural identity, and claims he is Majestian. He feels uncomfortable when Akeza, his client, claims otherwise:

> Akeza waved him off, reaching for another handful of peanuts. Typical Ngundan, avoiding questions. "Nothing. I guess Majestians think differently."
> "You thought I was Ngundan."
> "Ya. You are Ngundan."
> "I can't be both."
>
> (2023: 3)

Dustin believes in the idea that one can only have one cultural identity. As such, he decides to claim he is Majestian instead of considering his relationship with his Ngundan heritage.

Dustin's struggle with his own idea of cultural identity represents the hybrid negotiations of identity in the face of dominant discourses of assimilation. Growing up clinging to the idea that he was Majestian makes Dustin unable to acknowledge the possibility of a hybrid identity. If he asserts his Ngundan heritage, he thinks it will make him disappear, since he will never be Ngundan enough, and never Majestian enough:

Dustin shook his head. "I'm Majestian, but I look Ngundan. I can't be both Majestian and Ngundan. The two cancel out and I become nothing." He blinked, surprised he was being so honest.

(2023: 16).

Unable to fully identify with the cultural specificities of being Ngundan or Majestian, Dustin interprets cultural hybridity as lacking a cultural home. In this way, Dustin struggles to come to terms with an identity that is more complex than just being one thing or another and doesn't feel fully comfortable with being labelled one or the other.

On the other hand, Akeza firmly believes in Dustin's identity as a Ngundan, claiming,

"We are all Ngundan in the end, no matter how far we go," Akeza said. The family turned to her. She laughed, self-conscious. "Don't you think?"

(2023: 8)

When faced with the possibility of Dustin's hybrid cultural identity, she relies heavily on traditional ideas of what makes someone Ngundan to assert that this essentialised identity can never be lost:

"You don't get it," Dustin said. "If I'm too Majestian to be Ngundan and too Ngundan to be Majestian, then who am I?"

"Both," Akeza insisted. "I know a Ngundan when I see one. Fearless. Adventurous. Loyal."

"Anyone can be that."

"But not anyone can claim it as their birthright."

Dustin shook his head. "I don't get that way of thinking."

(2023: 17)

Akeza uses heritage and lineage as proof of an essentialised Ngundan identity that can never be lost. She finds it hard to believe that anything can shake this essentialised fact:

He unlatched his fist. "Can you even begin to understand what it's like to live here, looking like this? To be too different to belong, but too different to go back?"

Akeza frowned. "But you're Ngundan. You can always go back."

(2023: 26)

It's only when she reflects on her own experience as a Ngundan in Majestia that Akeza realises her Ngundan identity might not be as simply kept as she thought it would be:

Who would she be without Ngunda? The thought struck deep. Maybe she did understand how Dustin was feeling. Just a little.

(2023: 27)

Meanwhile, Dustin concludes that it's okay if he doesn't have a concrete grasp of his identity and he realises that it is constantly shifting:

"I'm also a Shapeshifter," he muttered, "changing into one or the other, never really one or the other."

(2023: 28)

He only comes to this realisation after reflecting on the ship he has been assigned to maintain. The inscrutability of the Shapeshifter allows Dustin to slowly accept the inscrutability of his cultural identity, not easily defined as one or another, but as a shifting hybrid.

For Akeza it dawns on her that the price of displacement from Ngunda and the rooted identity it provides is higher than she first thought:

"If I were to live here, would I eventually become someone who's too different to go back and too different to belong? Would I deserve to go back?"

Dustin avoided her eyes. "I'm sure you'd be fine. You're too Ngundan anyway."

"Have you thought about how your parents feel about who they are?"

"They're Ngundan, end of story."

"They haven't gone back to Ngunda in the twenty years they've raised you. How do you think they feel when they hear news of their family, new words and trends?"

Dustin gritted his teeth against a flash of anger. "I don't know. They've never told me."

"Your parents, Dustin, told me they don't feel quite Ngundan anymore and not quite Majestian."

Afrofuturism and Exploring Cultural Identity 147

"So they've told *you*." Typical, he thought. Typical for his parents to exclude him from everything and then act surprised when he excluded himself from them.

"They're strangers wherever they go now," Akeza said.

"At least they're from somewhere!" Dustin snapped. "They have a strong link to one place while I have none."

(2023: 28–9)

In this exchange, I wanted to highlight a misunderstanding between a newly arrived migrant and a child of newly arrived migrants. Akeza, the newly arrived migrant, notices how she might start to feel alienated from Ngunda if she stays away for too long, and how that alienation might manifest in the inability to relate to its future. Her identity would become tied to Ngunda's past. Dustin, the child of a newly arrived migrant, struggles to feel at home anywhere, as his cultural identity has never been rooted in one place. He refuses to accept that his parents might be struggling with a similar sense of homelessness, while it dawns on Akeza that she might one day suffer from it too.

The Shapeshifter vessel Dustin and Akeza fly in is a silent witness to their struggles. It carries them to the final destination of the story, and towards the resolution of their internal struggles. In this way, the Shapeshifter is a symbol of the hybrid constructions of identity that Akeza and Dustin grapple to terms with. It is a constant in their rapidly changing world. While they cannot be rooted in one place, the one certainty is that the ship they travel in will continue to shift and so will their destination.

"Fell Our Selves" shows that Afrofuturism is a useful framework for examining how one's self-identified cultural identity can shift in hybrid, futuristic imaginings. There is a whole collage of possibility for writers to continue to explore.

Parting Questions

Afrofuturism as a genre of exploration encourages writers to remix their pasts in order to imagine futures for people of African descent. I find it fitting to use this subgenre to explore the future of cultural identity. For migrants and their children, this is a hybrid future that shapeshifts much like the ships I have conceptualized in "Fell Our Selves." This novelette engages with a literal consideration of how being displaced from a place of origin might affect one's own self-identification. Science fiction is a useful genre for writers to continue exploring these ideas in more subtle ways.

Exploring cultural identity and its hybridity warrants further study in the speculative genre, which is suitable for engaging with innovative ways of considering the past and future. The dynamics of what return to a cultural homeland means needs further exploration in speculative fiction. This is because ideas of how one might identify with a cultural identity will continue to evolve as we consider how recent African migrants might identify, and how children of recent African migrants might identify.

The African diaspora continues to expand. New branches of meaning join the original definition of people descended from the forced displacement of African slaves to all corners of the world. What futures can we imagine for the newly displaced, their children, and their children's children?

References

Afful, Adwoa (2016), "Wild Seed: Africa and its Many Diasporas," *Critical Arts*, 30(4), 557–73.

Anderson, Reynaldo (2016), "Afrofuturism 2.0 & The Black Speculative Arts Movement: Notes on a Manifesto," *Obsidian: Literature and Arts in the African Diaspora*, 42(1–2), 228–31.

Bradley, Rizvana, and Damien-Adia Marassa (2014), "Awakening to the World: Relation, Totality, and Writing from Below," *Discourse*, 36(1), 112–31.

Burnett, Joshua Yu (2019), "'Isn't Realist Fiction Enough?': On African Speculative Fiction," *Mosaic: An Interdisciplinary Critical Journal*, 52(3), 119–25.

Byrd, Merry (2021), "The Sankofa Spirit of Afro-futurisms in Who Fears Death and Riot Baby," *Femspec*, 21(1), 45–71.

Carrera-Suárez, Isabel (2017), "Negotiating Singularity and Alikeness: Esi Edugyan, Lawrence Hill and Canadian Afrodiasporic Writing," *European Journal of English Studies*, 21(2), 159–73.

Cobo-Piñero, Rocio (2018), "From Africa to America: Precarious Belongings in NoViolet Bulawayo's We Need New Names," *Journal of the Spanish Association of Anglo-American Studies*, 40(2), 11–25.

Delany, Samuel R. (2020), "The Mirror of Afrofuturism," *Extrapolation*, 61(1), 173–84.

Dixon, Frederick Douglass (2021), "Literary Afrofuturism in the Twenty-First Century," *Rocky Mountain Review*, 75(1), 121–23.

Edoro, Ainehi (2021), "What is Africanjujuism," *Brittle Paper.* [online] Available at <https://brittlepaper.com/2021/07/what-is-africanjujuism/> [Accessed April 24, 2023].

Edugyan, Esi (2022), *Out of The Sun: Essays at the Crossroads of Race*, London: Serpent's Tail.

Feracho, Lesley (2017), "Engaging Hybridity: Race, Gender, Nation and the 'Difficult Diasporas' of Nalo Hopkinson's Salt Roads and Helen Oyeyemi's The Opposite House," *South Atlantic Review*, 82(4), 31–52.

Glissant, Édouard (1989), *Caribbean Discourse: Selected Essays*, Charlottesville: University Press of Virginia.

Glissant, Édouard (1997), *Poetics of Relation*, Ann Arbor: University of Michigan Press.

Hall, Stuart, and du Gay, Paul (eds.) (1996), *Questions of Cultural Identity*, London: SAGE Publications.

Holgado, Miasol Eguibar (2017), "Transforming the Body, Transculturing the City: Nalo Hopkinson's Fantastic Afropolitans," *European Journal of English Studies*, 21(2), 174–88.

Hopkinson, Nalo (1998), *Brown Girl in the Ring*, New York: Grand Central Publishing.

Lavender III, Isiah, and Lisa Yaszek (2020), *Literary Afrofuturism in the Twenty-First Century*, Columbus Col: Ohio State University Press.

Niyonsenga, Aline-Mwezi (2023), "Fell Our Selves," *GigaNotoSaurus.* [online] Available at <https://giganotosaurus.org/2023/02/01/fell-our-selves/> [Accessed April 24, 2023].

Okorafor, Nnedi (2011), *Akata Witch*, New York: Viking/Penguin Books.

Okorafor, Nnedi (2015), *Binti*, New York: Tor.com.

Okorafor, Nnedi (2019), "Africanfuturism Defined," *Nnedi Wahala's Zone Blog.* [online] Available at <https://nnedi.blogspot.com/2019/10/africanfuturism-defined.html> [Accessed April 24, 2023].

Pérez, Emma (1999), *The Decolonial Imaginary: Writing Chicanas into History*, Bloomington: University of Indiana Press.

Samatar, Sofia (2017), "Toward a Planetary History of Afrofuturism," *Research in African Literatures*, 48(4), 175–91.

Thomas, Sheree Renée (2016), "And So Shaped The World," *Obsidian: Literature and Arts in the African Diaspora*, 42(1–2), 3–5.

Willey, Ann (2013), "A Bridge over Troubled Waters: Jazz, Diaspora Discourse, and E.B. Dongala's 'Jazz and Palm Wine' as Response to Amiri Baraka's 'Answers in Progress,'" *Research in African Literatures*, 44(3), 138–51.

Womack, Ytasha L. (2013), *Afrofuturism: The World of Black Sci-Fi and Fantasy Culture*, Chicago: Lawrence Hill Books.

9

Tobi Ogundiran: Fabulist Imaginings in *Tales of the Dark and Fantastic, Nigeria/USA*

Bio

Tobi Ogundiran is the Ignyte award-winning author of the critically acclaimed *Jackal, Jackal*, a Publisher's Weekly Top Ten Summer Read, which has been described as "Grimm by way of Amos Tutuola; Stephen King meets Cyprian Ekwensi." He has been nominated for the Shirley Jackson, British Science Fiction Association, and Nommo awards. His short fiction has been collected in several Year's Best anthologies, and also featured on the hit podcast LeVar Burton Reads. His debut novella, *In the Shadow of the Fall*, about Yoruba gods and the beings that hunt them, is out from Tor.com in 2024. Tobi has called many places home, including Lagos, Russia, and now Oxford, Mississippi, where he's pursuing an MFA in Creative Writing. Find him online at tobiogundiran.com.

In this chapter, I will talk about the importance of naming and definitions, and explore myths and folklore that guide fabulist imaginings. I discuss surrealism, with examples from my short story collection Jackal, Jackal: Tales of the Dark and Fantastic *(2023).*

Keywords: Fabulist Imaginings, Folklore, Futurism, Myths, Surrealism

The Naming of Things (Genres)

In much genre discourse, science fiction as a literary category is retroactively sketched, its inception set around the works of Mary Shelley to H.G. Wells, eventually then entering the "Golden Age" with writers like Isaac Asimov and Robert Heinlein. This is a Western pedigree, which excludes non-white contributors to the genre. African-American writers such as W. E. B. DuBois and Ralph Ellison wrote what we understand today as science fiction, albeit science fiction of a different flavor to the works of their white counterparts—as scholar Lisa Yaszek suggests in an article on Afrofuturism, science fiction and the history of the future:

> … nineteenth [and twentieth] century Afrofuturist authors were bound together by a shared interest in representing the changing relations of science and society as they specifically pertained to African-American history—including, of course, the history of the future.
>
> (2011)

Recognizing this, critic Mark Dery coined the term "Afrofuturism," defining it as "speculative fiction that treats African American themes and addresses African-American concerns in the context of 20th century technoculture—and more generally African-American signification that appropriates the images of technology and a prosthetically enhanced future" (1994: 180).

Two things stand out to me in this definition: one, that Afrofuturism chiefly concerns itself with the African diaspora and experience, two, that it specifically concerns itself with science fiction, a subgenre of speculative fiction. The problem with definitions and categories is that they are constrained by whatever parameters define them, and by who defined them, inevitably excluding works that don't fit neatly into those parameters.

One could argue that such classifications serve a good purpose, as in the case of Afrofuturism, but there also arises the danger—one that has been made manifest—of lazily applying this term to any work of Afro or Afro-diasporic origin with vaguely speculative elements, without regard for said parameters. Publishers, readers, and even critics eschew the nuances of the term for more macro, obvious and, therefore, surface criteria.

Writing sci-fi/fantasy while Black? You write Afrofuturism, period. Afrofuturism, I fear, has gone the way of magical realism, becoming a catch-all term for works produced by authors of a certain cultural background. Afrofuturism has become a term slapped onto Afrocentric works, or work by those originating from Afro-descending people, without proper interrogation of the nuances of category or subject matter. In resistance to this umbrella classification, authors and scholars have created their own alternate terms.

An example of this is the Nigerian-American writer, Nnedi Okorafor, who coined the terms Africanfuturism and Africanjujuism. She describes Africanfuturism as a sub-category of science fiction that is,

> directly rooted in African culture, history, mythology and point-of-view … and … does not privilege or center the West, is centered with optimistic visions in the future, and is written by (and centered on) people of African descent while rooted in the African continent. As such its center is African, often does extend upon the continent of Africa, and includes the Black diaspora, including fantasy that is set in the future, making a narrative "more science fiction than fantasy" and typically has mystical elements.
>
> (Okorafor 2019)

Okorafor goes on to stress that "it is different from Afrofuturism, which focuses mainly on the African diaspora, particularly the United States" (2019). Her classification of Africanfuturism is more specific to what African science fiction writers might produce and, while it does a good job of describing what it is, it remains subject to the failings of classifications expressed earlier—some things inevitably don't fit.

But I find all this exercise in taxonomy a little exhausting. Do I write Afrofuturism, Africanfuturism, Africanjujuism? Who cares? The truth is I am not interested in labels; I'm much more concerned with expression.

On Myths and Folklore

I write speculative fiction with primarily African (Nigerian) characters, in an imagined African or Africa-inspired setting, or settings far removed from Africa, like Russia or Paris. Fantastic and otherworldly elements often feature subtly or prominently. If we're peddling terms, one might call my work Afro-centric, or even fabulist—I don't know that I think about genres and definitions when writing.

I hold firmly that writers are storytellers, and the deliberate act of criticism (or worrying about where my work fits in scholarly discourse of creatives, African or otherwise) is not the best use of my time. Such exercise can and will stifle creativity. I really don't want to sit down and think, "I shall now pen the next great [insert whatever genre/label] novel," worrying about parameters and other such things. What I'm most interested in is being a storyteller as the storytellers of yore, producing riveting tales that endure.

In the future I may very well veer into other genres and topics of interest but in this nascent stage of my career I find myself fascinated by myths and folklore of peoples, how groups all over the world share similar creation myths, or pantheons—this similarity arising with little to no interaction or cross-pollination. I am curious, in effect, about comparative mythology through a creative lens.

In writing, I seek to understand how fables and parables shape a people and how I might weave myths from different cultures to create something both new and instantly recognizable—you might call it postmodern: the infusion of new wine into old skins. Of course, the realization that this is what I do has only come in retrospect. When I sat down to compile my stories into a recent collection, I began to recognize patterns, motifs, and recurrent techniques employed in the creation of these stories.

To this end, please allow me to show you how I create fiction.

Many of the stories in my debut collection *Jackal, Jackal* (2023) weave African (particularly Yoruban) folktales with Western fairytales. But they also interrogate culture and cosmology centered on an imagined present or past. "The Tale of Jaja and Canti" has elements of the story of that famous wooden boy, Pinocchio, but set in a world heavily influenced by African cosmology. In this story, Jaja does not seek to become a real boy, but journeys all over the world to find his mother, a powerful entity best not sought out; the one who breathed life into him:

> Seated on the balcony of the house across the street is a man. He is slumped in his chair and has remained unmoving for several hours. The tattered frays

of his agbada spreads about his person like an old sailcloth, snapping in the wind. His equally tattered hat is positioned on his head such that you cannot see his face. He has maintained this position for nigh on a day (which is much, much longer than you think).

If you think him dead, you'll be wrong; if you think him alive, well …

Look closely.

You may find that the skin of his hand is the texture of old wood, the shrivelled grains of a tree long exposed to the elements. You may find that the wrinkles on his face are unmoving, the tight curls of his beard a little too solid, the globes of his eyes a little too elliptical.

Don't be alarmed, it is exactly as you think: he is made of wood.

After some five hundred-odd years of roaming the treacherous terrain of the Midworld, his journey has led him here. Now. Sprawled on that balcony as unmoving as a tree.

Waiting.

(2023: 9–10)

This excerpt opens the story and also the collection. While it begins the story, it is not necessarily the *beginning*; it is also the end, or almost the end. It harkens back to the practice of oral storytelling, prevalent in Africa, and in ancient cultures the world over. Long before the written word, stories were orally disseminated. You might imagine an audience gathered around a fire beneath the watchful eye of a full moon. A storyteller, a grand orator, rises to his feet. He addresses you, the audience, with gusto or silent wisdom, guides you with gestures, vocal variety and pauses through the immersive story. The experience and consumption of a story therefore eschews passivity as the narrator actively brings in the audience to engage with the characters, events, and morals of the story:

"Look closely."

"It is or isn't as you think."

Such manner of storytelling translates into written medium in fables and parables, folktales and fairytales. There is the presence of an omniscient narrator, privy to the thoughts and future of characters. She knows where the story starts and where the story ends, and she cleverly withholds or dispenses information until such time as they become necessary. She declares events yet to happen (which have bearing on the present) in an unsubtle foreshadowing;

she engages in asides, going off the story to wander down the tangent of another story. All this makes for a unique experience.

The illusion of an impartial narrator is done away with, for the narrator herself becomes a character in the story. It is nonlinear, irreverent, certainly irreverent to the stringent rules of modern storytelling. Perhaps the characters are flat, mere symbols for ideas; perhaps they're larger than life, vessels for the illustration of unimaginable feats; perhaps they're non-human. Such manner of storytelling has fallen out of favor in modern storytelling landscape, where pedants of Point of View sneer at age-old storytelling techniques. But they are old for a reason, and have endured for a reason.

And I find these pure and true not just to African storytelling but also to African spirituality. Let us look at the ending of "The Tale of Jaja and Canti":

> Standing on the balcony of the house across the street is a tree. It is a magnificent tree with each limb spreading out regally in the direction of the seven worlds. The leaves are tendrils of light hanging from the limbs like curtains of Dawn itself. The powerful roots are firmly entrenched in the earth of the Midworld. The tree has stood for a long time (which is longer than you think) and will stand for even longer.
>
> Look closely.
>
> Upon closer inspection, you may find carved into the trunk the lines of an ancient face, the delightful crinkles of old eyes, the suggestion of lips upturned in a contented smile.
>
> Don't be alarmed, it is exactly as you think.
>
> (2023: 16)

You may have noticed that the end mirrors the beginning somewhat, producing a sort of circular tale, which reflects the concept of time in many African cultures. Time, and experiences, and stories, are not linear but circular. The end is the beginning; as the beginning is the end.

The Evil Forest/Journey into the Unknown

The evil forest is a staple of Nigerian literature. It is a vast, endless, unknowable place; a place where the veil between realms grows thin. Unwanted babies are oft abandoned in the forest for the spirits therein. And sometimes, sometimes, they come back. In Amos Tutuola's novels *My Life in the Bush of Ghosts* (1954) and *The Palm-Wine Drinkard* (1952), he describes a narrator who goes into the bush (Nigerian Pidgin for forest), and the phantasmagorical nature of his adventures therein. He fights spirits, outwits eldritch beings. Tutuola, the apt storyteller, found the seeds of his tales from real-life experiences: from hunters of yore, who often ventured into the forest for game only to report days, sometimes weeks, later with the most riveting tales.

The forest, a theater for the fantastic, also plays a huge part in Daniel O. Fagunwa's *Forest of a Thousand Daemons* (1968), originally titled *Ògbójú Ọdẹ nínú Igbó Irúnmọlẹ̀* (1939)—one of the first novels to be written in any African language, and then translated to English by Wole Soyinka. There is the sense that anything is possible in the forest. You may wander for what feels like days and exit years later to find all your contemporaries long returned to dust. For me this is fascinating, delightful stuff. But it is not unique to Nigerian or African literature or myths. This reverence for the forest is prevalent in Western, Eastern, even Russian tales. And, having come to this realization, I began to seek an equivalent in cultures around the world to compare, to weld these disparate tales. I eventually settled on "Hansel and Gretel," a tale I enjoyed as a child. "Deep in the Gardener's Barrow," a story in *Jackal, Jackal*, is the result.

In the Story Notes of the book, I describe the story's inception:

> I've always been fascinated by forests. The cancer of steel and concrete and asphalt has covered the face of the modern world, and most city dwellers have lost touch with nature. But if you've ever been deep in a forest or jungle, untouched by the Anthropocene and its human elements, you can't help but feel in awe, overwhelmed even as you contemplate your existence in the grand scheme of things. I once ventured so deep into the forest, that otherworldly place where the trees grow so closely together, leaves and limbs knitting into a canopy so dense that sunlight had not passed through for years. And there, in that moment, I could not help but think, the forest is alive. But of course it was alive, in the sense that all organisms that respire and excrete are; but on the heels of that rumination came the disquieting thought, the forest is sentient. Thus this tale was born. The astute reader might find traces of that old fairy-tale Hansel and Gretel here, but it is only the skeleton around which this one was built.

(2023: 306)

Seeking to capture that otherworldly sentience of the forest, I wrote the opening paragraphs:

The trees were old, old things. They wore the mark of their years in the girth of their trunks, in the reach of their limbs, in the twist of their roots snaking across the forest floor in an ancient lattice-work. Iná could not make out the sky; the leaves choked it, obscuring it from view, so she could scarcely tell day from night, nor count the days they had spent fleeing in the forest. And that, perhaps, was the worst of all. The loss of time; the way one day bled into the other, unmooring her from reality.

Next to her, Tofi whimpered. "I'm tired. When do we rest?"

"Soon."

She cast back over her shoulders, half-expecting to see an ululating rider charge out of the gloom of twisted trees to strike her down at last. Kill her like they'd killed all the others. But no such rider appeared. In fact, it had been a while since she'd heard the guttural grunts of the raiders, the sounds of hooves churning the forest floor as they raced after her and Tofi. She stopped. Come to think of it, it had been a while since she heard anything—

"Can we rest?" asked Tofi. "I'm tired."

"Quiet," she hissed.

"But—"

"Quiet!"

Iná listened. There was no sound. The chirping of birds, the hoot of owls, the croak of frogs and the chirp of crickets, the whisper of wind through leaves, the groans of old trunks, the gurgle of a running stream— all the sounds of a forest alive was gone, leaving in its wake a cloak of silence that bore heavily down on her shoulders.

Iná felt the back of her neck prickle.

It seemed the trees had shuffled closer, which was ridiculous, because trees could not move. It seemed they were watching her, which was ridiculous, because trees have no eyes. The earth itself seemed to heave, almost as though the forest were breathing. Which was ridiculous—

"Because the earth has no lungs." She breathed through parched lips.

"What?"

"Nothing," she said, shaking her head. She was exhausted, nerves frayed from the pursuit and loss they'd endured. She was seeing things; her mind had come unhinged. "I think we can rest now."

(2023: 219–20)

Fabulist Imaginings 159

As in "Hansel and Gretel," this story has two children lost in the deep of the forest, and they eventually come upon a witch. Where the witch in "Hansel and Gretel" dwells in the forest, and is the primary antagonist, here the witch and the forest are not exactly divorced. The forest *is* the witch. In African myths, spirits both benign and malicious often dwell in trees. So I took all these ideas and wove them into a tale both new and familiar.

Another technique employed in my fiction is nested stories, wherein a smaller tale affects the larger tale or, in some instances, both tales are threaded as to affect each other in the telling. Fables often enter my stories in this manner, as evident in this excerpt from my story "Isn't Your Daughter Such a Doll" published in *Jackal, Jackal*:

> Ralia gave a dramatic sigh. "You poor thing. Well, it's lucky you have me. So the tale begins like this:
>
> "In a little village called Esie there lived a wicked king. He was rich and powerful and very unkind. The villagers feared him. Anyone who tried to stand up to him always disappeared without trace, and so the villagers learned with time not to complain, regardless of the harsh living conditions. There was very little food. The king took it all—and not that there was famine or anything like that—no. He just wanted them to suffer. He liked to watch them suffer."
>
> "He was very wicked." Celine remarked.
>
> "Yes," Ralia agreed, visibly pleased. "He took all the best lands for himself, all the best girls—he had a very large harem of beautiful virgin girls." (Celine giggled) "Anyway, one day he went about the village as usual, seeking the finest girls to collect for his harem, when he found this girl by the stream. She was singing. Her voice was magic and the king fell in love immediately. He took her and decided to make her his queen, not just place her in the harem like the others. The girl, of course, was upset. She didn't want to leave her family and friends and spend her days locked up in the palace. But her family begged her not to cause any trouble, because the king always made trouble-makers disappear. Did she want them to disappear? Did she? She answered no and that was that. She was taken to the palace and was made queen.
>
> "The palace was large, and she had thousands of servants who served her and attended to her needs, but she was lonely. Even though this wicked and terrible king did his best to be kind to her, she still felt

unhappy. Even though she was generally free to roam the palace, she was never allowed to leave and soon it became clear that she was a prisoner. The only time she was alone was at night, and so in the nights, she started to explore the palace, seeking for an escape.

"That was how she came across the door with no lock."

"A door with no lock … " Celine repeated in a hushed, dramatic whisper. She tried to envision a door with no lock and the vision of a wall rose in her mind.

"A door with no lock," Ralia repeated. "It was a magic door and it always changed positions. This night it was here, another night it was there, and the girl enjoyed roaming the palace every night, trying to find where the door would appear. Every night she found it, she grew more and more excited, until she was no longer content with just finding the door. She wanted to open it, to see what was behind it. She was convinced the way to escape and freedom was behind it."

Celine turned to face Ralia now, her eyes wide with excitement. "Did she open it?"

Ralia smiled. "The door sensed she wanted to enter and spoke to her. It said, 'I am a door, my name is Door. I am protector of the secrets within.' The girl answered, 'I am a girl, I am the Queen. Open, Door and admit me in!' and the door swung open."

Celine clapped and whooped with glee. "And what did she find!" she asked breathlessly.

"Hundreds and hundreds of small stone sculptures," said Ralia, "the girl realized with horror that they were the villagers who had disappeared, turned to stone sculptures by the king!" (Celine clapped a hand over her mouth) "She ran out of that room and roused the palace, screaming at the top of her voice of the atrocities behind the vanishing Door. The news of what the king had done soon spread around the village and all the villagers, in their fury, marched to the palace to kill the king."

"Yes!" Celine whooped.

"But the king fled and was never heard from again," Ralia finished. "Till this day, the Door remains in Esie, changing positions every night, hiding the hundreds of statues behind it."

"Wow," Celine breathed. Dusk had fallen; long shadows fell across the room. She could see the Door before her. The door without a lock, hiding humans turned to stone. "But it's not true, is it? It's a folk tale."

Ralia shrugged. Just then, Celine's mother called from the kitchen. "Dinner, my dears!"

(2023: 106–8)

At this point in the story, Celine and her friend Ralia have only just made up after having their first major argument. In the wake of their newly kindled friendship Ralia decides to tell Celine a folk tale to help "reconnect her with her African roots." (Celine is half-French and has never been to Nigeria.)

The queen in the story is actually Celine's mother who fled from Esie, and Ralia is a construct of the king who has traced his queen to Paris to have his revenge. In essence, both stories are braided, the fable of the wicked king and the girl with no door nested into the main storyline, but this fable is actually the incidence that sets off the cascade of events.

From the Story Notes:

There is a town called Esie in Kwara, Nigeria, filled with soapstone sculptures of people caught in mundane tasks: a mother nursing her babe, a hunter venturing into the forest, women pounding yam for dinner. Legend has it that they were once people who lived and breathed and yearned and loved. Never mind that saner minds have dismissed these as apocryphal; I seized on to the idea and would not let it go. It is said that every great story is born from an attempt to answer a "what if" question. So I asked myself, "What if, truly, the sculptures had been people?"

(2023: 301)

Humans are incredibly imaginative. We are curious and ask ourselves questions: Why does the cock crow at dawn? What strange tentacled beast prowls the deep sea? We come up with stories to explain natural phenomena, stories which form the bedrock of culture. Some of these stories endure, and others don't, but it is a testament to creativity that they exist in the first place.

Who is a writer, who is a storyteller, but one who merely observes the world and comes up with creative answers to existential questions? That, ultimately, is my interest.

Denouement

So, classifications … While I personally do not care for it, I understand and even appreciate the desire for classification. But it is more important to engage with each individual work on its own merit. We must actively discourage the casting of speculative fiction coming out of Africa under one umbrella. Once upon a time all Africans wrote postcolonial literature, and now some previously postcolonial works have been reclassified as speculative fiction, as Africanfuturistic. Although they're all fruits, you can't expect an avocado, an orange, and a mango to taste the same.

In the same vein, just because the African writer writes speculative fiction does not mean that they write or *all* they write is Africanfuturism/ Africanjujuism/Afrofuturism or whichever static futurism.

References

Dery, Mark (1994), "Black to the Future: Interviews with Samuel R. Delany, Greg Tate, and Tricia Rose," in *Flame Wars: The Discourse of Cyberculture*, 179–222, Durham: Duke University Press.

Fagunwa, Daniel O. (1939), *Ògbójú Ọdẹ nínú Igbó Irúnmọlẹ̀*, Lagos: Church Missionary Society Bookshop.

Fagunwa, Daniel O. (1968), *Forest of a Thousand Daemons: A Hunter's Saga*, London: Thomas Nelson & Sons, Panafrica Library.

Ogundiran, Tobi (2023), *Jackal, Jackal: Tales of the Dark and Fantastic*, Ontario: Undertow Publications.

Okorafor, Nnedi (2019), "Africanfuturism Defined," *Nnedi Wahala's Zone Blog*. [online] Available at <https://nnedi.blogspot.com/2019/10/africanfuturism-defined.html> [Accessed May 24, 2023].

Tutuola, Amos (1952), *The Palm-Wine Drinkard*, London: Faber and Faber.

Tutuola, Amos (1954), *My Life in the Bush of Ghosts*, London: Faber and Faber.

Yaszek, Lisa (2011), "Afrofuturism, Science Fiction, and the History of the Future." [online] Available at <https://web.archive.org/web/20110626153716/http://sdonline.org/42/afrofuturism-science-fiction-and-the-history-of-the-future/> [Accessed June 30, 2023].

10

Dilman Dila: A Vision for Direct Democracy in Yat Madit, *Uganda*

Bio

Dilman Dila's most recent book, *Where Rivers Go To Die*, is a finalist for the Philip K. Dick Awards (2024). He has been shortlisted for the BSFA Awards (2021), the Nommo Awards (2022), and the Commonwealth Short Story Prize (2013), among many writing accolades. His short fiction has appeared in *Africa Risen*, *The Best Science Fiction of the Year: Volume Six*, and in *The Best of World SF V.2*, among other anthologies. His films have won multiple awards. You can watch them and read his stories on his patreon.com/dilstories.

In this chapter, I will talk about speculative fiction as a doorway, the misconceptions in perceptions about what precolonial Africa looked like, and how my Yat Madit stories bring to life my vision for direct democracy— through a governance system modeled on nations without centralized governments or kingships, an AI that enables a vision for direct democracy.

Keywords: Acholi, Direct Democracy, Patriarchy, Precolonial Africa, "Yat Madit"

A Brief Introduction

Speculative fiction, to me, is a doorway to other worlds, full of wonder, decorated with the fantastical, and yet still grounded in the reality of our lives, our histories, our cultures. A creator projects their lived experience into this other world and, when people consume the material, it shapes their own perception of reality. With non-African ideals and aesthetics dominating popular culture, we are forced to see the world from that alienated (rather than lived) point of view, and, sadly, many works of African speculative fiction simply recycle these non-African ideas. You'll find stories with costumes of African peoples resembling those of ancient Greeks, or African warriors, with martial arts and sword skills of East Asian peoples. Or you'll find the obsession with centralized governance, and especially with kings and queens, which is the focus of this chapter. Of recent I've been taken up with governance systems, particularly one that features in a lot of my recent works. I call it Yat Madit. It first appeared in the eponymous short story "Yat Madit" in *Africanfuturism: An Anthology* (Dila 2020c), and it is my way of questioning the predominant centralized narrative about our histories.

In creating science fiction and fantasy, I look at the cultures I grew up in, mostly Luo and Bantu cultures within present-day Uganda, and I mine their knowledge systems for solutions to the myriad of problems—like bad governance—that affect us today. Yat Madit, a Luo phrase that translates to "big tree," alludes to the communal governance that existed in Acholi before colonialism, elements of which persist today, where you'll find citizens of a village under a tree discussing issues. Most communities have a landmark tree that functioned as the default meeting place, hence "big tree" is symbolic. I imagine it is possible to recreate such a system in the present world, given that digital technologies and social media have influenced politics, as seen in #MeToo, #EndSARS, and in the Arab Spring (Britannica 2023)—anti-government protests that spread across the Arab world in the early 2010s in response to corruption and economic inequality. In Taiwan, a similar phenomenon called the Sunflower Student Movement birthed vTaiwan (info. vtaiwan.tw 2023), a real-life experiment with direct democracy, powered by an open-source digital technology, as Carl Miller writes in a *Wired* article (2019). vTaiwan, Miller writes, "was an attempt to better unite parliament and crowd, changing how government listens to its citizen, and makes decisions. An attempt to reinvent democracy itself … move political debate closer to internet-powered governance: transparent, inclusive and, above all, consensus-seeking" (2019).

Vision for Direct Democracy in Yat Madit 165

It is not far-fetched to think of a future where citizens of a nation get rid of central governments, along with politicians and presidents, in favor of a direct democracy run on some kind of decentralized social media platform. This scenario plays out in the Yat Madit universe, and this book chapter is a rambling of my thought processes in building this world, and the background research I undertook.

On the Idea that "We Were Kings and Queens"

A glance at any map of precolonial Africa showing kingdoms and empires will reveal huge blank spaces, because the vast majority of African peoples were not under centralized rule. And yet, popular creative works about Africa center around kings and queens. Examples include the movie *Coming to America* (IMDb 1988), starring Eddie Murphy as an incognito African prince, and *Black Panther* (IMDb 2018) with its Prince T'Challa. This, I'll say, is because we have been sold a certain narrative about nobility, and it is best illustrated by an African-American phrase, "We Were Kings and Queens," which counters the message that Black history started with slavery.

Kings and Queens, in this African-American context, stands for civilization, intelligence, sophistication, power, riches, freedom, everything that racism made it seem was lacking in people of African descent. Using this symbolism, however, only emphasizes the wrong histories we have been taught, which glorifies aristocrats. Ancient Egyptian Pharaohs are deified, Mansa Musa is placed on a high pedestal while The Queen of Sheba and Shaka Zulu are elevated to legend status. Popular works of science fiction and fantasy continue to feed us visions of individuals who hold dominion not just over a country but over entire worlds. Examples include J.R.R. Tolkien's *The Lord of the Rings* (1954), which gives Sauron global dominance, and the film *Star Wars* (1977), which gives Darth Vader control over an entire galaxy. These illustrations feature worlds in a state of war and, in the medieval ages, when theorists like Dante Alighieri, in the book *On Monarchy* written circa 1312–1313, thought of world peace, they could only imagine it happening with the world under the rule of a single monarch. Later on, Immanuel Kant (1795), while not approving of a single world government, thought peace could only be possible under a federation of free states, an ideology that paved way for the United Nations (UN), and inspires futurism where similar federations, either of governments or corporations, reign over planets or galaxies.

However, societies that did not have centralized leaderships or concentrated power have been ignored, and stories like that of Atiko wither away. He was an Acholi rwot (a word that colonialists mistranslated as "chief," but more on that later) who blossomed in a decentralized system and ruled with the consensus of his people. Why are people like him not revered? Because of a Eurocentric view of the world with a racist classification of the "stages of civilization" putting urban-industrial societies with centralized rule at the apex, just above absolute monarchs, as writer Ron Eglash suggests in "African Fractals: Modern Computing and Indigenous Design":

> This view comes from the old idea of cultural evolution as a ladder, a unilineal progression from "primitive" to "advanced." In the ladder model the small-scale decentralized ("band") societies would be on the bottom rung ... and the most hierarchical (state) societies would be on the top rung.
>
> (1999)

Eglash continues to write that this is not a very accurate view of history, and authors David Graeber and David Wengrow echo these sentiments in *The Dawn of Everything: A New History of Humanity* (2021). They paint a picture of ancient human societies, where the world of hunter-gatherers is a decentralized one of bold social experiments and a carnival of political forms:

> Agriculture, in turn, did not mean the inception of private property, nor did it mark an irreversible step towards inequality. In fact, many of the first farming communities were relatively free of ranks and hierarchies. And far from setting class differences in stone, a surprising number of the world's earliest cities were organized on robustly egalitarian lines, with no need for authoritarian rulers, ambitious warrior-politicians, or even bossy administrators.
>
> (p. 15)

Graeber and Wengrow point to eighteenth-century European ideology as the birth ground of the idea of cultural evolution, or stages of civilization, and this, I believe, inspired colonialism because Europeans believed they were more civilized than the peoples in Africa, partly because many African people did not organize in hierarchies and thus existed in a "state of anarchy." In Uganda, British colonialists thought that Buganda, because it had an authoritarian monarch with a hierarchical governance model, was more civilized than, say, the Acholi, who had a communal governance system (Fisher, 1911). Modern scholars continue to refer to the kind of political organization that was predominant in Africa as "stateless and hence disorganized" (Noyoo 2014). Colonialism was justified as a civilization campaign, and it consequently destroyed heterarchical communal governance systems and replaced them with the authoritarian leaderships of today.

In a lot of my works, I imagine Africa hitting the reset button to undo centuries of colonial harm, or I fantasize about what life might have been like had colonialism not disrupted our societies. And since bad governance is Africa's biggest problem, and a direct legacy of colonialism, I find myself daydreaming a lot about a country where things work, where every village has a high degree of self-sufficiency and every citizen has free access to basic necessities of life. I dream about a true direct democracy where governance is by consensus, and it is communal, and not just because an individual "won" the ballot at the general elections. The world I dream about has grit and imperfections, but it is a world of justice, where people govern themselves and share resources equitably, and power is not concentrated in the hands of a few.

And, after going over a lot of old books, I finally found a model for this world in the pre-colonial political systems of the Acholi.

The Nature of Social-Political Organization in Pre-Colonial Acholi

The Acholi are a Luo speaking people found predominantly in northern Uganda and southern South Sudan. They did not always think of themselves as Acholi. Okot p'Bitek (2018: 385) says that the name Acholi maybe a corruption of Collo, the dominant clan in Shilluk, by Arab traders. They were called O-gangi by their neighbors, the Lango. The Acholi, however, identified not according to the language they spoke but according to their kaka. Okot p'Bitek refers to kaka as chiefdom, a label ascribed by colonialism, but I'll side with scholar John JaraMogi Oloya (2015) in insisting on using kaka rather than chiefdom, first because kaka "is the Acholi description for the form of relationship exhibited before colonialism at the highest governance level" (p. 138). Above that, it is problematic to categorize kaka as chiefdoms "because it underplays the very principle of the consociations, which were brotherhoods rather than rulers-subjects" (p. 170). The leader of each kaka was known as a rwot (plural is rwodhi, or rwodi) and I'll use that instead of the colonial term "chief." The word kaka translates to "clan" but, again, a lot of meaning is lost in the English translation. It's a tragedy that colonialists stratified our societies using an alien world view and language that distorted the meaning of words and institutions. Frank Girling, in "The Acholi of Uganda" (2018), laments over this;

> There is also a semantic problem to be faced. Acholi institutions have no ex-act equivalent in Britain and it is difficult to know in what terms to describe them. It might be misleading to use English words which inevitably carry with them a penumbra of associations belonging specifically to our own society. One alternative is to use the Acholi terms where they exist. And this, too, is unsatisfactory. These words cannot be translated exactly or defined briefly and the reader rightly becomes exasperated with trying to understand a text peppered with half-understood foreign words. If only, one thinks, anthropology had devised a vocabulary which was culturally neutral and had a general application!
>
> (p. 72)

To argue this from another angle, colonialist did not rename the political systems in the Middle-East and Asia. The "sultan" retained their title and were not re-branded as kings, or chiefs, and their realm remained a "sultanate." Yet, in Africa, the colonialist called entire nations "tribe," and this derogatory label sticks to date, so you hear of the "Yoruba tribe" or the "Buganda tribe."

Though there were anywhere from thirty to over seventy different kaka in Acholi at the time of colonization (Oloya 2015: 173), they all had a common history, culture, and customs. So, if a person migrated from one kaka to another, they would be bound by the rules and customs in the new kaka, which would be similar to their place of origin. Okot p'Bitek lists anecdotes of persons being made leaders upon arriving in a certain location, mostly as refugees of succession disputes from Bunyoro, because they carried certain symbols of authority, like the two-headed all metal spear, and it lends to my argument that the different kaka were bound by shared beliefs, morals, customs, and laws. If over seventy different peoples practiced the same kind of governance, then they were bound into a form of statehood by their shared intrinsic values, beliefs, and customs. They were a nation, not in the Eurocentric view of a state, but still a nation. Girling (2018) makes a strong statement when he says that, "In the case of the Acholi they were certainly not 'stateless' in 1860, and there is no evidence to indicate that they ever had been" (p. 68).

So the Acholi were a nation, and J.J. Oloya, who I regard an authority in its political system, gives us, in his PhD thesis, a detailed description of the structure of Acholi political organization:

> The Acholi macon's different governing entities, namely: i) dog odi (dog ot for singular), which were the foundation or the households, ii) dye-kal or paci, were groups of odi that were lineages or corporate families – identified by a common wang oor or the evening bonfire and patrilineal shrine or kac; (iii) dog gangi (gang for singular) – collections of these related paci/dye-kal that recognized a common eponymous ancestor. Gangi were the modern villages, and first level of ethnic identity. In ethnic terms, this was the communal level of governance .... (iv) kaka, which were the consociations of a number of gangi agnates and therefore, the second level of ethnic identity .... Dog in Acholi refers to a unit and literally translated as "mouth of" and therefore, an entry point. Thus, dog kaka refers to kaka, a political unit. ...
>
> (2015: 15)

To summarize, Oloya presents two main political arenas in Acholi. The first being the communal governance realm, with the elementary families (dog odi), the hamlets (dye-kal), and the villages (gangi), and the second arena was "the macro-level of the traditional governance system of the Acholi that came about through the consociations of the *gangi* agnates ... It had much to do with shared governing interests, that is, choices and expectations, influenced by common sense and the environment." And he adds that "If dye-kal was corporate, gang was a communal level, while kaka was the political level of authority" (2015: 151).

Just to emphasize, these three, homestead, village, and kaka, were not hierarchical. That is to say, the homestead was not subordinate to the village which in turn was not subordinate to the kaka. Rather, they existed in a level plane, where the kaka had a duty to ensure the homestead was happy and well taken care of, and the members of a homestead could make a decision that could affect the kaka, for the governance was communal, rather than that of subject-ruler.

This concept is best understood through the study Ron Eglash (1999) did on African fractals, where he found repeating patterns in the architectural designs of many African people. If we apply the fractal theory to the Acholi, the kind of governance in the kaka level was a reflection of governance in the household level, and vice versa. That is to say, you could have a good understanding of how the governance worked in the kaka by examining its functionality in the homestead, or in the village. This fractal nature of governance is illustrated during the installation rituals of a new rwot. The rituals that his wife, the dak ker, underwent was similar to the rituals of a first pregnancy (Girling, 2018: 177). The dak ker, or the wife of the kaka, was a position of great significance to the governing of the kaka, as her last born becomes the heir, and she had a say in pronunciations of war, among other duties.

While homesteads were agnatic (paternal), the villages, it should be noted, were not made up of family groups. They were simply fortuitous groups of people who built their houses together (Grove 1919). Oloya states that the majority of gangi agnates "were made of mixed lineages" (2015: 144), and he quotes J.P. Crazzolara on Lwoo traditions (2015: 148):

> An individual, possibly with his wife, who wanted to join up with a smaller or a larger group or clan, was always accepted and wholeheartedly welcomed, even if he originated from a different or hostile tribe.
>
> (Crazzolara 1951: 71)

This kind of fluidity meant that very few kaka were mono-ethnic. Crazzolara noted that the nine gangi agnates that formed kaka Lamogi represented three distinct language groups, making it a fierce group with the combined war technologies and bodies of warriors representing these diverse groups. It meant kaka Lamogi, compared to other prominent kaka, "was more decentralized at the ethnic level and therefore dispersed. This feature of 'diffused power' gave even the British some hardship in controlling them" (Oloya 2015: 247).

The various kaka did not form a federation, as each was independent of the other. There were also rivalries between the kaka, which was exacerbated with the arrival of first the Arab slave traders, and then the colonizing Europeans (Adimola 1954; Driberg 1923).

In Yat Madit world, I take the first political arena Oloya describes, the village, to be the most important if every citizen is to have a meaningful say in running the government. Village here is not restricted to rural areas, but is the smallest administrative unit in Uganda's local government structure. This is sometimes called a "zone." Governance at village level directly affects the day-to-day affairs of an individual, impacting things like where their child goes to school, their health center, the roads to their homes. A person then is more concerned with the distribution of resources within their village than at national level. The villages form a federation within the state, each being a semi-autonomous entity with a high degree of self sufficiency. The village leader becomes a co-president, to use a Ugandan way of speaking, as they share presidential powers and duties with about 8,000 other people. These co-presidents form themselves into committees to replace ministerial positions. The idea is that, since the highest political office is that of village leader, it is easier for people to keep their leaders from authoritarian tendencies.

In a way, Yat Madit mixes communal governance and representative politics, decentralization, and centralization, for there are certain aspects of the modern world that cannot be decentralized, like the national army, though they would report to a committee made up of hundreds of people and closely monitored by citizens.

On the Formations of Power Structures

A strange thing about the kind of governance in ancient Acholi is that it was linked to, and it heavily influenced, centralized monarchies in neighboring polities, especially Bunyoro. Interestingly, the British used these centralized systems in their colonial conquests, while dismissing their origins. A study of the history and the folklore of Bunyoro shows that when a power vacuum occurred, Luo migrants stepped in and established the Bito dynasty (p'Bitek, 2018: 391). Many other kingdoms in present-day Uganda, including Buganda, which the colonialists used and praised as being the most civilized in the region, share foundation stories with this dynasty. Ronald R. Atkinson in *The Roots of Ethnicity: The Origins of the Acholi of Uganda Before 1800* (1994) emphasized this when he wrote that Luo-speakers spread throughout East Africa, establishing "more centralized political organization for many of East Africa's peoples" (p. 78).

Okot p'Bitek (2018: 391) described rituals that illustrated the institutionalized and special relationship between the Bito rulers of Bunyoro and the Luo. To the present day, as Anywar reported in Uganda's national daily newspaper *The New Vision* in 2006, the installation ritual of the Bunyoro omukama and that of the kaka Payira rwot involve emissaries being sent from one to the other. Author A. Southall in "The Alur Legend of Sir Samuel Baker and the Mukama Kabarega" (1951) noted that the rwodi of Alur, who practiced decentralization, claimed kinship with the omukuma (centralized monarchy) of Bunyoro. The Alur also claim that their wanderers could go to Bunyoro and be given leadership roles by the king, "evidence that in Bunyoro, as in Buganda, there were 'bureaucratic' chiefs appointed directly by the king without any hereditary title ...." And Okot p'Bitek added that the Luo did this (create centralized administrations) by peaceful processes, and he quotes Southall:

> ... for the Luo colonisers had a more highly specialized political institution than the people they dominated .... The impression they made must be attributed to the superiority in the scale of their social and political organization, and the self-confidence which gave them their reputation as rainmakers, arbitrators and administrators, and preserved their sense of destiny to dominate.
>
> (2018: 413)

We should note here the misuse of the word "colonisers" for the Luo were not a colonizing force. They did not think themselves superior to other people, and in many cases, like in Bunyoro, they lost their language and adopted that of the Banyoro. Okot p'Bitek paints a picture of the Luo moving across the Nile into Bunyoro, establishing the Bito dynasty, and then re-crossing the Nile back into their homeland to establish kaka polities, but it leaves me baffled. Why did they not create a similar centralized kingship in their homeland? Why did they create centralized governments among other people, but retain a decentralized and communal system in their home? Graeber and Wengrow call this phenomenon schismogenesis (2021: 56).

D. O. Ochieng in "Land Tenure in Acholi" (1955) suggests a gradual diffusion of power from the center, that in the beginning Acholi was ruled by one rwot, who had absolute power over his subjects. However, as the population grew, and upon the deaths of rwodhi, people would disagree over who should be the new leader, and the minority would then move away with their chosen leader to start their own thing somewhere else. This gave rise to kaka, and the kaka broke up in this way over time, and each kaka in its new region was a separate sovereignty. The rwot then needed the elders to help govern, and this meant relying more and more on elders for decisions:

> When his powers were bit by bit delegated to a group of clan elders, so also the rwot began to lose the control he had hitherto exercised over what was, by custom, his land, while the people began to have more and more say. His other rights, however, continued to be respected by the people.
>
> (Ochieng 1955: 59)

Thus, the rwot ceded some of his powers to the elders and to the people, and the bigger the population grew, the more power shifted away from the center to the elders in the respective villages, thus forming the kaka heterarchical governance structure.

Though Ochieng does not mention the original rwot, and though Acholi traditions and folklore do not support this hypothesis, which makes me think there is very little truth in Ochieng's writing, it still gave me ideas about a diffusion of power from the center—that power does not only evolve from the margins to the center; it can also be dissolved. And, in the Yat Madit, we have a revolutionary shift from a presidency to direct democracy.

On the Ideas of Democracy and Direct Democracy

What we know as democracy is defined by a practice in ancient Greece, as a government of the people, by the people, for the people. We are told today that democracy functions with regular election of leaders, who then make decisions on behalf of the entire population. But is this really it?

If I'm to arrive at my own definition, it would involve direct democracy, and in Yat Madit every citizen is considered a parliamentarian. I'm, however, aware that it is nearly impossible to attain such pure democracy. I refer to Yat Madit as a system of direct democracy, more to ease the reader's perception, but I think it sits somewhere between representative and direct democracy, with the key characteristic being rule by consensus. Perhaps we should give it a name of its own, something like "big tree democracy."

In Acholi, the rwot was "elected." When we think of elections, we imagine casting ballots and counting votes to decide a winner, and this seems to be the accepted standard to call a system democratic. In Africa, Western institutions and governments do not care about the process. The most powerful political party can exercise violence to get votes, but Western institutions will disregard it because, often, they want to maintain the status quo and protect their interests. All that matters is how "peaceful" the end result is, if the loser accepts defeat or resorts to legal rather than guerrilla means to address any grievances.

Elections in pre-colonial Acholi did not involve campaign rallies and ballots and voting. Most likely, it was not a one-off affair that happened periodically. The actual selection would be sparked off by the death of a rwot but, by then, the "election process" would have been happening for many years, and the final process would see elders arriving at a consensus on who should succeed the rwot.

The Acholi practiced a succession system based on ultimogeniture (a principle of inheritance), where the youngest son of the dak ker, the wife who had undergone installation ceremonies with the former rwot, became heir (Atkinson 1994: 90). But succession was not automatic. Qualities such as intelligence, generosity, and manners were more important than birthright. The son who best typified these qualities was the most likely choice, and there was a preference for choosing younger rather than older men. This is why I say the "election process" would happen over many years, as the community would study the sons of the rwot to decide which one was capable of replacing the father. Author R. M. Bere in "Awich—A Biographical Note and a Chapter of Acholi History" published in the *Ugandan Journal* (1955: 50) suggests that "succession moved, with the generations, into different branches of the 'royal' families, sometimes even to someone not of the blood" who showed the qualities expected of a rwot.

Patrick Otim (2020), in an article titled "The Fate of a Transitional Chief in Colonial Acholiland: Iburaim Lutanyamoi Awich, 1850s–1946," writes how Awich, a famous rwot of kaka Payira, and a notable figure in Uganda's anti-colonial resistance, became a leader, yet he was not the youngest son of the dak ker. One of his brothers might have become rwot (I'm struggling not to use the word "crowned" for they did not wear crowns, nor did they have thrones, and the symbol of authority was vested in a royal drum), but Otim quotes a scholar, J. O. Dwyer (1972), saying that Awich's elder brother "was not considered qualified" to replace his father. No satisfactory reason is given, though other historians like Bere (1946: 76–8) note that Awich's father, rwot Ocama, took him to important meetings like that between rwot Ocama and the British colonial agent Sir Samuel Baker, an indication that Awich, rather than other brothers who might have a claim by birthright, was being groomed to succeed his father, most likely because he exhibited leadership qualities. Given his accomplishments in resisting British imperialism, I'll say he was a great rwot.

Succession conflicts were rare in extant Acholi traditions because the sons of rwodi had no political, economic, or military bases from which to contest a succession decision. They were not chiefs under the rwot, nor did they have any other means to attach to themselves to either territory or large groups of people. Sons not chosen to succeed, therefore, had no special resources with which to oppose the decision. Disappointed sons could usually do no more than move away to a new place with their followers. This contrasts with Bunyoro and Buganda, where sons were territorial chiefs and often used their office and subjects as bases to fight for the throne when their father, the monarch, died.

Needless to say, this partly inspired me in thinking of the village leader's office as being the highest political position in the country. If we can't do away

176   *Afro-Centered Futurisms*

with representative politics, then it's better to elect a person who has lived in your village for a long time and whose manners and qualities are well known, and not just a person who appears in your timeline seeking votes. The idea is that a committee made up of thousands of people, whose leadership qualities are known in their respective villages, will be a foundation for good governance.

Welfare of Every Individual and Equitable Distribution of Physical Wealth

Perhaps succession conflicts were rare because "there seems never to have been any differentiation between members of the aristocratic and of the commoner communities" (Bere 1955: 50). Again, note the use of an English word distorting the meaning of kal, which was often the lineage of the founding family of the kaka, but they were not "aristocrats." Though the rwot was expected to hail from any of these families, the same author noted on this same page that the rwot could also be chosen from outside the bloodlines. The rwot, thus, was not an overload. Bere describes the rwot's main role as *won lobo*, or owner of the land, not in the sense of personal proprietor, but as a trustee, holding all the kaka's land on their behalf according to the customs (Bere 1955: 53).

The rwot did not appropriate wealth from his kaka and, while those under his jurisdiction might give him tributes, he was obliged to share this with others who were less advantaged, for he had a responsibility to ensure that everyone in his kaka was well catered for. The rwot was expected to be a rainmaker, a useful power to have in the dry environments of northern Uganda. Rainmaking could have been a scientific activity, which colonial forces disregarded as magic. Little that has been written about the practice, but it involved burning a special kind of crystal that was deadly to touch without an antidote, and this makes me think of "cloudseeding"—I'll leave that intricate discussion for another day. For now, I take the rwot's duty to make rain as symbolic, since rain was considered a blessing, and thus the rwot had a duty to bless his people. Of this, author Ronald Atkinson in his ethnoseries book *The Roots of Ethnicity: The Origins of the Acholi of Uganda Before 1800* (1994) wrote; " … rwodi provided food to eat, a place to settle, or military protection or assistance for those in difficulty" (p. 85). He continued: "The rwot thus was the focal point in a redistribution of goods and services within the polity" (p. 94). And John JaraMogi Oloya adds; "In other words, the importance of an agnate was measured by their ability to provide food and protection to members as well as ensuring social justice to all" (2015: 158). Girling offers an example, while describing the installation rituals of the rwot:

> On the three days he sat before his hut the Rwot was formally exhorted by the old men and old women of the domain. They came up to him where he sat and addressed him in words such as these: "Care well for your father's people"; "Be generous and feed your father's people"; or "Do not trouble the wives of your father's people, as your father did". It is said that these exhortations were very much feared by the rulers, and that Olia, the Rwot of Attiak, who committed suicide in 1923, did so because of impotency caused by having failed to obey the admonitions he received at the time of his installation.
>
> (2018: 178)

Since there was strength in numbers, larger kaka, in terms of population, were seen as more successful, and would provide a better sense of security to its members, and so the rwot had to work hard to ensure unity in the kaka, and he could only do this with the consensus of its members.

On the Rule by Consensus and Antipathy to Concentrated Authority

A key feature of the Acholi political system, that I can't comprehend fully because a lot has been lost to time, and distorted by our current worldview, is that rule was by consensus. This might seem obvious, because we might think that current governments rule with consent, but there are problems with electoral democracy in a capitalist system. I should perhaps illustrate consensual rule with a couple of quotes.

Hesketh Bell, the colonial governor of Uganda from 1905 to 1908, noted that the Acholi people were "unwilling to submit to domination by chiefs"

(Barber 1965: 32). At that time, the colonialists were considering expanding their territory, and it was a policy of indirect rule to use local authorities. Yet in the Acholi region, the article quotes Bell, "There are no powerful local authorities through which we might transmit our directions." The British colonialists thought it would be a major headache for them to institute a completely new political system. They had conquered other Bantu peoples neighboring Buganda, whose system of governance was easy to replicate for these other Bantu peoples had similar systems. But the "northern tribes," which included the Acholi, were seen as economically and politically weak, because they did not have "an effective central organization, which made it powerful enough to capture the attention of the British" (Barber 1965: 32). Only much later did anthropologists like Atkinson study the Acholi concept of governance, noting that " … the degree of power available to rwodi was limited, as they shared both authority and decision making with the heads of the chiefdoms' constituent lineages … Shared authority and a large degree of sub-group autonomy and identity merged in the Acholi chiefdoms with limited forms of centralization and stratification" (Atkinson 1994: 78).

But Atkinson did not see merit in this kind of governance system, relegating it to a mere anthropological curiosity, and colonialists like Bell thought it a backward system that ought to be stumped out for it was useless to them. And it's not until recently that scholars like J. J. Oloya have come to recognize the significance and uniqueness of the Acholi communal governance system, and what lessons we can draw from it to find solutions to the problems that affect the continent today. Oloya notes:

> The social-political forms and characteristics of the Acholi macon epitomised networks of cascading levels of interwoven governing arrangements where male-based elders of the different agnatic communal groups, appeared to have led non-elders dominantly through regulations rather than command … An authoritarian won gang, which was also common, resulted in breakaways of the corporate families from the territorial settings of the gangi (Girling 1960: 63). (p. 157)
>
> In other words, unlike in the case of despotism, where systems had outright authority over the others, here the dominant experiences were based on a mutually reinforcing demand for coalition (Atkinson 2010: 84–87). As such, kaka were "coalitions of the willing."
>
> (p. 163)

I struggled to understand what consensus would look like in complex modern societies, until I read about the real-life experiment with direct democracy, vTaiwan, using the digital platform Pol.is. As Miller writes, "vTaiwan has allowed citizens to sidestep the gruelling divisions that define online politics. vTaiwan didn't necessarily try to resolve the areas of bitter disagreement, but instead to forge a way forward based on the numerous areas most people agreed on" (Miller 2019). This contrasts with today's alleged "democracies," where politicians make inflammatory statements meant to further divide the population, rather than seeking areas of consensus to work upon in building a better country for everyone.

On the Question of Patriarchal Societies

A question that often emerges is whether the kaka system oppressed women, for the stereotype we have is that ancient Acholi was a patriarchal world in which women had no voice. However, the recording of this world, as handed down to us, starts around about the time the Acholi began to interact with foreigners. First the Arab and Swahili traders who came for slaves and ivory, and then, ultimately, colonialists who introduced European ideals of patriarchy based on Christian values, and this heavily distorted the nature of the Acholi society, for the worse. This is not to say that ancient Acholi society was completely fair to women, and I'm not trying to gloss the past and downplay the real oppression women suffered, for it was still a patrilineal society. However, to get a sense of whether women had a voice or influenced governance issues in the kaka, we need to investigate how they treated women. Though they are generally described as a patriarchal society, and there is no written record of a woman ascending to the position of rwot, we perhaps need to look at the nuances in their culture, at their belief systems, and we might develop a sense that, perhaps, they were not a patriarchy. It was patrilineal, but women had a lot of rights and freedoms. Sadly, a great injustice was done to this culture by looking at it through patriarchal eyes of Christian Europe.

To start off, let us look at the Lango, who were neighbors of the Acholi and shared a common culture and language. Jack Driberg, a colonial official, in *The Lango: A Nilotic Tribe of Uganda* (1923) recorded the existence of people called "mudoko dako," which translates to "a man who has become a woman" (p. 210). They are known as transgender today, and they face persecution, but back then, a mudoko dako could get married and be accorded all the duties and rights of a wife. These rights included "her own hut for cooking and sleeping and her own fields and granaries" (Girling 2018: 100). Just to emphasize, a woman owned and slept in a hut separate from that which her husband owned and slept in. Very little was written about jo mudoko dako, because Christian colonialists outlawed them and all that I can find is a footnote in Driberg's book. So I'm not sure what happened in the case of child bearing, since a marriage was not considered complete until after the bride bore a child. Nor do I know what the scenario was in the event of a person assigned female at birth transitioning to malehood. If colonialists had not looked down upon such people, perhaps they would have left us a more comprehensive record.

Can we still consider a society patriarchal if they accord such rights to trans people?

It stirred my imagination, and it formed the premise of my interactive graphic novel, *Jopolo* (2020a), which I showcased during the South African National Arts Festival in 2020, and which I am developing into a role-playing-choose-your-own-adventure kind of game. It is about a mudoko dako and their quest to have a child, for they feel their husband loves his other wife more because she can bear children. And so they travel to the stars where, they heard, people like them can get pregnant. This, perhaps, is the biggest critique of ancient Acholi, for women were expected to bear children. Only after a bride gave birth would she cease to be regarded as a daughter, or a kind of maid, in her mother-in-law's homestead, and enjoy all the rights and honors of a wife. A lot of the rare cases of suicides in ancient Acholi that anthropologists came upon were among childless wives (Girling 2018: 104).

Perhaps the most illuminating article about the place of women in this society is found in a publication by E.T. N. Grove on the customs of the Acholi in *Sudan Notes and Records* (1919):

> Theoretically the girl is the absolute property of her father before marriage and of her husband after. Practically a girl nearly always marries the man of her choice and leaves him for another if he bores or maltreats her. The men are usually pretty philosophical about their wives leaving them, saying that

if a woman does not want you, it is better to get your money back and find one who does.

Divorce is thus pretty common, the new husband paying his dowry to the father of the girl who then hands it back to the old husband.

(p. 157)

Though this sheds a lot of light on gender relations and marriage, I find a big problem with this text for it uses words that distort the picture. A person cannot be the absolute property of another, as was the case in slavery, and yet have the freedom to choose whoever she marries, and even to divorce whenever she feels *bored* (my emphasis). This writer was a European, coming from a world that perpetrated slavery and was most likely a Christian, and so he could not understand a system where a woman has rights and freedom in a patrilineal world.

Okot p'Bitek (1964), in an article in *Transition Magazine*, threw more light on the matter. He noted that very few men could afford to be polygamous—only chiefs and notable individuals in society had many wives, but both men and women could have multiple sexual partners and lovers. And he notes that, though brothers, fathers, and husbands were very strict on ensuring women did not sleep around, when caught, the man she was sleeping with suffered greater punishments, even death in the case of adultery, than the woman.

However, we should note other forms of marriage where the woman's choice, or mutual consent of both parties, did not matter. Girling (2018: 157) describes the marriage where a woman could be forced to marry, including if captured in a war, or if two men who were friends wanted to cement their relationship with a marriage. Girling downplays the consent of a woman, but he was interacting with the Acholi late in the 1940s, when Christianity and colonialism had already changed the society a great deal.

The colonialists further distorted the culture of dowry, which they mistook to mean "wife purchase." Unfortunately, because, of the power they held over Africans, both religious and political, these misconceptions eventually became institutionalized, and Africans now see themselves and their cultures through the eyes of their colonizers. This explains the rabid homophobia in the continent, for example. Girling (2018) wrote a lot about dowry, sharing several anecdotes that paint a picture of it being a kind of gift, and its purpose was a transfer of wealth within communities. Maybe we should critique it from what it was used for, mainly by brothers to marry wives of their own, and a woman would refer to her brother's wife as "ci lim-a," the wife of my bride-wealth (Girling 2018: 119). Also note that a father could not use bride-wealth to marry wives of his own. If a man was too poor, or did not have agnatic relations who could collect for him the bride-wealth, and for whatever reason could not afford to gift the family of the bride, then he could appeal to the rwot, who would provide the wealth with which the man could marry. What constituted the bride-wealth was also determined by the perceived wealth in circulation within the community at that time. When cattle were abundant, they paid in cattle, and when an epidemic wiped out cattle, it changed to goats. When money was introduced, then it increasingly was demanded as bride-price, and the culture became commercialized, prompting Okot p'Bitek to write the novel *Lak Tar* (*White Teeth*) in 1953.

To summarize my sentiments on bride-wealth, I'll refer to Grove's (1919) article in *Sudan Notes* quoted above, with men being pretty philosophical about their wives divorcing them. Today, bride-price (as this is what it has become) is used as an excuse to keep women in abusive marriages. Of course, back then, dowry was not commercialized, which means it was pretty easy to give back to a husband upon a divorce, but over time much changed for the worse for women. First, Christianity introduced the concept of virgin brides and, growing up, we kept hearing stories where parents emphasized the virginity of a girl, painting the picture that this was always the case. Yet old texts reveal otherwise (p'Bitek 1964). Today, because "bride-price" is commercialized, it's problematic for the girl's father to pay back, especially since a divorcee is not considered a virgin anymore—and if she has already given birth to children, her "value" goes way down and a second husband would be hesitant to pay back the first husband. This is compounded by Christian ideals which prohibit divorce, meaning women are forced to endure abusive and violent marriages.

I'll wind up this section by citing two ways women were protected from maltreatment in marriage in the traditional past. We've already seen that they had the freedom to walk away, even if they did not get a second husband. Girling (2018) shares many examples of women going back to their father's home and being accepted, and the dowry returned to end the bad marriage.

But a woman had a powerful weapon to keep a husband from mistreating her: *Kir*. This was the wife's curse, which would always start with her crying out "Oh! Am I not a human being?" Okot p'Bitek (2018: 500–1) writes that this curse "posed a permanent threat for husbands with a tendency to trouble their wives. Everyone knew that if a man persisted in troubling his wife she might commit kir." And when she did, she would force elders from both her husband's and her own families to convene an emergency meeting to resolve the situation in fear that this curse might cause deaths in the family. Though some level of wife beating was tolerated in the name of "training" a woman, the argument I'm making is that the traditional belief system, including on the efficacy of curses, offered a woman some kind of protection from spousal abuse. This protection was washed away with Christianity breaking up, discounting, and even making illegal, this belief system, and today's weakly enforced laws cannot deter a husband from mistreating his wife.

The Role of Women in Governance in Kaka System

Let's look back to governance, since we have seen that the society did not regard women as second-class citizens, and I can't find any traditional reason why women would be excluded from participating in governance decision-making in such a society, given that most administrative and economic duties revolved around social functions and ceremonies, farming, and perhaps war. That said, women were actively included in governance, and we can see how by examining their power in the household. As Girling suggests,

> The household is one of the basic institutions of Acholi social life and its structure is, in a sense, a paradigm of the whole political order.
>
> (2018: 95)

Girling offers a comprehensive description of the power structures in a homestead, and one thing that stands out for me is that each married woman had her own hut, separate from that of her husband, and she carried the title of "hut-owner." Each woman hut-owner had her own fields to grow grains, and her own granaries to store the grains, and she was responsible for the distribution and consumption of these grains. This is a stark contrast to today where women are institutionally excluded from ownership of property and resources, and, as such, excluded from decision making. Furthermore, as John JaraMogi Oloya writes. The homestead

… was made up of the male children and their fathers. It also included the women married to it and the daughters. It was an operational level of corporate governance …. a woman married into it would bring additional power sometimes, depending on the political power of her agnate.

(2015: 151)

And, he adds that it was at this level that

… the management practices—the levelling of patrilineal practices and influences—interfaced with the realities and power of "foreign" culture from the women married into it. Often, these practices were contested, contradicted, and often reconfigured to reflect the elements of lived experiences that are moderated by marriages. In other words, dye-kal provided opportunities for democratic practices, innovations and change.

(p. 226)

And about governance at the village, he writes that administrative tasks were shared with members of the corporate level, and he cites several individuals involved, including "the sister of one's father" (p. 156), while at the kaka macro-level, Oloya quotes Girling that,

The wife of rwot, dako ker or daker in short, sanctified men to war when she approved of war that was sanctioned by the society (see: Girling, 1960: 86–7).

(p. 146)

Which would give women considerable power in declarations of war.

I found the best example of women involved in governance in Okot p'Bitek's description of the institution of the queen mother in Bunyoro, which was ruled under a different political system with an absolute monarch. But, as we have seen earlier, the Acholi influenced the politics of Bunyoro a great deal, and they were responsible for providing wives to the *omukam*a (king) of Bunyoro.

The institution of queen mother played a vital role in the politics and administration of a chiefdom or kingdom. It counterbalanced the forces that tended to reinforce the powers of the king, thus curbing the dictatorial tendency of the monarch.

(p'Bitek 2018: 394)

This ultimately means men had a moral duty to obey their mothers, and so, while a man would be a ruler, there were female forces at play dictating how he ruled. I don't think the absence of queens, or visible female leaders, means a culture excludes women from governance. An example would be present day Pakistan, which has had female presidents, and yet still oppresses women, or the USA, which has had a Black present, and yet still suffers from institutional racism. The way a culture treats its women indicates the level of influence and participation women have in governance.

A Final Critique of My Own Works

I apply learning about the past as a journey of discovery in my Afrocentric futuristic stories. I ache to rewrite stories that were influenced by the misconceptions of our history. My short story, "How My Father Became A God" in *Terra Incognita* (2015), is premised on bride-wealth as wife buying, yet the story is set in a time before bride-wealth had become commercialized. Today, I'd rewrite this story to find a different reason for a little girl to flee from her brothers rather than because her siblings wanted to marry her off to an old man, for this reason only reinforces false and negative stereotypes about the past, which, in turn, influences our perception of the present. I'd also revise *The Future God of Love* (2020b) from its depiction of romance that does not reflect dating in the past. I'd perhaps tweak the nature of the two main characters and their romance to reflect the time period, and the story would be less misogynistic, and would certainly not feature a younger woman seducing an older man.

My novella *A Fledgling Abiba* (2019) is set in a city, and describes a powerful king of sorts—perhaps the last time I'll have such an individual in a story set in an ancient African world. I am currently developing a TV series, in the world of the interactive graphic novel *Jopolo* mentioned in this chapter. At first, it revolved around a powerful king and the death of his son, the heir, but, since learning more about the kaka system, I've re-written the script from scratch, setting it in a world without kings, without succession struggles, without a centralized leadership, because I believe it's the only way we can imagine a better civilization for us all. Just as we have been fed stories of kings and emperors, and made to believe centralized leadership is inevitable for humanity, I believe telling the other kind of story will one day make decentralized leadership the de facto kind of governance for all peoples.

I'll end this chapter with a quote in the *Wired* article by Miller, from Tang, one of the architects of vTaiwan:

> "Once people get the idea that you don't need a government to do governance, then people get into the true spirit of collaborative governance," she says. "It may take a generation or more for people to see the state as a useful illusion and only use that illusion whenever convenient."
>
> (2019)

I keep revising and re-interpreting the world of Yat Madit, which is set in the future and so gives me a bit more freedom of imagination than when writing about the past. But I want to be as true to the past as possible, even though I'm not creating anthropological works, because it's dangerous to continue propagating the negative and stereotypical views that we have been fed about ourselves. Ultimately, the way we see the past influences how we see the present, and the future.

References

Adimola, A. B. (1954), "The Lamogi Rebellion 1911–1912," *The Uganda Journal*, 18(2), 166–77.

Alighieri, Dante (1312–13), "On Monarchy," OLL [online] Available at <https://oll.libertyfund.org/page/dante-on-monarchy> [Accessed July 2023].

Anywar, Godfrey (2006), "The Bunyoro, Acholi Brotherhood," *The New, Vision*. [online] Available at <https://www.newvision.co.ug/news/1139025/bunyoro-acholi-brother-hood> [Accessed July 24, 2023].

Atkinson, Ronald Raymond (1994), *The Roots of Ethnicity: The Origins of the Acholi of Uganda Before 1800*, Ethnohistory Series, Philadelphia: University of Pennsylvania Press.

Atkinson, Ronald Raymond (2010), *The Origin of Acholi of Uganda*, Kampala: Fountain Publishers.

Barber, J. P. (1965), "The Moving Frontier of British Imperialism in Northern Uganda 1898–1919," *The Uganda Journal*, 29(1), 27–43.

Bere, R. M. (1946), "Awich—A Biographical Note and a Chapter of Acholi History," *The Uganda Journal*, 10(2), 76–78.

Bere, R. M. (1955), "Land and Chieftainship Among the Acholi," *The Uganda Journal*, 19(1), 28–30.

Britannica (2023), "Arab Spring." [online] Available at <https://www.britannica.com/event/Arab-Spring> [Accessed July 25, 2023].

Crazzolara, J. P. (1951), *The Lwoo. Part II: Lwoo Traditions*, Verona: Museum Comboniaum/Instituto Missioni Africane. [online] Available at <https://www.cambridge.org/core/journals/africa/article/abs/lwoo-part-ii-lwoo-traditions-by-j-p-crazzolara-fscj-verona-museum-combonianum-no-6-missioni-africane-1951-pp-323/519B0AB440A2595689622F375D137B62> [Accessed July 24, 2023].

Dila, Dilman (2015), "How My Father Became A God," in Nerine Dorman (ed.), *Terra Incognita: New Short Speculative Stories from Africa*, South Africa: Short Story Day Africa.

Dila, Dilman (2019), *A Fledgling Abiba*, Guardbridge: Guardbridge Books.

Dila, Dilman (2020a), *Jopolo*, first exhibited at National Arts Festival, South Africa.

Dila, Dilman (2020b), *The Future God of Love*, Edinburgh: Luna Press Publishing.

Dila, Dilman (2020c), "Yat Madit," in Wole Talabi (ed.), *Africanfuturism: An Anthology*, Brittle Paper. [online] Available at <http://brittlepaper.com/wp-content/uploads/2020/10/Africanfuturism-An-Anthology-edited-by-Wole-Talabi.pdf> [Accessed July 24, 2023].

Driberg, J. (1923), *The Lango: A Nilotic Tribe of Uganda*, London: T. Fisher Unwin Ltd. [online] Available at <https://www.loc.gov/item/2021666779> [Accessed July 24, 2023].

Dwyer, J. O. (1972), "The Acholi of Uganda: Adjustment to Imperialism," PhD dissertation, Columbia: Columbia University.

Eglash, Ron (1999), "African Fractals: Modern Computing and Indigenous Design," *ResearchGate*, New Brunswick: Rutgers University Press. [online] Available at <https://www.researchgate.net/publication/257314589_Ron_Eglash_African_

Fractals_Modern_Computing_and_Indigenous_Design_-_New_Brunswick_NJ_Rutgers_University_Press_1999> [Accessed July 24, 2023].

Fisher, A. B. (nee Ruth Hurditch) (1911), *Twilight Tales of Black Baganda*, London: Marshall.

Girling, Frank (1960), *The Acholi of Uganda*, London: HMSO.

Girling, Frank (2018), "The Acholi of Uganda," in Tim Allen (ed.), *Lawino's People: The Acholi of Uganda*, Berlin: LIT Verlag.

Graeber, David, and David Wengrow (2021), *The Dawn of Everything: A New History of Humanity*, New York: Farrar, Straus and Giroux.

Grove, E. T. N. (1919), "Customs of the Acholi," *Sudan Notes and Records*, 2(3), 157–82.

IMDb (1988), *Coming to America*. [online] Available at <https://www.imdb.com/title/tt0094898/> [Accessed July 24, 2023].

IMDb (2018), *Black Panther*. [online] Available at <https://www.imdb.com/title/tt1825683> [Accessed July 24, 2023].

info.vtaiwan.tw (2023), [online] Available at <https://info.vtaiwan.tw/> [accessed August 11, 2023].

Kant, Immanuel (1795), *Perpetual Peace: A Philosophical Sketch*. [online] Available at <https://www.gutenberg.org/files/50922/50922-h/50922-h.htm> [Accessed July 24, 2023].

Miller, Carl (2019), "Taiwan Is Making Democracy Work Again. It's Time We Paid Attention," *Wired*. [online] Available at <https://www.wired.co.uk/article/taiwan-democracy-social-media> [Accessed August 11, 2023].

Noyoo, Ndangwa (2014), "Indigenous Systems of Governance and Post-Colonial Africa: The Case of Barotseland," Conference paper on African Indigenous Knowledge Systems, Indaba Hotel, Fourways, Johannesburg, May 8–9.

Ochieng, D. O. (1955), "Land Tenure in Acholi," *The Uganda Journal*, 19(1), 57–6057–605.

Oloya, John JaraMogi (2015), "How Did Governance in Acholi Dovetail With Violence?," *Academia*. [online] Available at <https://www.academia.edu/33922296/HOW_DID_GOVERNANCE_IN_ACHOLI_DOVETAIL_WITH_VIOLENCE> [Accessed July 24, 2023].

Otim, Patrick (2020), "The Fate of a Transitional Chief in Colonial Acholiland: Iburaim Lutanyamoi Awich, 1850s–1946," *Canadian Journal of African Studies*, 55(1), 1–21 [online] Available at <https://www.researchgate.net/publication/340179522_The_fate_of_a_transitional_chief_in_colonial_Acholiland_Iburaim_Lutanyamoi_Awich_1850s-1946> [Accessed July 24, 2023].

p'Bitek, Okot (1953), *Lak Tar*, Kampala: Eagle Press.

p'Bitek, Okot (1964), "Acholi Love," Transition, 17: 28–33.

p'Bitek, Okot (2018), "Religion of the Central Luo," in Tim Allen (ed.), *Lawino's People: The Acholi of Uganda*, Berlin: LIT Verlag, 379–518.

Southall, A. (1951), "The Alur Legend of Sir Samuel Baker and the Mukama Kabarega," *The Uganda Journal*, 15(2), 187–190.

Tolkien, J. R. R. (1954), *The Lord of the Rings*, London: George Allen & Unwin Ltd.

11

Nerine Dorman: A Gaze at Post-Colonial Themes That Re-Envision Africa, *South Africa*

Bio

Nerine Dorman is a South African author and editor of science fiction and fantasy living in Cape Town, with short fiction published in numerous anthologies. Her novel *Sing Down the Stars* (2019a) won Gold for the Sanlam Prize for Youth Literature in 2019 and The Percy Fitzpatrick Award for Children's and Youth Literature in 2021. Her YA fantasy novella, *Dragon Forged*, was a finalist in the Sanlam Prize for Youth Literature in 2017, and she is the curator of the South African Horrorfest Bloody Parchment event and short story competition. Her short story "On the Other Side of the Sea" (2017a) was shortlisted for a 2018 Nommo award. Her novella *The Firebird* won a Nommo for "Best Novella" in 2019. In addition, she is a founding member of the SFF authors' co-operative Skolion.

In this chapter, I will talk about my experiences of dissonance in wanting to belong, and what Africa, the land of my bones, means to me—I gaze at post-colonial themes through my fiction to re-envision what Africa might have turned out to be, had it stayed "untouched."

Keywords: African, Afrikaans, Culture, Colonization, Post-Colonial

What Makes an African?

Ever since I was young, I knew I wanted to write about the landscape that lives in my heart and bring it to life. One of my earliest memories involved peering at the mysterious books on my parents' bookshelf filled with stories locked behind (then) incomprehensible typography. What magic was this? How could I, too, make such objects that can reach through space and time be considered precious enough to hoard? I grew up on a steady diet of Western fantasy and science fiction, with influences ranging from and including J. R. R. Tolkien, Robin Hobb, Neil Gaiman, Anne McCaffrey, C. J. Cherryh, Poppy Z Brite, Storm Constantine, Kate Elliott, Jacqueline Carey, Cat Hellisen, and Katherine Kerr. It was, however, when I first encountered Neil Gaiman's *The Sandman* graphic novels—see "Sandman Overture" (2023) on his website—with their incredible range of intertextuality between history, literature, and comic books, that I felt as if I could give myself permission to tell a story that was uniquely my own, uniquely African, and take my first steps into creating these magical cultural artefacts that others might cherish.

But what makes an African? I can only speak of my own lived experience—a woman descended from many peoples. Many years ago, when I was still in primary school, my class was asked to do a genealogy project, and I was fortunate in that I could interview my mother, my grandparents, and other relatives. A fascinating picture emerged that included Dutch settlers from the fifteenth century, French Huguenots from the seventeenth century, Asian, and even a whiff of Khoe courtesy of Krotoa's people. Her people lived in the shadow of the Hoerikwaggo, Table Mountain, otherwise known as Camissa, sweet waters (Cape Town Museum 2021)—where I would be born late in the twentieth century, many hundreds of years later. Granted, I have yet to validate my family's oral history with an actual genetic study, but when it comes to storytelling, it's the story we tell ourselves that matters, and not so much the raw materials of physicality.

Stories are an important act of remembrance, of connecting with those who've gone before, and reaching out to the ones who will come after us. When the mortal remains are gone, it's the story that endures while there are those who will speak the words.

A Gaze at Post-Colonial Themes   193

What my family's story teaches me is that my past is a tapestry. I cannot oversimplify my identity by saying "I am just this," or "I am just that," because what is evident is that I have been birthed out of a cauldron of many stories and pasts, and what holds weight is now: how I speak, how I think, and how I choose to act. What roles I play within different contexts, be it homemaker, graphic designer, author, writing coach, woman … While I speak a language handed down by past colonial powers, I have my mother tongue, too, a language birthed on the lips and tongues of those who were enslaved, who transformed the words of their colonial masters and made it their own (Willemse 2017).

And it's in the roots of the language that I've gained a realization. If Afrikaans, a creole language with its roots in languages drawn from all over, can be considered a southern African language, then I, too, can consider myself African. To transform the common insult I've had hurled at me for decades, I can't go home to my own country because *this is my home.*

Africa is the land of my bones. The skin and the cultural background are merely accidents of birth.

Who Am I? What Makes Writing Recognizably African?

Perhaps the most insulting rejection I ever received from a publisher came during the early years of my career, with a novel I've since withdrawn from the market called *Camdeboo Nights.* It is a young adult contemporary fantasy novel that represented my second novel-length foray into depicting themes drawn from a meeting of West and Africa. While the French publisher who initially rejected the manuscript shall remain unnamed, the words in his email remain forever etched in my memory—"this novel is not recognizably African."

I smarted from his assessment for a long time, but it got me thinking. I wrote that story based on *my* lived experiences as a South African, in a country that is a true melting pot of cultures whose people have seen colonization by Dutch, annexation and colonization efforts by the British, and a resulted nation distorted by these social upheavals and consequent years of systemic, institutionalized racism.

What I suspect people often forget is that culture is not a static thing. We meet each other and share stories. We trade material and intellectual goods and, through this exchange, we ourselves change, become something more, something new. Sometimes, old ideas fall by the wayside, eulogized in songs, poems, and stories. Sometimes new ideas are birthed into being by the marriage of new and old.

When that publisher told me that my story was "not recognizably African," I laughed.

What? Does he think that Africans live in mud huts and ride elephants to school? Does he not realize that we have electricity and use smartphones? Look at the statistics:

> GSMA Intelligence data showed that there were 108.6 million cellular mobile connections in South Africa at the start of 2022, equivalent to 179.8 per cent of its population.
>
> (Further Africa 2022)

My lived experience as an African means that I inhabit a world where most people have access to many of the benefits that modern Westerners take for granted. We have electricity, telecommunications, retail experiences, education, public transport—all in a built environment that, although it might not be as "modern" or "sophisticated" as its counterparts across the pond, is still recognizably part of the twenty-first century.

The sheer cultural jingoism of a Westerner to assume that what we take for granted in our day-to-day lives is "not recognizably African" is not just absurd but insulting too. It displays a complete disregard and lack of understanding of what many Africans' lived experience is. A cursory Google of "fiction set in Africa" will often throw up many covers displaying warm, sunset tones, featuring silhouettes of wildlife and thorn trees against an orange setting sun. This is not the lived experience of many Africans, some of whom live in coastal cities or in rolling wheatlands, to mention but two locales.

Africa is more than the image popularized in media of the annual wildebeest migration on the Serengeti, of lions feasting on a zebra, of people wearing traditional garb performing gumboot dances for an audience.

How Africans choose to define their lived experience varies so much even within a single country, that it is impossible to offer a generic stamp of a one-size-fits-all definitive description. If you want to know what makes African writing (or, indeed, any cultural object created by an African) "recognizably African," *ask an African*. You will get many different answers. All of them are equally valid.

A Sense of Space: Transforming Our Environment

In much of my writing, I take my readers from that which is known, and draw them into the unknown. Considering how popular media often distorts or misrepresents what others perceive as being African, I often start with what may be familiar to Western readers. In my earlier writing, when I was still finding my feet, so to speak, I stuck to the age-old advice of "write what you know." So stories such as those in my series *Books of Khepera* and *Those Who Return*—details of these are on my website (2023)—begin in Cape Town, the city where I was born and where I've lived my entire life.

Cape Town, itself, has a long, complicated history embedded in colonialism and the slave trade, and, situated where it is, at the tip of Africa, it has also been a meeting place of many cultures, as first the Portuguese, then the Dutch, and the British, left their mark as they encountered indigenes. Colloquially known as the "Tavern of the Seas," Cape Town has served as a stopping and staging point for many a journey, be it around the tip of Africa by sea or overland into what a few centuries ago was most certainly "terra incognita."

Depending on where you go in the city, you will see Europe's stamp on the architecture—be it the Castle of Good Hope, a seventeenth-century bastion fort (Castle of Good Hope n.d.) with its characteristic pentagonal shape; or the late Victorian style of historical areas like the Simon's Town's so-called "Historical Mile" (The Heritage Portal 2017); and gloriously eclectic styles in between, whether it's a Brutalist mansion in Bantry Bay sculpted out of concrete, or a modest home in Langa pulled together from whatever building materials were handy.

And yet these imports have become something unique to the space, transformed by the people living in them as much as the people within the spaces are transformed. And the stories told within these spaces are as unique to the area. To excise all traces of the West that have grown on African shores over the centuries is to erase a fundamental past of African identity, no matter how painful a reminder it is of the way a potential future was overwritten by Western interference. We will never know what may have been, had the Portuguese, the Dutch, and the British never set foot on these shores. But we can imagine. We can tell stories that ask the magical question of "what if?"

A Culture Distorted by Colonializm

There is a wonderful Afrikaans idiomatic expression that I learnt from my mother that doesn't truly translate into English. It goes along the lines of *"en nou sit ons met die gebakte pere"* (and now we sit with the baked pears). Perhaps it is close in meaning to not crying over spilled milk, but it's more a case of asking oneself, "What are we going to do with these pears?" We can't unbake them. Perhaps they are no longer palatable—what have we learnt from this disaster? Much as we can't disentangle ourselves from the events of the past, if we attempt to erase them, we set ourselves up for repeating the mistakes of our forefathers. We can choose to be nourished by that which is bitter; out of a sense of injustice, we can weave stories of bravery, of strength against great adversity—stories that inspire others to be better, to *do* better. We transform that which has been planted on our shores, and it changes, taking on an identity that often blends many sources.

Our past informs us, offers a starting point from which we can rebuild. It can offer the necessary friction or perhaps the rubble that we can use as a platform.

In that sense, I believe my writing is transformative. In many of my stories, I have characters working with the hand they have been dealt. They are products of the society that birthed them, and they must find a way forward within a society that is often distorted by the lingering effects of a colonial past, be it the remaining architecture or people who are still struggling to gain a sense of community and personal identity, who have emerged from a society deeply scarred by centuries of systemic racism. These are wounds that do not go away overnight.

In some of my stories, characters soldier on, simply not addressing or engaging with these issues—when I consider the actions of occultist Jamie in my *Books of Khepera* or magician Ash in my *Those Who Return* books. The protagonists' concerns are metaphysical, focused on alternative realities that are separated in place and time from the present. And yet both are Capetonians, brought up in privileged white communities. They are outsiders by choice, who exist in liminal spaces that are nonetheless informed by the history and physicality of the Mother City. Their own biases toward others are clear in their actions, which are often far from altruistic, nor compassionate. Through their eyes, we catch glimpses of the continued social disparities that exist. It is not a heartening sight. Nor is it meant to be. If my protagonists were not flawed, did not suffer lapses of judgment that led to them making grave errors, there would not be much of a story to tell now, would there be?

And yet there are characters who try their best, despite inheriting a legacy of racial prejudice from their parents. Marietjie, the white Afrikaans protagonist from my short story "Shame" (Dorman 2017b) is one such. Although she was raised by parents who never worked through their own racial prejudices, and whose worldview remained narrow and unchallenged in the small, fictitious Karoo town where they've lived their entire life, Marietjie has nonetheless grown past her upbringing. She's moved to Cape Town, where she's met and fallen in love with a Zulu man, Thulani, whose presence and bearing challenges Marietjie's parents' preconceptions. As it should. And, although his compassion eventually proves his undoing that unwittingly brings doom to an entire region, for this is a tale of horror poised on the brink of a "zombiepocalypse," he is nonetheless a central figure in this narrative. Marietjie, through Thulani, is allowed a glimpse into the lives of the majority—a world previously closed to her, thanks to her sheltered upbringing. She gains a small taste of the awfulness of racial prejudice that still festers in South Africa and no doubt other parts of the world, and she is faced with the bigotry of her family and cultural identity.

"Shame" is an uncomfortable, perhaps cautionary, tale that has no happy, uplifting ending, yet it confronts issues that often go unaddressed in contemporary South Africa, using the vehicle of an existential disaster to foreground them. The zombie plague can be considered a metaphor for these unexamined issues that manifest as a sickness that permeates and affects all strata of a society, with no regard for social status.

Re-envisioning Africa: Our Stories Matter

In writing many of my stories, I prefer to normalize diversity instead of foregrounding it. In an ideal society we won't need to point out that we have certain quotas of races, cultures, or genders. People are considered as individuals, and uniquely so, existing in their own right. They simply happen to represent a particular group. In my discussions with BIPOC (black, indigenous, people of color) authors in terms of situations where I act as mentor, I've often encountered the statement, "I want to feel seen"—which in an industry that has historically been dominated by Western-centric and white cultural themes, is vital. I envision a reality where diversity is the norm and is taken for granted, as it should be.

It is my belief, as storyteller and editor, that all people, no matter creed or culture, deserve an opportunity to express themselves within a media environment that is representative of the incredible diversity we have globally. Creating within the context of African literature, is no different.

In my YA space opera *Sing Down the Stars* (2019a) I took my story to the far future, to an interstellar society populated not only by humans, but a multitude of other sentient, space-faring species. While biases might still be encountered, depending on the situation and context, the diverse communities interact with each other based on an objective, universal approach—at heart a civilization based on secular humanist principles. There are no races demonized as per Tolkien's orcs with such broad racial descriptive references as "swarthy southerners" to suggest an inescapable racial trait aligned with "evil." Conflict, when it arises, is borne out by individuals' inherent traits and actions. While characters are inescapably a product of their environment and culture, they inhabit a milieu that has largely moved on from outdated, harmful racial and gender stereotyping. Granted, it is always possible to encounter outliers, but these are the exception, not the norm.

It has been a long-held dream to envision a future where we can look past the notions of inherited guilt, of children who are freed from having the pay the wages of their parents' sins. Children should not have to suffer for accidents of their birth—this is a powerful message. And while many of my characters still suffer some form of oppression, for instance the orphan Nuri in *Sing Down the Stars* (2019a), who, like Oliver Twist, is forced to steal for a crime boss, she overcomes this rough start in her life that has nonetheless equipped her with skills that help her win through to success, despite the incredible odds stacked against her.

In another of my works, *The Company of Birds* (2019b), I have delved deeply into southern African history by setting up a society distorted by the effects of colonialism and systemic racist policy in a secondary world setting. The milieu displays firmly entrenched patriarchal and colonial attitudes, with communities divided and disadvantaged in a manner that echoes the injustices perpetrated by whites against Black Africans in South Africa during the 1980s. This novel is an exploration of how a disempowered, essentially deplatformed woman, Liese ten Haven, whose unpopular and unexpectedly liberal worldview, given the society in which she has been raised, has turned her into an outsider within her own community. As the story progresses, not only does she discover that she is in possession of a dangerous, forbidden magical power, but also she is drawn into a resistance movement by helping to repatriate a magical child back to her people. In this manner, she strikes a blow at the heart of an oppressive system while also helping to right an ancient injustice within the framework of the themes of reconciliation and restoration.

Wanting My Dreams to Be Seen

Perhaps the most gnawing desire I felt before I turned my hand to penning my own stories, was reading tales that reflected my dreams and the world that I am familiar with. The adage of "write what you know" that is expressed within a West-centric publishing model means that many of the stories we encounter in retail outlets and in libraries, and see talked up on social media, reflect the lived reality of Western authors living in cultural centers in the US and Europe. Only in recent years have I started seeing African authors sharing *their* narratives in terms of speculative fiction making headway, with names such as Nnedi Okorafor, Eugen Bacon, Wole Talabi, Tendai Huchu, Oghenechovwe Donald Ekpeki, and more coming to mind.

Africans have been telling stories for eons. Until recently, it feels, the world has simply turned a deaf ear.

This brings me back to the reasons why we tell stories, often, because we ask that simple, magical question: "What if?" Those two, short words lead us down many winding paths, which for some may end in tragedy while for others result in a transfigured existence, despite a troublesome start. Both stories matter: the tragedies, perhaps because they act as cautionary tales warning us how our actions may play out with unintended consequences, and the transfigurations because they remind us that our troubles can be used as kindling to start the fire that can send us to the stars.

Personally, these have been the two primary objectives in my writing, to show protagonists who engage in a form of personal alchemy to become more than what they were before they set out on their journey. These sorts of stories speak to me on an archetypal depth, resonating with the power of Joseph Campbell's Monomyth that I believe lies at the heart of all stories:

> … it will be always the one, shape-shifting yet marvelously constant story that we find, together with a challengingly persistent suggestion of more remaining to be experienced that will ever be known or told.
>
> Throughout the inhabited world, in all times and under every circumstance, the myths of man have flourished; and they have been the living inspiration of whatever else may have appeared out of the activities of the human body and mind. It would not be too much to say that myth is the secret opening through which the inexhaustible energies of the cosmos pour into human cultural manifestation. Religions, philosophies, arts, the social forms of primitive and historic man, prime discoveries in science and

technology the very dreams that blister sleep, boil up from the basic, magic ring of myth.

(Campbell 1993: 11)

In "On the Other Side of the Sea" (Dorman 2017a), my two young protagonists are sisters who embark upon what, at face value, might strike readers as a standard quest. It is implied that they are the children of a despotic white dictator who has been cast down. The girls have flown from their ivory tower and are journeying to an almost mythical harbor where a vessel is waiting to take them West, back to where they are supposed to have come from. They carry their deceased mother's ashes as they flee across a harsh, post-apocalyptic landscape.

For a brief while, they find respite in the homestead of a kindly black woman who offers them shelter. The older girl is naturally suspicious, but the younger one, more willing to accept her changed circumstances by embracing a new life, is less wary. However, at the elder girl's urging, they are soon on their way again and, upon reaching their journey's end, it's to find an abandoned port town and, most telling, no fabled ship sailing West. It is at this point that the biggest differences in outlook become more obvious. The older girl falls into despair—her entire life's mission, to regain a way of life that has been taken from her, is faded. The younger girl accepts that holding onto this unsustainable past is but an illusion. She can let go of her past by symbolically casting her mother's ashes into the ocean, and then start the return journey to the village, where she will integrate with the community and be an active, participatory member of that community going forward.

I intended this story to function on a literal and a metaphorical level, to discuss the way in which white people can let go of their preconceived notions of being somehow apart and superior, courtesy of South Africa's apartheid legacy within the difficult changes inherent in a post-colonial society. The story was about a way for them to shed their hubris and accept that they are integral to rebuilding a land ravaged by the effects of institutionalized systemic racism. In many ways, this is my story about claiming an identity as an African, *despite* the cultural baggage that I carried with me for many years growing up, feeling neither fish nor fowl in terms of where I belong. I have no homeland to go to. That ship has sailed centuries ago. Africa is my home. This claiming of an African identity comes with a degree of personal humility, of acknowledging the painful past associated with my ancestors and an acceptance of moving forward, of being able to participate in a new cultural movement where I am but one small part in a greater community, no better or no worse than the next person. My ancestors' sins are not mine, and I can be better than they were.

The theme of belonging and community, is also an important theme in my short story "Arriving from Always" (2021), which was written at a time when we were experiencing great uncertainty about the future during the COVID pandemic. Initially intended for an anthology that sadly did not see the light of day, the brief, from the editor, had been to write a story about an Africa in the near future where there is a glimmer of hope. And so, despite feeling decidedly bleak at the time, I'd written about a woman returning home to her community to pack up her recently deceased mother's things.

At the time of writing, we simply didn't know what the long-term impact of a global pandemic would be and, being an author prone to writing dystopian futures, it was all too easy for me to envision a near-future that has seen a balkanization of larger nations resulting in a conglomeration of loosely connected, smaller city states managed by private corporate entities rather than democratically (or otherwise) elected governments.

My near future depicted a South Africa with even more decaying infrastructure than it has now, with communities insular and self-contained. I reimagined the valley where I live in the Cape Peninsula as being an isolated zone, no doubt influenced by our current divisions into different areas that experience rolling blackouts at carefully choreographed daily stages.

Perhaps living in a country constantly on the brink of some form of localized unrest has, in a way, provided me with plenty of fodder to feed my muse. In dealing with governance that is either incompetent or with resources spread too thinly to have benefit for all, it's easy to imagine how future, intensively siloed communities can and must stand together out of necessity if their people are to endure, if not thrive. Ubuntu, a concept that is uniquely African, is a word too easily bandied about, but do we truly practice it? Nelson Mandela stated this about the spirit of Ubuntu, a philosophy of "I am because you are":

A traveller through a country would stop at a village and he didn't have to ask for food or for water. Once he stops, the people give him food, entertain him. That is one aspect of Ubuntu, but it will have various aspects. Ubuntu does not mean that people should not enrich themselves. The question therefore is: Are you going to do so in order to enable the community around you to be able to improve?

(Sylvia-Educomm 2012)

This sense of the individual thriving, thanks to the community around them, is the hope for the future that I express in my short story "Arriving from Always" (2021)—my protagonist realizes this, almost too late, when the assassins from the rival corporation hellbent on a hostile takeover, come for her. She is able to fend them off but understands that her future lies with her community, her people, who have assimilated the past and are moving forward in a way that blends all aspects of culture at their disposal—the remnants of Western technology with the spirit of African people standing together to build a future on their own terms, despite what is happening in the larger world. Community matters; family, whether found or related by blood, matters when the rest of the world is tearing itself apart. We may not be able to control the actions of governments and global powers, but we can collaborate with the people within our community to navigate a better future and, we can hope, weather whatever challenges catapult our way, be it climate change, pandemics, or thuggery.

Sharing My Africa with the World

Over the years, I've had opportunities to write tie-in fiction for several intellectual properties. These include a story that appeared in the *Midian Unmade: Tales of Clive Barker's Nightbreed* anthology (Howison, and Nassise 2015), which is a selection of short stories inspired by Clive Barker's novella *Cabal* (1988), which also served as the inspiration for the cult horror movie *Nightbreed* (IMDb 1990).

I was always offered the opportunity to write tie-in fiction for the popular table-top roleplaying game *Vampire: The Masquerade*, with my short fiction appearing in *The Endless Ages Anthology* (Gates 2016). Additionally, I had the incredible privilege of working with the creator of the Wraeththu mythos, Storm Constantine, and had many stories published in her *Para* short story anthologies of fan-written fiction (Immanion Press n.d.).

In all these contexts, I elected to write short fiction set in Africa, developing experiences of Africans either within a contemporary fantasy setting (as per the *Midian Unmade* and *The Endless Ages* anthologies) or in a post-apocalyptic, transhuman futuristic fantasy setting, as per Constantine's Wraeththu mythos. In all these worlds, I have always felt that Africa is underrepresented, so it has offered me a quiet thrill to have stories set in Africa featured for an international audience. Surely, as Africans, if we can grow up and understand the Western settings through our consumption of media, we can surely build bridges that flow the other way, by inviting non-African readers to cross over and discover the world that we are familiar with?

In Conclusion: The Dangers of Oversimplification

It is my hope that, in creating a bridge between Western and African lived realities, I can combat the very real dangers of oversimplification. Africa, as is so often portrayed in mass media, is more than a broad vista of a savannah with thorn trees and orange sunsets. My experience of Africa is that of a transformative environment, that blends many cultures and many stories that often don't fit in well with the comfortable narratives of what African literature "should be," according to mass media and popular misconceptions.

It's taken me years to understand and accept that my voice, even as a minority, is as valid as any other African's. To judge another based on the color of their skin or the land where their ancestors were born decades, if not centuries ago, is to rob the individual of the validity of their own unique experiences as an inhabitant of Africa. Nor can or should we invalidate the stories of those who have flown from the continent to set root in foreign soil, for they carry that piece of Africa with them. We are mothers, sisters, daughters, teachers— more than can be summed up in one word. Our thoughts and dreams are fired in a crucible, a veritable alchemical process that might combine personal experience, a myth here or legend there, a smidgen of history that we blend and transmute to form the gold of our stories that can be carried forward to the future as an act of self-remembering and sharing.

It is my dream, my hope, my passion, that I can continue to weave together all the many threads of my life and the lives of the people around me, past, present, and future, to continue making stories that carry a mythic resonance that is uniquely my own.

References

Barker, Clive (1988), *Cabal*, New York: Poseidon Press.

Cape Town Museum (2021), "Krotoa, Translator, Negotiator & Peacemaker (1642–1674)." [online]. Available at <https://www.capetownmuseum.org.za/they-built-this-city/krotoa> [Accessed August 10, 2023].

Castle of Good Hope (n.d.), [online] Available at <https://www.castleofgoodhope.co.za/> [Accessed August 10, 2023].

Campbell, Joseph (1993), *The Hero with a Thousand Faces*, London: Fontana Press.

Dorman, Nerine (2017a), "On the Other Side of the Sea," *Omenana Magazine*. [online] Available at <https://omenana.com/2017/09/17/side-sea-nerine-dorman/> [Accessed August 10, 2023].

Dorman, Nerine (2017b), "Shame," *The Manchester Review*. [online] Available at <https://www.themanchesterreview.co.uk/?p=7674> [Accessed August 10, 2023].

Dorman, Nerine (2019a), *Sing Down the Stars*, Cape Town: Tafelberg.

Dorman, Nerine (2019b), *The Company of Birds*, Stafford: Immanion Press.

Dorman, Nerine (2021), "Arriving from Always." [online] Available at <https://omenana.com/2021/07/22/arriving-from-always-by-nerine-dorman/> [Accessed August 10, 2023].

Dorman, Nerine (2022), *Dragon Forged*, Cape Town: Ba en Ast Books.

Dorman, Nerine (2023), "Writing." [online] Available at <https://nerinedorman.blogspot.com/p/about-my-stories.html> [Accessed August 15, 2023].

Further Africa (2022), "African Countries with the Highest Number of Mobile Phones," *Further Africa*. [online] Available at <https://furtherafrica.com/2022/07/19/african-countries-with-the-highest-number-of-mobile-phones/> [Accessed August 10, 2023].

Gaiman, Neil (2023), "Sandman Overture." [online] Available at <https://www.neilgaiman.com/works/Comics/Sandman+Overture/> [Accessed August 15, 2023].

Gates, Jaym (ed.) (2016), *The Endless Ages Anthology*, Atlanta: White Wolf Publishing.

Howison, Del, and Joseph Nassise (eds.) (2015), *Midian Unmade: Tales of Clive Barker's Nightbreed*, New York: Tor.

IMDb (1990), *Nightbreed*. [online] Available at <https://www.imdb.com/title/tt0100260/> [Accessed August 15, 2023].

Immanion Press (n.d.), *fiction*. [online] Available at <https://www.immanion-press.com/fiction> [Accessed August 10, 2023].

Sylvia-Educomm (2012), *Ubuntu Told by Nelson Mandela*. [online] Available at <https://www.youtube.com/watch?v=HED4h00xPPA> [Accessed August 10, 2023].

The Heritage Portal (2017), "Simon's Town Historical Mile," *The Heritage Portal*. [online] Available at <https://www.theheritageportal.co.za/thread/simons-town-historical-mile> [Accessed August 10, 2023].

Willemse, Hein (2017), "More Than an Oppressor's Language: Reclaiming the Hidden History of Afrikaans," *The Conversation*. [online] Available at <https://theconversation.com/more-than-an-oppressors-language-reclaiming-the-hidden-history-of-afrikaans-71838> [Accessed August 10, 2023].

12

Denouement: Autoethnography—The Self-As-Research, Eugen Bacon, *Tanzania/Australia*

The question of what compels writers to write and then to write particular stories is one that writers, readers and critics have been asking for centuries.

(Gandolfo 2014)

In this closing chapter, I will talk about the autographic nature of the writings herein, then—with self-examples—canvas the process of writing autobiographical creative fiction, how a narrative can offer the potential for catharsis, purpose, even a sense of identity, to both the writer and reader.

Keywords: Auto-Ethnography, Otherness, Self-As-Research, Power of Narrative, Reflexivity

The Self-As-Research

we cartwheel from the sky   precious metals in gold platinum silver   shimmering down into summer fields full of maize and arrow roots everyone has forgotten   the more we hit the fertile ground one and all refuse to notice the less visible we become to those clutching with bare hands a naked disbelief in referents or ghosts though they are unsure why/   we speak to them in a language of radical futurism but by the time we seep into their hearts someone has dialed emergency services and a brigade   not an exorcist   arrives with

maps and graphs for sandbags
of migration and hybridity

our ancestors—bless them
could never argue with
—'Mis/Identity'

(Bacon 2022: 168)

This book invites you to share an African perspective from those with lived experience of the continent: how and why we write our Black speculative fiction. Each chapter is, to an extent, autoethnographic—it's a gaze into the process and practice of writing the self, of leveraging on narrative to find meaning and a sense of identity, belonging, a sense of place in an imbalanced world.

Let me give a self-reflective autoethnographic account that draws from my own personal feeling of discontinuity and an awareness of being between worlds as an African-Australian migrant, and focus on the self-knowledge that emerged from the act of writing a short story in the wake of grief. I use narration—the act or process of storytelling—to understand my own narrative strategies, how I tell a story, where each telling might be unique.

In earlier chapters of this book, we saw how other authors situate "Africanness" and connections to Mother Africa in storytelling, thus, in essence, ethnographically and autoethnographically exploring the self and identity through fiction. Suyi Okungbowa in his introduction reiterates our pining, as Afrodescendants, for better ways to exist, how we define and reshape our own realities by telling stories that reimagine our pasts and futures, our effort to see the future in our present. Shingai Kagunda, in her chapter says, we don't just want a seat at the equality table, because the table itself is flawed: "the only honest way to move towards Black futures is to burn down the table, scatter its ashes, and build something else."

We must create ourselves into a new existence, imagine our own pasts, presents, and futures different from what someone else (colonialists, slave traders, and those who persist in the circle of inequality) imagined for us. As we chart in self-conversations and essays our processes and approaches to writing, offering excerpts in our individual chapters herein, we are, in essence, participating in an autoethnographical interrogation.

Autoethnography is a method that combines characteristics of autobiography and ethnography—the study of "a culture's relational practices, common values and beliefs, and shared experiences" for the benefit of "insiders (cultural members) and outsiders (cultural strangers)" (Ellis, Adams, and Bochner 2011: 3).

Researcher Dwight Conquergood acknowledges ethnography as a distinctive research method whose participant–observation fieldwork privileges the body as a site of knowing (Conquergood 1991: 189). In ethnography, the idea of the person shifts from that of a fixed, autonomous self to a polysemic site of articulation for multiple identities and voices (p. 185). The researcher is "betwixt and between worlds," a self-made refugee, in a "postmodern existence of border-crossing and life on the margins" (p. 185). Simply put, ethnography is the art and science of describing a group or culture (Rice and Ezzy 1999: 153).

As a subset of ethnography, autoethnography uses the self as research (or data). Autoethnography is "an approach to research and writing and ... seeks to describe and systematically analyse (graphy) personal experience (auto) in order to understand cultural experience (ethno)" (Ellis, Adams, and Bochner 2011: 1). "Auto" refers to the individual or self and "ethno" is from the Greek term ethnos in reference to race, people, or culture.

The authors in this book share, in diverse chapters, how the self (our heritage, history, experience, identity ...) is also data, research or subject, subversive in the Afro-centered futurisms in our stories. Take Stephen Embleton who borrows from his South African heritage and his knowledge, experience, and research of Zulu, Nguni, Namalaen, even Hailom myths, folktales, and pantheons. He uses his heritage, history, experience, identity, and more, to weave language and "way of being" into his fiction based on—in his words— "the people and cultures, and real-world systems (political, familial, and linguistic) around me."

Nigerian-British writer of speculative fiction Nuzo Onoh need not reach too deep in search of her Igbo ancestry; it is intrinsic, a natural occurrence of her being, having lived amongst the Igbos for a great part of her growing up. She leverages on this to explore philosophy, culture, or cosmology through fiction that embodies "African spirituality in all its fascinating complexities." Meanwhile, Cheryl S. Ntumy weaves elements of Ghanaian culture into imaginary settings, religion, and magical systems to reimagine contemporary

Ghanaian views on community and spiritual devotion (for example, her inborn cultural connection shaping the way she tells her stories).

Xan van Rooyen positions their queer fiction alongside fluidity of identity, in a rejection of the rigidity of gender labeling, pondering "what if?"—with the self as research, and imagining normalized queerness in African-inspired worlds. Elsewhere, in discussions on how Afrofuturism compares to Africanfuturism or Africanjujuism, Aline-Mwezi Niyonsenga in her chapter of this book contemplates her own state as a child of an African migrant living outside the continent and ponders how or where she fits in the exploration of black futures. "Is it Afrofuturist to consider the future of one's cultural identity?" she crucially asks in interrogating the liminal space in which she occupies, where her cultural identity is all and none of Quebecois, Canadian, Rwandan, and Australian. She uses autoethnography to explore her identity through fiction, where protagonist Dustin in her novelette "Fell Our Selves" (2023) struggles with their shifting sense of cultural identity, and tries to gain a greater understanding of "self" and "future" in what Niyonsenga calls "hybrid negotiations of identity in the face of dominant discourses of assimilation."

Tobi Ogundiran shares in his chapter how he situates his fiction on his origins: Nigeria (Yoruban), or places he has lived, such as Russia, to create what he calls imagined or Africa-inspired characters, and stories that fuse African folklore with Western fairy tales. In a similar vein, Dilman Dila draws from the cultures he grew up in, mostly Luo and Bantu cultures within Uganda, and the influences this heritage has infused in him to write stories (as in his world of Yat Madit) that seek answers in fiction to real-world problems. In his chapter, he suggests, "A creator projects their lived experience into this other world, and when people consume the material, it shapes their own perception of reality."

Nerine Dorman speaks to her acknowledgment that she has been birthed out of a "cauldron of many stories and pasts," she is, like me, a sum of many, and has always wanted to bring alive the landscape that dwelled in her heart. Her skin and cultural background are "merely accidents of birth," but Africa is the land of her bones. She writes from her lived experiences as a South African to answer her own question: Who am I?, where others have doubted her Africanness because of her skin and cultural background, where, as she says, "culture is not a static thing." Where else is home for her, if not Africa, and what makes something "recognizably African"? Her transformative stories are of characters "working with the hand they have been dealt," products of the society that gave birth to them, irrespective of their being neither "fish nor fowl" in terms of where they belonged.

Hosting my own fiction on Afrocentric roots, memories of my grandmother in a village of mangos and tilapia on a Lake Victorian island marry with the backdrop of the arty Melbourne, and the breadth of the land down under, to craft African-Australian fiction that's a mirror of my own cross-cultural hybridity. In an example of autoethnographic research, I would like to focus this chapter on personal narrative reflexivity, sharing how I draw from my own personal feeling of discontinuity and mirror an awareness of being between worlds as an African migrant in Australia in the short story "Still She Visits" published in my short story collection *Danged Black Thing* (2021). Coupled with writing that offers self-knowledge in the wake of grief, I demonstrate here how I am applying the self as data, subject or research.

I intersperse excerpts from the story that follows the emotional journey of our protagonist Segomotsi, an African migrant in Australia, who loses her sister to HIV. In mirroring into the creative fiction aspects of my own experience (loss), my relationship with fictional Segomotsi was symbiotic. I needed her as much as she needed me. As I developed her character and transferred to her my direct experiences, she responded. Without answering all my questions, Segomotsi came along with new meaning that helped me understand and process my grief. My overall intention here is to expose a written artifact (fiction) on death, an artifact that is, to me, also a metaphor for life.

Behind the Story

As a writer you take on aspects of your characters and if you are not careful the world you are creating begins to blend with the world you actually inhabit.

(Tsiolkas 2008)

I wrote the short story "Still She Visits" following the death of my sister Flora in Tanzania. The emotion in this fiction is raw, honest—I connect with it personally. It is partly autobiographical—the story of an African migrant in Australia, a tale of hybridity, where hybridity is the experience of being between worlds or in two worlds, of changing identity to fit in with either world, of "otherness."

What is otherness? Scholar, translator, writer, and poet Dominique Hecq, in her article "Writing the Unconscious: Psychoanalysis for the Creative Writer" (2008) well defines the term "otherness" as "a necessary category in the process of self and cultural definition within a social system" (p. 10). Hecq elaborates that, depending on context, otherness may refer to "an object of desire, identification, or rivalry in psychical, existential and political terms" (p. 10). My context of otherness is that of identification, where there exists a self and an other.

Existential thinker Simone de Beauvoir writes about the opposition between a sovereign self—a subject—and an objectified other (2010 [1949]: 11). As human beings, we are each individually situated in our unique relationship with the world, a relationship whose distinctive situation is not closed with respect to other cultures we experience. As an African-Australian migrant, I am a person who is experiencing hybridity, where my sense of "otherness" is a result of immersion in multiple or mixed cultures. It is this otherness, the hybridity, that robs me of a true sense of belonging.

"Still She Visits" was a writing of the self, and it started with a skeleton: a narrative about grief. The rest was experimental. The writing became generative. The written became visible, more deliberate than speaking. Later, I understood how protagonist Segomotsi mirrored facets of me. Where at first the writing investigated, gradually it unbundled self-revelations. It motivated me to question my identity—the self and the unself; in the wake of my sister's death, who was I?

In this chapter, my self-reflexive discussion draws on literary writing (the creative) and autoethnographic research. In integrating excerpts of "Still She Visits," my chapter explores the process of writing fiction and the context of art as research. I recognize the dual role of an artist and a scholar in the arts—a collaboration that engenders knowledge while creating art. Enza Gandolfo

(2014) writes on empathy and emotion in the writing process, and speaks of therapeutic benefits of writing; there is power in narrative—for example, in writing about ancestry, about belonging/misbelonging … even about trauma, as we explore here.

The Power of Narrative

Narratives and narrative strategies are crucial devices that explore and facilitate the nature of being human. There is power in biographical and autobiographical writing. As an instance of discourse in an autobiography Paul John Eakin asks: "Who is this 'I', then?" (1992: 3). The self or subject is the principle referent in autobiographical writing. There is potency in reflective work, albeit fictionalized, if it offers healing to its narrator(s) and recipient(s) through the act and process of storytelling.

In story writing, characters and their creators share a symbiotic relationship. Judith Butler explores the link between survival and speakability—the courage to speak out—and the discourse of freedom (1997: 147). The act of writing "Still She Visits" was a "speaking out". My approach to the compositional space was with a sense of urgency, with a knowing that writing was an active speaking that emerged from a neutral position of unknowing, or a subjective position of knowing.

Dominique Hecq looks at the potential usefulness of psychoanalysis for the creative writer, and at writing in particular. She suggests that she writes to answer incipient questions troubling her mind, or to relieve some form of anxiety where cause may not yet be symbolised. She states, "I write because I must do so, exhilarating, detestable or painful though this might be" (Hecq 2008: 4). Different realities, different drives compel different authors.

In her article "Becoming Writing, Becoming Writers," Julia Colyar examines writing as a product, process, form of invention, and instrument of self-reflection (2009: 421). To Colyar, writing "is a symbolic system which articulates what we know, but it is also a tool whereby we come to these understandings" (2009: 422); it is a method of inquiry as a means of illustrating (2009: 424).

I use the concepts of storytelling in this chapter to shed insight into the writer as reader. A writer is connected with the character(s), with the story. Creation does not detach me, the author, from the work. Even the most reclusive writer connects with something. Integration with the work positions the author within a Freudian "process of sublimation": refining basic drives, such as those of grieving, and converting them into creative impulse (Carter 2006: 72).

"Still She Visits" was a partly autobiographical piece, albeit fictional. It offered an immersive gaze at angst where the written was visible, more deliberate than speaking (Vygotsky 1934 [1962], cited in Colyar 2009: 429). Using the character Segomotsi, the story subconsciously, and then consciously, unraveled forms of grieving and guided its players (author, character, reader) towards reconciliation with loss and self. It was a story manipulated to find healing.

When my sister Flora died, I turned to what I knew: writing. My writing was a search, a journey, a coming through. Text shaped my silence. It shouted my chaos. When I write, I often start with a skeleton, a general idea, and then the writing shapes itself. Characters tell their story and the story's ending, like Segomotsi's, astonish me. To fully explore my grief in this story, it was essential to move the narrative geographically away from me. I divorced myself from my Tanzanian heritage and found a point of reference in Botswana:

YOU REMEMBER when you were eleven or twelve, hands fumbling with a folded cloth. The tingle of a sore nipple, the claws of muscle cramp. Each pang in your pelvis was a sword that hacked away your childhood.

Your mother waltzed into your grave-sized room. It was tiny enough to hold two coffins and a row of ghost feet. It always felt haunted. Mamm brought in her rage and suspicion in a growl that said, "What mischief are you plotting?" even though the words were different: "Tidy your room yet?" Furrows on her forehead, her no-nonsense gait ... all now just a memory in fragments.

It was your little sister Mokgosi – her name means "a call for help" – who used her body to shield your secret from your mamm. Why it had to be a secret, you don't know; maybe it was to stop your mother from fraying your ears with threats about boys. How they took everything you gave, then broke you even though you were empty. How they sauntered whistling to a forever

Denouement 215

place, leaving you with mouths to feed, tiny mouths that couldn't tolerate hunger.

(Bacon 2021: 107–8)

And:

Segomotsi – your name means "a comfort" in Setswana. Few people here know you by that name; they call you Seggie Slacken – the Aussie you married.

It's years since you travelled home. Botswana will be a stranger, the village of Lejwana even more. But with your parents gone, and without your sister Mokgosi, what's left to call home?

(p. 109)

Applying the self as research in "Still She Visits," my autoethnography crossed genres and moved beyond literary and sociological borders. This is a concept that anthropologist Clifford Geertz in his book *The Interpretation of Culture* (1973) refers to as "webs of significance" in which humans are suspended, where culture forms the webs and their analysis forms an interpretive science in search of meaning (p. 5).

In the "lived experience" of studying my own grief (autoethnography) and that of Segomotsi's (ethnography) in this chapter, I am going beyond examining relational practices, common values and beliefs; I am now studying my own experience analytically, retrospectively, and selectively. It is a contemplative exercise that allows me to write about an "epiphany," one that stems from, or is made possible by, being part of or by possessing a particular identity (Ellis, Adams, and Bochner 2011: 4). In the writing, I am attempting to explain how the cultural constructions in which I live influence my response to the experiences of loss and grief. The practice of observing my trauma means that, while I am its author, an "other" outside the work, I am not divorced from the creative fiction. Rather I interact with it. I am coming at you, the reader, from an insider's perspective.

The protagonist Segomotsi is "between cultures." The narrative continues cultural anthropologist Renato Rosaldo's social analytical discussion on cultural borderlands in modern cities, encounters with "difference" that pervade the everyday in urban settings (1993: 28). To Segomotsi, here and back home offer different webs of meaning:

> A girl waits opposite you at the shrink's office. She flicks through pages of a brand-new issue of Women's Interest. She's chewing gum. Flick, chew. The receptionist ignores you both.
>
> You consider the receptionist, her face sharp as a pin, her nose and ponytail equally harsh. Back home, you would chat to strangers like old friends: ask about their cows, their goats, their children. Here, folk don't do that.
>
> The psychiatrist who retrieves you has dimples. Her pensive face is complete with lines: forehead lines, crow's feet at the sidelines, marionette lines that run straight upwards from the corners of her mouth. Her room is pristine, bland colors unable to touch your moods. Her leather couch is familiar, wears an easy look like the coin-slotted massage sofa at the Jam Factory in South Yarra.
>
> You ignore Mokgosi, her hollow eyes, oozing entrails, sitting in the corner of the room. The settee in which you recline, face up to the bland ceiling, smells synthetic. Nothing like the dusky cowhide on Uncle Kopano's chairs in Lejwana, unbleached skin and hair that smells of wet mud. This leather is coffee colored, café latte.
>
> (pp. 109–110)

Like Segomotsi, my "lived experience" is that of having roots in multiple cultures. By crossing borders and acquiring "multiple identities and voices" (Conquergood 1991: 185), as a writer I find myself existing in the "zones of difference within and between cultures" (Rosaldo 1993: 28). "Still She Visits" borrows from cultural anthropologist Renato Rosaldo's work on cultural citizenship, ethical versus cultural relativism, and how cultures are not separate: "they are not confined to their own individual museum cases," but rather "exist side by side in the same space" (Rosaldo 1993: 14).

As a migrant, I offer this fictional narrative as insight into the reality of a person who crosses borders to new worlds (that become home), who shifts from a "fixed, autonomous self" to "multiple identities and voices" (Conquergood 1991: 185). The narrative offers knowledge of being "betwixt and between worlds," a self-made refugee in a "postmodern existence of border-crossing and life on the margins" (p. 185).

Narrative Strategies

Where "narration"—derived from the term "narrate," or to tell—is the act or process of giving an account or a story, as of events, experiences, etc., "narratology" in literary criticism is the analysis of narrative texts (Schmitz 2008: 43). In interrogating "Still She Visits" here, I am using narratology to understand the role of subjectivity in the inflection of a character's being, their becoming, existence, or reality, predominantly its role in influencing how characters shape their dimensions and what constitutes their being. I am also using narratology to understand some of my own narrative strategies—the unique ways in which I tell a story.

I discuss in this section a number of narrative strategies that I applied in writing the short story and these include characterization, point of view, the self as subject, and a transformation curve to the storyline that leads to resurrection, which is also a healing.

Characterization

Characterization in "Still She Visits" was an important device to develop the narrative. The psychiatrist, Dr Bland, offers perspective. Her role removes me, the invisible narrator manipulating Segomotsi, from the subjectivity of grief:

> "How are you?" Dr Bland. Her voice matches the insipid room.
> "How is she in this room?" you say.
> "How is who in the room?"
> "There. Can't you see?"
> "What would you like me to see?"
> "She looks like death but smells fresh and sweet like gazania."
> Silence.
> "She was like that in life, you know. Bright yellow, hot orange, cheery purple, her temperament, sometimes the clothes she got from mtumba – second hand. Face of the sun, unfussy, everything she wore just fit right."

218 *Afro-Centered Futurisms*

Silence.

"Dainty, but she was the stronger of us two. With a mother like ours who had to fight for everything she got, so much that she mistook her children for combat, you needed a Mokgosi standing with a water bottle and a towel in your corner. So here she is, fully here, to fight my demons – only now she's one too. All wretched to look at, but there's strength in her scent. Sweet mango. Sometimes durian."

(p. 110)

In this excerpt, the character of Dr Bland is impersonal. Like her namesake, her voice is bland. She does not have to engage in dialogue. Her mild nudging, or silence, provokes the protagonist to engage and share feelings of alienation, experienced at the workplace, with a complete stranger. The doctor's role almost neutralizes the emotiveness of an otherwise subjective autoethnographic piece.

Point of View

As a you narrative (also termed second-person point of view, with "you" as the personal pronoun), "Still She Visits" attempts a teasing out of fact versus fiction, and employs metalepsis (figurative substitution) to disorient or reorient the reader's "frame of expectation" (Fludernik 2011: 101). The short story, in its use of the personal pronoun "you," directly addresses an invisible reader, inviting them to examine how they identify with the text and unfolding events. This approach to writing encourages a writerly/readerly relationship that is not divorced but prosperous, with co-existence between the writer and reader:

Mokgosi who always stood by your side, but you're the one who got away. It was curiosity for the world and a scholarship that put you on a plane, and away, away you flew.

"What's she looking at?" asks Dr Bland.

"You."

"What's she thinking, do you know?"

"I guess – why you? She was always there for me."

"And how do you feel right now?" asks Dr Bland.

"Cross," you say.

"Cross – because your sister is looking at me?"

"Because work sucks. Been thinking to leave."

Silence.

"Employee assistance programme, bereavement leave on tap, cards, flowers … " you say.

"I'm glad you took EAP – that's why you're here," says Dr Bland.

"How can a plant so rugged be so beautiful? It grows in extreme heat, tolerates any drought, climbs out of the hardest earth to splay in vibrant colors … " You choke.

Dr Bland hands you a tissue.

(pp. 111–12)

Informed Insider: Cathartic Autobiography

The short story also explores the potential of the self as subject, where cathartic autobiography introduces a transformation curve—in this case the stages of grief. Through the eyes of Segomotsi, in her weekly visits to the psychiatrist, I gazed upon my own hopelessness, agony, and rage, alone in Melbourne, removed from my family and tradition back home in Africa. In writing the self into a larger story across boundaries and borders into a space of resistance between the individual and the collective (Denshire 2014: 834), I embraced the self as subject and became an informed insider and an outside participant.

A Resurrecting Ending

In "Still She Visits," for the trauma narrative to be effective, there were no Macbeths—the protagonist in William Shakespeare's play "The Tragedy of Macbeth." The curtain did not draw instantly upon or a little after a death. First there was death, then came a resurrecting finish:

A week.
Silence.
Silence.
"Tell me anything." Dr Bland.
"Anything."
She smiles.
Silence.
Silence.

"I know to see when I'm drowning," you say.
"Good. Make sure you keep swimming."
You smile.
Silence.
Silence.

(p. 119)

A Self-Reflective Conclusion

Discussing "Still She Visits," this self-reflective speculative story where the protagonist must combat with her own demons and the ghost of her dead sister, fits the kind of writing that Colyar terms "a method of inquiry as a means of illustrating" (2009: 424). In its subsections, this chapter here exposes a written artefact (the fiction) on death, an artefact that is also a metaphor for life. Both the chapter and short story are products, processes, forms of invention, and instruments of self-reflection (2009: 421). Together, they articulate what I know, and are tools whereby I come to understanding (2009: 422). Through protagonist Segomotsi, I was able to comprehend and process my grief. In this grieving, I questioned my identity as an African-Australian migrant, and how the fact of mourning in solitude emphasized my "otherness."

This does not imply that each piece of my writing is the seed of a personal event. Yet the writer as reader is connected with the character, with the story. Creation does not detach. Even the most reclusive writer connects with something. As Gandolfo says, the artist "cannot stand at a distance—observing, watching—they have to become part of the person, thing, and event that they are creating" (2014: 21). Integration with the work positions the author within a Freudian "process of sublimation": refining basic drives, such as those of grieving or aggression, and converting them into creative and intellectual activity (Carter 2006: 72).

"Still She Visits" is a narrative of grief, a burning story that remains cathartic. It offers knowledge, ever evolving. I still question why Flora died. Why she could not save herself, or be saved, in an era when the AIDS pandemic is meant to be manageable through anti-retroviral treatment. Contemplating Judith Butler's linkage of survival and speakability—the courage to speak out—and the discourse of freedom (1997: 147), I hark back to the considered words of a colleague who once told me, "Writing is your lifeline. But never think it is your life." When I wrote "Still She Visits," the writing heartened speakability—it gave voice to grief. It bandaged my wounds from the sharpest blade of new trauma. The short story was my lifeline. Like any story, there is room to expand, to develop. But in its simplicity, this written artifact evidences my metaphor for life, showcases that I write … to find. "Still She Visits" is a story that continues to offer me a means of dealing with inner contradictions. It is a creation of art whose effect is real.

This brings me back to the authors of this book, the creation of art that carries meaning. So why do the authors in this book write? What compels us to craft Afro-centered futurisms in our stories?

It is the power of narrative. The very act of storytelling allows liquefaction— it's a fluid intercourse of the literary, the sociological and the psychological. In our fictions, we leap hurdles, step through walls, transverse borders.

We write to find.
We write to be.
We write to save ourselves.

We write because we must do so, exhilarating, unsettling or aching though this might be, whichever our reality, whatever our drive, compulsion. In writing, we find the courage to speak out. We are informed insiders offering our perspectives in a range of narrative strategies.

Our speculative fiction is a safe space in which to explore our ideas, to query and grasp whichever singular or collective sense of belonging, to find linkages that yarn our pasts, presents, and futures.

We write because we can. But also, because we must.

References

Bacon, Eugen (2021), "Still She Visits," in *Danged Black Thing*, Melbourne: Transit Lounge Publishing, 115–19.

Bacon, Eugen (2022), "Mis/Identity," in *African Literature Today 40: African Literature Comes of Age*, New York: James Currey, 168.

Butler, Judith (1997), *Excitable Speech: A Politics of the Performative*, Abingdon: Routledge.

Carter, David (2006), *Literary Theory*, Harpenden: Oldcastle Books.

Colyar, Julia (2009), "Becoming Writing, Becoming Writers," *Qualitative Inquiry*, 15(2), 421–36. [online] Available at <http://qix.sagepub.com/content/15/2/421> [Accessed July 15, 2023].

Conquergood, Dwight (1991), "Rethinking Ethnography: Towards a Critical Cultural Politics," *Communication Monographs*, 58 June. [online] Available at <www.csun.edu/~vcspc00g/603/RethinkingEthnography-DC.pdf> [Accessed July 15, 2023].

de Beauvoir, Simone (2010 [1949]), *The Second Sex*, trans. Constance Borde, and Sheila Malovany Chevallier: Alfred A. Knopf.

Denshire, Sally (2014), "On Auto-ethnography," *Current Sociology*, 62(6), 831–50.

Eakin, Paul J. (1992), *Touching the World: Reference in Autobiography*, Princeton: Princeton University Press.

Ellis, Carolyn, Tony E. Adams, and Arthur P. Bochner (2011), "Autoethnography: An Overview," *Forum: Qualitative Social Research*, 12(1). Available at <http://nbn-resolving.de/urn:nbn:de:0114-fqs1101108> [Accessed July 15, 2023].

Fludernik, Monika (2011), "The Category of 'Person' in Fiction: You and We Narrative-multipilicity and Indeterminancy of Reference," in Greta Olson (ed.), *Current Trends in Narratology*, 101–41, New York: De Gruyter.

Gandolfo, Enza (2014), "Take a Walk in Their Shoes: Empathy and Emotion in the Writing Process," *TEXT*, 18(1). [online] Available at <http://www.textjournal.com.au/april14/gandolfo.htm> [Accessed July 15, 2023].

Geertz, Clifford (1973), *The Interpretation of Culture*, New York: Basic Books.

Hecq, Dominique (2015), *Towards a Poetics of Creative Writing*, Bristol: Channel View Publications.

Hecq, Dominique (2008), "Writing the Unconscious: Psychoanalysis for the Creative Writer," *TEXT*, 12(2). [online] Available at <https://www.textjournal.com.au/oct08/hecq.htm>. [Accessed July 15, 2023].

Niyonsenga, Aline-Mwezi (2023), "Fell Our Selves," *GigaNotoSaurus*. [online] Available at <https://giganotosaurus.org/2023/02/01/fell-our-selves/> [Accessed April 24, 2023].

Rice, Pranee L., and Douglas Ezzy (1999), *Quantitative Research Methods: A Health Focus*, Melbourne: Oxford University Press.

Rosaldo, Renato (1993), *Culture & Truth: The Remaking of Social Analysis: With a New Introduction*, Boston: Beacon Press.

Schmitz, Thomas A. (2008), *Modern Literary Theory and Ancient Texts: An Introduction*, Oxford: Blackwell Publishing.

Tsiolkas, Christos (2008), Interview: Interviewed by Belinda Monypenny and Jo Case. Available at <http://www.readings.com.au/interview/christos-tsiolkas> [Accessed July 15, 2023].

Vygotsky, Lev S. (1962 [1934]), *Thought and Language*, trans. E. Hanfmann, and G. Vakar. Cambridge: MIT Press.

Acknowledgments

To **Suyi Okungbowa**—thank you, dear brother, for not hesitating one minute when I timidly approached you with the idea of this book, requesting that you help to frame it with a non-introduction. Without a blink you said, "Of course, I'd be happy to!" You bolstered my daring and passion when you said, "This is some really exciting stuff for the field, and I'm glad you put this project on the map." You were my confidante, counting the titling. You said "there's room for work in deeper capacities in the future." I can't wait to see what might arise from what we've started.

To author contributors of this groundbreaking book, **Aline-Mwezi Niyonsenga**, **Cheryl S. Ntumy**, **Dilman Dila**, **Nerine Dorman**, **Nuzo Onoh**, **Shingai Njeri Kagunda**, **Stephen Embleton**, **Tobi Ogundiran** and **Xan van Rooyen**—thank you for sharing something of you in your chapters. Your longings, hopes, and dreams for Future Africa.

To **Jennie Goloboy** of Donald Maass Literary Agency—thank you for taking on this vital project, meticulously negotiating the agreement with the publisher through fulfilment.

To **Don** of Donald Maass Literary Agency—thank you for briefly taking the reins and reminding me of the maddest literary crush with a genius who's also a philanthropist with a passion for books and the long-term careers of the authors your agency represents.

To **Amy Martin**, Acquisitions Editor, Literary Studies, Bloomsbury Academic—thank you for your enthusiastic belief in this project and your support in getting it approved by the Bloomsbury Board.

Acknowledgments   225

To series editors **Toyin Falola** and **Abimbola Adelakun**, Black Literary and Cultural Expressions (BLACE)—thank you for supporting this pioneering book, and the staggering endorsement (Toyin!) to the Bloomsbury Publishing Board of Directors for approval. From manuscript to publication: thank you for making true your words: "In an era characterized by the growing appreciation for diverse viewpoints, it is imperative to guarantee the inclusion and representation of all voices within the realm of literature."

To publishing assistant **Hali Han** and the rest of the publishing crew at Bloomsbury, from agreements to copyediting to proofing to indexing to payments, etcetera, etcetera, etcetera as in *The King and I*—thank you. We see you.

To African trailblazers, Angélique Kidjo, Chimamanda Ngozi Adichie, Fela Kuti, Julius Kambarage Nyerere, Margaret Ogola, Miriam Makeba, Nelson Mandela, Ngũgĩ wa Thiong'o, Sadia Zulfiqar, Sefi Atta, Steve Biko, Wangari Maathai, Winnie Mandela, and more, yesterday, today, and tomorrow—thank you for teaching us to cry freedom in whichever dialect.

To you, dear reader—thank you. This book is for you.

To me, in the words of RuPaul, "If you don't love yourself, how in the hell you gonna love somebody else?"—Mami, good on you, darling!

—Eugen Bacon

Index

Achebe, Chinua 67–8, 79, 91
Achebe, Nwando 123
Acholi cultures 163–89
Adhiambo, Mercy 122
Adichie, Chimamanda Ngozi 42–3
Āfer (pl. *Āfrī*) 11–12
"Africa and the Art of the Future"
    (Edugyan) 138–9
Africa is not a country xiv, 132
African Americans 65, 98–9
    formerly Negro Spirituals 65
African cosmologies 138
    see also cosmologies and languages
        building
African definitions *see* identity
African diaspora 137, 139–42, 148
African folklore 2, 16–17, 28–31, 142–3,
    153–6
"African Fractals: Modern Computing and
    Indigenous Design" (Eglash) 166
African history
    as fact 78–83
    LGBTQIA+ communities &
        homophobia 119–36
    queer imaginings in Africanfuturism
        119–36
African science fiction and fantasy 2–3,
    142–3, 151–62, 192
African Speculative Fiction Society
    (ASFS) 10
"African Spiritual Phenomena and the
    Probable Influence on African
    Families" (Knoetze) 67
African spirituality 59–76, 97–117
African voice 46, 62–4
"The African Writers Series and the
    Future of African Writing"
    (Embleton) 29
Africanfuturism 3, 9–11, 14–15
    and African history 119–36
    African spirituality 59–76, 97–117

and African voice 46, 62–4
AfrikaIsWoke.com 114
cosmologies and languages building
    15–16, 23–39
difference between Africanfuturism &
    Afrofuturism 98–101
"Godmother" by Ntumy 109–14
Igbo philosophy 60–2
queer imaginings 17, 119–36
Africanfuturism: An Anthology 10, 100,
    163–89
"Africanfuturism Defined" (Okorafor) 100
Africanjujuism 14–15, 26, 31–2, 42–3,
    153, 162
Africanness 4–6, 17–18, 192–3
Africentric/Africentrist 12–13
Afrikaans 193, 196, 197
    see also South Africa
AfrikaIsWoke.com 114
Afrocentric 42, 44–5, 50, 55–7
Afrocentric futurisms
    case for 11–15
    consciousness in action 15–18
Afrodescendant xii, 1–4, 10–19, 208
Afrofuturism xii–xiv, 2–11, 14–15, 17
    AfrikaIsWoke.com 114
    autoethnography, self-as-research 210
    Black-futurisms vs. systems of
        domination 78, 98–101
    blending science fiction and fantasy
        142–3
    coined by Dery 3–4
    and cultural identity as process of
        becoming 137–50
    cultural identity as a process of
        becoming 137–48
    definitions 138–9
    diaspora subjectivity 143–7
    difference between Afrofuturism &
        Africanfuturism 98–101
    dystopia and the Afro-irreal 41–58

Index

"Evidence" by Alexis Pauline Gumbs 89–90
fabulist imaginings, dark and fantastic tales 152–3, 162
faith and fantasy 97–117
faith and fantasy, spirituality 108, 110, 114–15
"Godmother" by Ntumy 109–14
naming 42–6
naming of things 152
positionality 140–1
power of African spirituality 62–6, 71, 73–4, 97–117
purpose, pros and cons 139–40
remixing cultural identity 141–2
shapeshifting concepts 139, 143–7
"Afrofuturism, Africanfuturism, and the Language of Black Speculative Literature" (Wabuke) 9
"Afrofuturism or Africanfuturism: Is the Difference Important?" (Kiunguyu) 108
Afrofuturism: The World of Black Sci-Fi and Fantasy Culture (Womack) 2, 140
Afro-irreal, Afro-irrealism 3–4, 16, 41, 46–51
Afromarxists 85
   see also Black Marxism
Afropantheology 3, 14–15, 78
Afrosurrealism 3–4, 14–15, 17, 84–5, 89, 93–4
Agojie women 130
Ajima, Onah Gregory 102
Akata Witch (Okorafor) 139–40
Alighieri, Dante 165–6
Alozie, Bright 121
"The Alur Legend of Sir Samuel Baker and the Mukama Kabarega" (Southall) 172
AmaNdebele 26–7
Among the Niger Ibos of Nigeria: 1912 (Basden) 69–70
ancestors, ancestry 16, 64–7, 89–90
   ancestor veneration 66–7, 69, 70, 71, 101–2
   see also spirits, gods, and the ancestors
& This is How to Stay Alive (Kagunda) 17, 80, 88–9, 92

animalism 66–7
Anlo-Ewe cultures 103, 105–6
anti-LGBT+ legislation 119–36
antipathy to concentrated authority 176–7
Anyi people 105, 108
Arab Spring 164
"Arabfuturism" 6–7
Arimah, Leslie Nneka 101–2
Ark of Bones and Other Stories (Dumas) 3–4
"Arriving from Always" (Dorman) 18, 202, 203
Asanti, Molefi Kete 12, 13
ASFS (African Speculative Fiction Society) 10
Asimov, Isaac 152
Atkinson, Ronald 172, 176–7
atlantic slave trade 81
authority 176–7
   see also power structures
autoethnographic xv, 208, 211
"Awich—A Biographical Note and a Chapter of Acholi History" (Bere) 174–5
Azania, Malcolm *see* Minister Faust
Azuka (Past glory, the past is greater) 60–2

Bacon, Eugen x–xv, 3–4, 16, 41–58, 61, 63, 73, 200, 207–23
Balogun, Uche 99–100
Bambara, Toni Cade 93
Baraka, AMiri 3–4
Basden, George Thomas 69–70
becoming 137–50
   see also identity
Bell, Hesketh 177–8
Bere, R. M. 174–5
Biden, Joe 129–30
p'Bitek, Okot 167–9, 172–3, 181–5
Bitter (Emezi) 93
Black anarchists 78, 166–7
Black and Brown bodies 83, 84, 85–6
Black futurisms, vs. Systems of Domination 17, 77–96
Black liberation movements 2
Black Marxism 81–2, 85, 92–3
Black Marxism (Robinson) 81–2
Black Panther: Wakanda Forever (2022) 71

228   *Index*

"Black Panther: Wakanda is Not Africa"
(Balogun) 99
Black Panther (2018) 7–8, 16, 25, 64–5,
67–74, 98–9, 165
Black Radical imagination 78, 86, 87–8, 89
Black Speculative Arts Movement (BSAM)
142
Black Speculative fiction xii, 46, 55, 63,
73–4, 78, 114–15, 137–8, 139, 208
"Black to the Future" (Dery) 3–4, 7, 13–14,
44, 64–6, 98, 152
Black-futurism
purpose, pros and cons 93–5
vs. systems of domination 17, 77–96
see also Afrofuturism
Blackness, "Black self" 4–8
see also identity
Boakye, Bridget 122
Bones & Runes (Embleton) 24–5, 26–7,
29–30
Books of Khepera (Dorman) 195, 197
Botswana 25, 109, 121, 214–15
Boyd, Sarah 98–9
*Boy-Wives and Female-Husbands:
Studies in African Homosexualities*
(Murray) 120–1
Brazilian Candomble 65
Brians, Paul 61
bride-wealth 181–2
Brown Girl in the Ring (Hopkinson) 143
Bruce, Delan 98
bush-doctors 73
Butler, Judith 213, 220–1
Butler, Octavia 7, 16, 57, 64–5
By Blood of Rowans (van Rooyen) 128

Café Irreal 47
Caliban and the Witch (Federici) 81–3, 85
calligraphy 26–7
Camdeboo Nights 193
Campbell, Bill 45
Campbell, Joseph 200–1
capitalism 85–6, 90–3
see also power structures
"captive body" 83
cathartic autobiography 219
"centricity" 12–13
see also Afrocentric futurisms

Cesaire, Aime 91
Cesaire, Suzanne 91, 93–5
characterization, narrative strategies 217–18
Chasing Whispers (Bacon) 16, 47–50
Chibados people from Angola 106–7
Christian values 62, 124–5, 179, 182
exorcisms, possession 67, 104
patriarchy 87–8, 179–83
see also colonization
Chronicles of the Countless Clans (Ntumy)
16–17, 101–8
Chrysalis (Lorde) 87
cisgender authors and transgenderism
128–9
Cobb, Jelani 8
Cole, Joe Robert 8
collective identity 2–3
Collins, Patricia Hill 12–13
colonization 83, 107, 139–40, 165–7, 181–2
decolonizing queerness 125–32
formation of power structures 171–3
post-colonial Africa 191–206
"sodomy laws" 124–5
see also Christian values
Coming to America (1988) 165
The Company of Birds (Dorman) 18, 199
Conquergood, Dwight 209, 216
continent versus diaspora 10–11
Coogler, Ryan 8
"Corrective Rape: The Homophobic
Fallout of Post-Apartheid south
Africa" (Smith) 123–4
cosmologies and languages building
15–16, 23–39
building from imagined worlds 31–8
creating linguistic cosmologies 24–6
power of a single word 26–8
real-world cosmologies 28–31
COVID pandemic 202
Crazzolara, J.P. 170–1
Crenshaw, Kimberlé 81
cross-disciplinary artistic movement,
Futurism 6–7
Crowther, Samuel Ajayi 25
Cuban Regla de Ocha 65
cultural identity 17
as process of becoming 137–50
see also identity

Index

culture
- Acholi cultures 163–89
- Anlo-Ewe cultures 103, 105–6
- distortions 196–8
- Igbo cultures 60–2, 66–73, 122
"A Cyborg Manifesto" (Haraway) 126

Dahomey kingdom 130
dance 67, 68–9, 104–5
A Dance for the Dead (Onoh) 66, 67–73
"Dangerous Muses: Black Women Creating at the Forefront of Afrofuturism" (Thomas) 45
The Dawn of Everything: A New History of Humanity (Graeber & Wengrow) 166–7
de Beauvoir, Simone 212
decentralized systems 165, 166, 171–3, 186
decolonization 6–7, 8, 56–7, 134
decolonized futures 143
decolonizing queerness 124, 125–32
"Deep in the Gardener's Barrow" (Ogundiran) 157–9
"A Deep and Terrible Sadness" (Bacon) 47–8
Delany, Samuel R. 3–4, 138
    see also "Black to the Future"
denouement 162, 207–23
deoxyribonucleic acid (DNA) 16, 64–7
Dery, Mark 3, 7, 13–14, 44, 64–6, 98, 152
DeSantis, Ron 82
"The Deviant African genders That Colonialism Condemned" (Elnaiem) 107
diaspora subjectivity 142–7
"Did Europe Bring Homophobia to Africa?" (Alozie) 121
Diene, Mame Bougouma 61
Dila, Dilman 46, 87, 163–90
Dillon, Grace 6–7
Diop, David 84
direct democracy 163–89
The Dispossessed (Le Guin) 51
Ditema tsa Dinoko writing system 26–7
divination 103–4
    see also spirits, gods, and the ancestors
Dixon, Frederick Douglass 141
dominant power structures 90–3

Dorman, Nerine 191–206
Dow, Unity 121
dreaming 199–203
Driberg, Jack 179–80
dualisms 60–2
DuBois, W. E. B. 152
Dumas, Henry 3–4
Dvorsky, George 126–7
Dwyer, J. O. 175
dystopia 51
dystopian futurisms 16, 41, 51–5

An Earnest Blackness (Bacon) x–ix, 43–4, 56–7
Eckstrand, Nathan 72
Edoro, Ainehi 15
Edozien, Chiké Frankie 125
Edugyan, Esi 138–9
Egbunike, Louisa 2–3
Eglash, Ron 166, 170
Ekpeki, Oghenechovwe Donald 43–4
Ekwukwe, planet in the *Sauútiverse* 37
election processes 174–5
Ellison, Ralph 152
Elnaiem, Mohammed 106–7
Embleton, Stephen 15–16, 23–40
Emezi, Akwaeke 93
The Endless Ages Anthology 203–4
#EndSARS 164
equitable distribution of physical wealth, direct democracy 176–7
Èṣù (deity) 25
Ethno-gothic 42–3
ethnography, autoethnography 207–23
"Evidence" (Gumbs) 89–90
Evil Forest metaphors 156–61
Ewe people 103
exorcisms, possession 67, 104

fabulist imaginings 151–62
    see also imagination, imagined worlds
fact
- and fantasy 101–8
- history as 78–83
Faghfori, Sohila 60
Fagunwa, Daniel O. 157
faith and fantasy 97–117
Family Watch International 125

230 *Index*

Fanon, Frantz 91
"The Fate of a Transitional Chief in Colonial Acholiland: Iburaim Lutanyamoi Awich, 1850s–1946" (Otim) 175
Federici, Sylvia 81–3, 85
"Fell Our Selves" (Niyonsenga) 137, 139, 142, 143–8
Female Monarchs and Merchant Queens in Africa (Achebe) 123
feminism 78, 87–8, 179–83, 213, 220–1
Ferrando, Francesca 126
festivals 68–9
First World War 52
A Fledgling Abiba (Dila) 185–6
fluidity of gender and/or sexuality 17, 107, 120, 123, 127–9, 170–1, 179–80, 210
folklore/folktales 2, 16–17, 28–31, 140, 142–3, 153–6
Forest of a Thousand Daemons (Fagunwa) 157
Freedom Dreams: The Black Radical Imagination (Kelley) 78, 86, 87–8
Freudian "process of sublimation" 214
The Future God of Love (Dila) 185
futurism(s) 6–7, 13–14
    see also Black futurisms

Gaiman, Neil 192
Gandolfo, Enza 207, 212–13, 220
Geʼez form 26–7
gender
    expressions and sexualities 106–7
    feminism 78, 87–8, 179–83, 213, 220–1
    fluidity, and/or sexuality 17, 107, 120, 123, 127–9, 170–1, 179–80, 210
    homosexuality 106–7, 119–36
    non-binary 123, 127, 128, 130–1, 133–4
    stereotypes 198–9
    transgenderism 123, 127–31, 179–80
    see also women
Ghana 25, 99, 102–3, 106, 109
Ghanian 101, 109–10
Girling, Frank 168, 169, 181, 182–4
"Godmother" (Ntumy) 109–14

Graeber, David 166–7
The Great Camouflage: Writings of Dissent (Cesaire) 93–5
Grove, E. T. N. 180–1
Guerrier, Fabrice 15
Gullah-Geechee root-healing 65
Gumbs, Alexis Pauline 89–90

Haitian Vodou religion 65
"Hansel and Gretel" (Grimm) 159
Haraway, Donna 126
Hecq, Dominique 212–13
Heinlein, Robert 152
"The HEretic Harmonic" (van Rooyen) 130–1
hierarchy, hegemony see power
history 78–83, 119–36
homosexuality 106–7, 119–36
"Homosexuality Un-African? The Claim is an Historical Embarrassment" (McKaiser) 121
Hopkinson, Nalo 7, 42–3, 45, 143
"How My Father Became A God" (Dila) 185
hybrid identity 139, 143–8
hybridity 6–7, 141, 143–8

identity 2–3, 17, 137–50, 193–5
    autoethnography 207–11
    non-binary 123, 127, 128, 130–1, 133–4
    see also gender
"The Igbo Clan" (Ogobegwu) 70
Igbo cultures 60–2, 66–73, 122
Igede dance 68–9
"Ihekanwa" (Nnedimma) 101–2
Ikechukwu, Nwafor Matthew 66–7
Ikeke, Omorovie 71–2
imagination, imagined worlds 31–8, 78, 151–62
    alternative ways of existence 1–4
    Black Radical imagination 78, 86, 87–8, 89
    queer imaginings in Africanfuturism 119–36
    role of 86–90
inclusive expression 1–21

"Indigenous Futurisms" (Dillon) 6–7
informed insider, narrative strategies 219
intersectionality 81
"Introduction to Anlo-Ewe Culture and
    History" (Ladzekpo) 105–6
Intruders short story collection 99–100
Iruka (Supreme future, the future is
    greater) 60–2
"Is the Post-Human a Post-Woman?
    Cyborgs, Robots, Artificial
    Intelligence and the Futures of
    Gender: A Case Study" (Ferrando)
    126
isiBheqe soHlamvu writing system 26–7
"Isn't Your Daughter Such a Doll"
    (Ogundiran) 159–61

Jackal, Jackal (Ogundiran) 16–17, 154,
    157–9
Jemisin, N. K. 8, 45
Jennings, John 42–3
Jones, Timothy W. 120
Jopolo (Dila) 180, 185–6
Juah-āju, sun in the *Sauútiverse* 36
Juju-priests 73

Kagunda, Shingai Njeri 46
kaka systems 167–79, 183–6
Kant, Immanuel 165–6
Kanu, Ikechukwu Anthony 72
Kelley, Robin 78, 86, 87–8, 92–3
Kimuhu, Aileen Waitaaga 124
"King Mwanga II of Buganda, the 19th
    century King Who Was Gay"
    (Boakye) 122
kings and queens, concepts 165–7
Kirby, Jack 8
    see also Black Panther
Kiunguyu, Kylie 108
Knoetze, Johannes J. 66, 67
KwaZulu-Natal 25, 31

Ladzekpo, C. L. 105
Lagos 25, 37, 44
Lagosian 45
Lak Tar (*White Teeth*) by p'Bitek 182
"Land Tenure in Acholi" (Ochieng) 173

The Lango: A Nilotic Tribe of Uganda
    (Driberg) 179–80
language
    African voice 46, 62–4
    linguistic cosmologies 15–16, 23–39
    "queer" as a word 120
Lavender III, Isiah 45, 46, 63, 141
Le Guin, Ursula 51
Lee, Stan 8
Lee, Stan, *see also Black Panther*
LGBTQIA+ 119–36
    see also homosexuality
liminal 41
*Literary Afrofruturism in the Twenty-First
    Century* (Lavender III & Yaszek) 45,
    46, 63, 141
The Lord of the Rings (Tolkien) 165
Lorde, Audre 87–8
"Lost in the Echoes" (van Rooyen) 131–2
Lwoo traditions 170–1

McKaiser, Eusebius 121
McNamarah, Chan Tov 121–2
Mage of Fools (Bacon) 16, 46, 51–5, 74
magic realism/magical realism 138, 140,
    143
Mahwé, moon in the *Sauútiverse* 37
Majali, Sulaïman 6–7
Makanjuola, Olumide 125
*Mama's Baby, Papa's Maybe: An American
    Grammar Book* (Spillers) 83
*Mandela's way: Fifteen Lessons on Life,
    Love, and Courage* (Stengel) 133
Manifesto of Futurism (Marinetti) 6
Marinetti, Filippo 6, 13–14
marriage 122, 181–3, 184–5
Martin, Win 98–9
Marvel studios 8
    see also Black Panther
Mashigo, Mohale 8, 9, 12, 99–100
Mathebula Nongoloza 121–2
medicine, healing rituals 67, 73
"Memories of the Old Sun" (Bacon) 49–50
metaphor 154–61
#MeToo 164
*Midian Unmade: Tales of Clive Barker[x
    2019]s Nightbreed* anthology 203–4

migrant 137, 139–40, 142, 147–8
migratory subjectivities 137, 139
Miller, Carl 164, 179, 186
Minister Faust 8, 13, 45
"The Mirror of Afrofuturism" (Delany) 138
monomyth 200–1
Mother Africa 25, 55–7, 208
Movement for Black Lives 92–3
Mugo, Micere 91
Murray, Stephen O. 120–1, 123
Mussolini, Benito 6
Mut, goddess of Motherhood 121
Mwanga II of Buganda 122
My Life in the Bush of Ghosts (Tutuola) 156–7
myths 153–6
   see also African folklore

naming, naming of things 4–11, 42–6, 152–3
narrative strategies 217–21
   characterization 217–18
   informed insider 219
   point of view 218–19
   resurrecting ending 219–20
   self-reflective conclusion 220–1
Naylor, Gloria 45
Ndloun, Lisa Yvette 3–4
Negritude Movement 84–6
Nelson, Alondra 7
nested stories 159–61
New Yam festival 68–9
Ngwu tree 72
Niyonsenga, Aline-Mwezi 137–50
Njinga Mbanda, queen 123
Nnedimma, Mbaeze 101–2
non-binary 123, 127, 128, 130–1, 133–4
Nsibidi form 26–7
Ntumy, Cheryl S. 46, 97–118
Nwankwo, Chimalum 2–3
Nyerere, Julius 85–6, 225

"objectivity" 80
O'Brien, Brandon 43–4
Ochieng, D. O 173
"Of Feathers and Flowers" (van Rooyen) 127, 129

Ogobegwu, Toni Akose 70
Ogundiran, Tobi 151–62
Okarafor, Nnedi 133
Okorafor, Nnedi 3, 9, 12, 26, 42–3, 61
   Africanfuturism 9–10
   "Africanfuturism Defined" 100
   Akata Witch 139–40
   Binti 139–40
   Geʾez form 26–7
   naming of things 153
Okungbowa, Suyi 1–22, 43–4
Oloya, John JaraMogi 167–8, 169, 170–1, 176–7, 178, 183–4
Olupona, Jacob 66, 70, 73
On Monarchy (Alighieri) 165–6
"On the Other Side of the Sea" (Dorman) 18, 201–2
Onjerika, Makene 46
Onoh, Nuzo 46, 59–76
Onwualu, Chinelo 45
origin 5
Órino-Rin, planet in the *Sauútiverse* 37
othering, 'otherness' 212, 215, 220
Otim, Patrick 175
"Our Mother, Creator: The Sauúti Creation Myth" (Embleton & Talabi) 31–8
oversimplification 204–5
   see also stereotypes

The Palm-Wine Drinkard (Tutuola) 156–7
Pan-Africanism 2, 46, 78, 91, 99
pastorpreneurs 109
patriarchy 87–8, 179–83
   see also feminism
Pérez, Emma 143
Pinaa, planet in the *Sauútiverse* 37
Pinochio 154–5
"Poetry is not a Luxury" (Lorde) 87–8
point of view, narrative strategies 218–19
positionality 140–1
possession 67, 104
post-colonial Africa 191–206
postgenderism 125–32
"Postgenderism: Beyond the Gender Binary" (Dvorsky) 126–7
power of narrative 213–17

power, power structures 90–3, 171–3, 176–7
  Black futurisms vs. Systems of Domination 17, 77–96
  of narrative 213–17
  patriarchy 87–8, 179–83
  of a single word 26–8
  pre-colonial Africa 18, 93, 106, 138–9, 167–71, 174
  queer imaginings 120–1
  spirituality 16, 61

Queer Africa: Selected Stories (Edozien) 125
queer imaginings 17, 119–36
  beginnings 120–5
  decolonization 125–32
  future of 132–4
  postgenderism 125–32
  "queer" as a word 120
Quimbada people from Angola 106–7

racial stereotypes *see* stereotypes
"The Rakwa wa-Ya'yn" ("The Song of Our Mother's Children") by Embleton & Talabi 31–8
reflexivity 211
relationship or affinity with the continent of Africa 5
remixing cultural identity/remix/ remixology 139, 140, 141–2, 148
representation 84–6
resistance to dominant power structures *see* power structures
"Resisting Homophobia: The Colonial Origins of Anti-Gay Laws" 121
resurrecting ending, narrative strategies 219–20
"Reviled, Reclaimed and Respected: The History of the Word 'Queer'" (Jones) 120
"Ricepunk Manifesto" (Wijeratne) 6–7
ritual 67, 73, 106–7, 121
Robinson, Cedric 81–2, 92–3
The Roots of Ethnicity: The Origins of the Acholi of Uganda Before 1800 (Atkinson) 172, 176–7
Roscoe, Will 120–1, 123

Rose, Tricia 3–4
  see also "Black to the Future"
Rule of Consensus 176–7
Rwanda 137, 140–3

sacrificial rituals 67
Samatar, Sofia 2–3, 45, 140–3
same-sex relationships *see* homosexuality
San people, Zimbabwe 121
The Sandman (Gaiman) 192
Sauúti Collective, *Sauútiverse* 15, 31–8, 63, 130–2, 133
  language and the five planets 35–7
  understanding the 32–5
Saving Shadows (Bacon) xi
science fiction and fantasy 2–3, 142–3, 151–62, 192
self-as-research, denouement 207–11
self-reflective conclusion, narrative strategies 220–1
Senghor, Leopold 84
sense of space 195–6
sexual violence 123–4, 164
"Shame" (Dorman) 18, 197, 198
shapeshifting concepts 139, 143–7
"Shatterling" (van Rooyen) 128
Shawl, Nisi 7, 45
Sing Down the Stars (Dorman) 18, 198–9
slavery 83, 139–40, 165–7
  see also colonization
Smith, Lydia 123–4
"And So Shaped the World" (Thomas) 138
social media 165
social-political organization in pre-colonial Acholi 167–71
"sodomy laws" 124–5
"Song of Myself" (Whitman) 115
Soul Searching (Embleton) 26–8
South Africa
  Afrofuturist/Africanfuturist spirituality 99
  autoethnography, self-as-research 209
  case for inclusive expression 18
  cosmologies and languages building 25, 26, 31
  direct democracy in Yat Madit 180

234   *Index*

post-colonial themes 194, 197–9, 201–2
queer imaginings in Africanfuturism 121, 123–4, 127, 132–3
Southall, A. 172
Soyinka, Wole 85
speculative fiction 2–3, 6, 9, 55
  African spirituality 64, 66
  ASFS 10
  BSAM 142
  fact and fantasy 101–2
  see also Afrofuturism; Black Speculative fiction
"Speculative and Science Fiction", *African Literature Today* 2–3
Spillers, Hortense 83
spirits, gods, and the ancestors 25, 66–8, 103–4, 121
spirituality 59–76, 97–117
  pre-colonial Africa 16, 61
Star Wars (1977) 165
"state of anarchy" 166–7
Stengel, Richard 133
stereotypes 61, 179, 185, 186, 198–9
"Still She Visits" (Bacon) 211–21
straight-washing 123–4
Sunflower Student Movement 164
Supreme Beings 103–4
  see also spirits, gods, and the ancestors
surrealism 3–4, 14–15, 17, 84–5, 89, 93–4
systems of domination 17, 77–96
  see also power

Taiwan student movements 164, 179, 186
Talabi, Wole 10, 15, 31–8, 46, 61, 100
"The Tale of Jaja and Canti" (Ogundiran) 154–6
Tales of the Dark and Fantastic 151–62
Tamale, Sylvia 121, 122, 133
Tanganyika 52
Tanzania xv, 25, 52, 85, 122, 212, 214
Tate, Greg 3–4
  see also "Black to the Future"
"The Muse of History" (Walcott) 79–80
"There is Magic in African Literature" (Embleton) 28–9
They Gave Us Stealth and Cunning (Ntumy) 103–4

They Made Us Blood and Fury (Ntumy) 103, 104–5, 107
Things Fall Apart (Achebe) 67–8, 79
thinking otherwise 78
Thomas, Sheree Renée 7, 45, 138–9
Those Who Return (Dorman) 195, 197
"Three C's of Colonialism: Civilization, Christianity, and Commerce" 62
Tifinagh form 26–7
time, past and future concepts 60–2
"Toward Arabfuturism/s" (Majali) 6–7
"Toward a Planetary History of Afrofuturism" (Samatar) 2–3, 140
traditional beliefs 28–32
  see also folklore/folktales
transatlantic slave trade 139–40
  see also colonization
"Transgender Rights and Issues" 129
transgenderism 123, 127, 128–31, 179–80
transmogrification 66–7
"Trends in Black Speculative Fiction" (Bacon) 55
Trump, Donald 129–30
Tsamaase, Tlotlo 46, 61
Tutuola, Amos 156–7
typography/calligraphy 26–7

Ubana, Eyong Usang 102
Ubuntu concepts 69, 133, 202–3
Ugobude, Franklin 105
ujamaa 51–4, 85
umbrella terms 11–12
United Nations (UN) 165–6
unknown, the 156–61
US military 129–30
utopianism 51, 55, 64–5, 122

van Rooyen, Xan 119–36
virgin bride concepts 182
Vocabulary of the Yoruba Language (Crowther) 25
voice from the grassroots xii
vTaiwan 164, 179, 186

wa Thiong'o, Ngũgĩ 46, 91
Wabuke, Hope 9, 12, 65–6
Walcott, Derek 79–80, 91
Walking the Clouds anthology 6–7

"We Were Kings and Queens" 165–7
welfare of every individual, direct
      democracy 176–7
Welsh, Kariamu 13
Wengrow, David 166–7
"Where Scary Traditions Allow Women to
      'Marry' Women" (Adhiambo) 122
white supremacy 138, 141
Whitman, Walt 115
"Who Will Greet You at Home?"
      (Arimah) 101–2
"wife purchase" 181–2
Wiimb-ó, planet in the *Sauútiverse* 37
Wijeratne, Yudhanjaya 6–7
Wild Seed (Butler) 16, 64–5
Wilson, D. Harlan 48, 50–1
Winda N., Chintya 67–8
witchdoctors 73
wokeism 114
Womack, Ytasha L. 2–3, 7, 138, 140
The Woman King (2022) 130

women
      anti-LGBT+ legislation 121–4
      "captive body", in times of slavery 83
      feminism 78, 87–8, 179–83, 213, 220–1
      in kaka systems 170, 183–5
      marriage 122, 181–3, 184–5
      Mut, goddess of Motherhood 121
      naming, Afrofuturism 45
      queer imaginings 121–4, 127, 128–32
      sexual violence 123–4, 164
Wood, Nick 45
'write what you know' 195, 199–200

Yaszek, Lisa 45, 46, 63, 141, 152
"Yat Madit" (Dila) 18, 163–89

Zanzibar 52
Zezépfeni, planet in the *Sauútiverse* 36
Zohdi, Esmaeil 60
Zuúv'ah, sun in the *Sauútiverse* 36
Zvawanda, Stephen 101–2

www.ingramcontent.com/pod-product-compliance
Ingram Content Group UK Ltd.
Pitfield, Milton Keynes, MK11 3LW, UK
UKHW022051230125
454015UK00003B/25